Making Meetings Work

W9-BKG-711

Making Meetings Work

Achieving
High Quality
Group Decisions

SECOND EDITION

John E. Tropman

University of Michigan, Ann Arbor

SAGE Publications
International Educational and Professional Publisher
Thousand Oaks ▪ London ▪ New Delhi

For information:

Sage Publications, Inc.
2455 Teller Road
Thousand Oaks, California 91320
E-mail: order@sagepub.com

Sage Publications Ltd.
6 Bonhill Street
London EC2A 4PU
United Kingdom

Sage Publications India Pvt. Ltd.
B-42 Panchsheel Enclave
Post Box 4109
New Delhi 110 017 India

Printed in the United States of America

Library of Congress Cataloging-in-Publication Data

Tropman, John E.
Making meetings work: Achieving high quality group decisions /
by John E. Tropman.— 2nd ed.
    p. cm.
Includes bibliographical references and index.
ISBN 0-7619-2705-0 (P)
  1. Meetings. 2. Group decision-making. I. Title.
AS6 .T743 2003
658.4′56—dc21

                          2002012831

This book is printed on acid-free paper.

03   04   05   06   10   9   8   7   6   5   4   3   2   1

Acquisitions Editor:	Al Bruckner
Editorial Assistant:	Mary Ann Vail
Copy Editor:	Gaye Lucas
Production Editor:	Diane S. Foster
Typesetter:	C&M Digitals (P) Ltd.
Proofreader:	Sally M. Scott
Indexer:	Molly Hall
Cover Designer:	Michelle Lee

Contents

Acknowledgments

I want to express appreciation to the many people who have made this second edition possible. Let me start, though, with the first edition. Armand Lauffer was instrumental in making the connection at Sage and has always been supportive. The wonderful folks at Sage—especially Marquita Flemming—helped throughout the process. And I must mention all the individuals who contributed "data": the people who participated in discussions about effective meetings, who let me observe their meetings, and who reflected on the meeting process. All of them made an immeasurable contribution.

What has been rewarding since the publication of the first edition is the communication I have had with readers from around the country. Many of them have tried to put into practice the ideas presented here and have shared their experiences with me. Time after time, they have expressed amazement at how much better they have become at the "meetings game." And even more, how much this proficiency has expanded the quality of their decision making. That feedback has been very rewarding. I have made notes of their suggestions over the years and have incorporated them in this expanded version.

Putting together a book involves lots of work. Roxanne Loy and Diane Devlin of the School of Social Work Faculty Support Office helped get me a disk of the book from which I could work. Then Terri Torrko worked her magic—she is an editorial genius—and not only improved the material but found errors that had previously been missed. Thank you.

I also want to thank my wife, Penny, with whom I discuss all these concepts and whose insight and observations add an immeasurable richness to the volume. My children, Sarah, Jessica, and Matthew, are adult professionals who have also contributed their insights from health care, grants management, information science, music, and orchestra management.

As our family has grown with grandchildren Jared, Evelyn, and twins Daniel and Ethan, time to be with family seems ever more important. The more efficient and effective my own meetings are, the more time I have to "grampolate."

And the better decisions that we make in our meetings, the better the decisions we'll have to pass along to future generations.

—*John Tropman, Ann Arbor, MI*

Introduction

Playing the Meetings Game

A lot of books have been written about bad meetings. I have written a few myself. Usually, these books focus on what goes wrong, frequently with caricatures of troublesome types in meetings—there is Sally Stall and Tim Talkalot, and the list goes on. But for many people, meetings are like the weather—everyone talks about it, but no one does anything about it. Poor meetings, like bad weather, are accepted. Many have come to accept the "fact" that they will be largely boring, unproductive, and generally a pain in the neck. Meeting complaints have become an accepted mantra, chanted hundreds of times a day throughout the world. Like back pain, people think bad meetings just have to be endured.

Meetings are often approached in a casual and unprepared way; indeed, such casualness is even occasionally praised as openness and flexibility, usually by people who thrive in that kind of environment. That is like not cutting your grass and calling it a "meadow." Gerard Egan, author of the book *Working the Shadow Side* (1995), talks about the unproductive meeting's costs and downsides as one of the big issues in contemporary organizations.

This book takes a completely different approach—a best-practices rather than a worst-practices perspective. It talks about good meetings. It looks at how things can be made right. Over the past several years, I have had the opportunity to identify women and men who run great meetings. Through the Meeting Masters Research Project at the University of Michigan (funded in part by the 3M Meeting Management Institute), I observed, talked with, interviewed, and participated in meetings with meeting experts in the United States and Canada to find out what they did to make their meetings excellent and productive. At the same time, I had ample opportunity to observe the work of nonexperts in the meeting arena.

WHO ARE THE MEETING MASTERS?

These experts stood out when I asked people for suggestions about whom to observe. They stood out because they ran meetings that stood out. My research showed that these excellent meetings almost always contained four features:

1. Their meetings were characterized by decision accomplishment. Decisions got made in these groups. Participants appreciated the sense of closure that almost always occurred.

2. There was little decision rework. The group did not have to get together to decide again something that had already been decided or, as likely, had been avoided.

3. The decisions were *good*. There was a feeling, buttressed by reality as time passed, that the work of the group was of high quality. These were not just decisions made to "get something done." They were thoughtful and reasoned, and they were actions that made a difference to the bureau, company, or agency.

4. People had fun! These were meetings that participants looked forward to. There was a sense of enjoyment and involvement. Participants felt that their time was well spent. They felt the meeting they were in was the "real" meeting. It was an authentic team experience.

These experts came from the three main sectors: government, the for-profit sector, and the nonprofit sector. They came from all kinds of organizations, including universities, big and small companies, religious organizations, and the military services.

One of my conclusions is that the techniques they used are useful everywhere. Many of the experts thought that *their* meetings were different—that what worked in a company would not work in a nonprofit organization or that what worked in the military could not work for a temple board. Despite their view of the uniqueness of their setting, I observed that these experts in different settings were using essentially the same techniques. Underneath the unique features of each organizational type, there was much in common. It is this common part that I am sharing in this book. It is a book of distilled "best practices."

There is something even more amazing. These practices are simple. Anyone can apply them. If you practice them, you will, as one expert said, at least "be able to get as little done as you do now in half the time!"

SEVEN PRINCIPLES AND FOURTEEN COMMANDMENTS

Although similar in producing great results, these experts were dissimilar in their consciousness of techniques. Some did what they did with much awareness. Others just used common sense. No one phrased them as I have here. My job was to do a fair distillation of what they were up to in ways that could reach a wider audience. Generally, the wisdom of these experts can be distilled into 7 principles (discussed in Part I) and 14 commandments (discussed in Part II).

Managing for Meeting Success

Part II provides techniques on how to become a meeting master. Research on the meeting masters revealed that they paid very detailed, very explicit attention to 14 separate areas of management (Chapters 2 through 15). Indeed, the complexity of what they did seemed very surprising, considering the apparent simplicity of the results. Yet as anyone who is any good at anything knows, dozens of details go into the apparently effortless performance. Let us look at some of the techniques they used in meetings specifically to get a general view of the entire picture before looking at the detailed examination.

MANAGING STRUCTURE AND PROCEDURE

In Chapters 2 through 5, we see how the meeting masters set up a structure for meetings that was understandable, clear, and involving. They had procedures for accessing the agenda so that participants knew what would be discussed. They had procedures for getting clear written materials out to participants. The meeting itself was organized well. Target goals were set for each item and for coming to closure. Participants knew approximately when and how this would happen. Time guidelines were followed.

MANAGING PARTICIPANT TRUST

Chapter 5 also shows how participants in the meetings with meeting masters could trust the process. The meetings began, and ended, on time. The participants could assume that if an item was on the agenda, they would actually get to it. Every so often emergencies occur, to be sure, but by and large the knowledge of structure and the knowledge of procedures—their presence and its helpfulness—were major contributors to their successful meetings. This procedural array was constructed by the meeting masters. It was adapted from commonly accepted procedures, but specially configured, for the particular group. The meeting master was able to do this whether he or she was a chair or a member participant.

MANAGING THE BEFORE AND AFTER

Chapter 6 looks at how meeting masters know that a lot has to happen before the meeting. Not only do materials have to be prepared and participants' schedules coordinated, but the meeting room must be prepared and a variety of details completed. Viewing the meeting as a performance or, alternatively, as a dinner party, meeting masters and people who work with them ensure that anything that can make the setting a welcoming one has been done. This procedure also involves checking with individuals in the interstitial period to ensure that reports that are supposed to be ready are ready, checking on whether scheduling has been completed after the agenda, and so on. After the meeting, following up with the progress of the meeting's agreed-on efforts is very important. Although meeting masters do not make pests of themselves in this regard, the occasional question and inquiry is often enough to keep momentum moving.

MANAGING REHEARSALS, PERFORMANCES, AND AUDIENCES

Chapter 7 examines the preparation, performance, and audience aspect of meetings. In the nonmeeting period, there are rehearsals of items (although these also come in the meeting period, too). Individuals sometimes need the chance to talk over an item privately—this is a kind of rehearsal. Sometimes small groups need to meet. But if the meeting masters felt that there would be benefit from such rehearsal, they actually arranged it. This part was difficult to discover because, of course, one never saw it in a meeting—one saw only the results. Individuals thus became more familiar with issues, more capable of discussing them, and less emotional about them.

For those who were consistently ill prepared, the meeting master arranged for a base-touching phone call to stimulate preparation in advance of the meeting. In short, all kinds of things occurred as a way of rehearsing and playing with things through dealing with items not so that they would not be dealt with at the meeting. Rather, the reverse is possible—they could be dealt with at the meeting.

Similarly, the meeting was viewed as a performance or a play. The setting had to be organized and preparations made. But like a coach before a game, the meeting master reminded participants that the upcoming meeting was important, that it was going to deal with some key items, and that participants must be ready to contribute ideas and solutions. The meeting master enhanced participants' motivation and readiness to "do battle with the issues." Sometimes others were invited to observe the meeting. In retrospect, I concluded that this was simply a way to further hone the performance aspect of the meeting, although it was never argued as such. It was also suggested as important because this guest needed to hear our discussion, or we needed to hear from that guest. The observers did not participate very much at all. They might ask an occasional question or two, but that was all. Their presence, however, dramatically improved participants' behavior.

MANAGING THE EMOTIONAL ELEMENTS IN MEETINGS

One of the key elements in any kind of group activity is the presence of emotion, feeling, or affect. In many settings in organizations, there is a pretense that emotion is not present. There is a fiction that the defeated person does not feel bad, and that the victorious person does not feel glad—"Hey, nothing personal." Of course, "nothing" couldn't be further from the truth.

Everything that involves people is personal. The meeting masters recognized this truth and acted on it. They found ways to help people feel good about their meeting participation. (These methods are discussed in Chapter 8.) There was the occasional stroke, the praising comment, the carryback of a compliment from someone else, shared in public.

There were also questions and observations of a more critical nature. All these criticisms were made in private. Losers on an issue, if there were losers, were praised for their contributions. Winners were gently reminded that, as in football, excessive celebration was unseemly. In short, the meeting master was sensitive to participants' feelings as a result of the proposals and comments made during the meeting. The meeting master was constantly on the go, dropping a word here, dropping a word there, intervening here, intervening there. None of this seemed untoward or heavy-handed or overdone; rather, it was similar to the busy maître d', checking every table, being helpful.

MANAGING IDEAS AND PROPOSALS

If managing affect and emotion is the interpersonal side of the meeting master task, managing ideas and proposals is the intellectual side, which is the subject of Chapter 9. Meeting masters are skilled, in a variety of ways, at opening up proposal ideas and keeping proposals and ideas moving. First, they always seemed rather supportive of new ideas, although not necessarily of any specific new idea. In those meetings, there was always the sense that one could suggest something a little bit off-the-wall, a little bit bizarre, and would receive protection from the meeting master. That did not mean, by any stretch, that the masters always agreed, but they always welcomed the new idea and always seemed to find it a place.

Frequently, meeting masters linked a new idea with an older item, thus giving a new idea a refurbished reputation and a rejuvenated part in a final solution. They combined ideas or suggested a piece of this and a piece of that. They seemed to sense when intellectual fuel was expended and when tabling was in order, despite their great interest in closure. Meeting masters also seemed to know when to press for closure, even though it appeared participants were exhausted—that with just a little bit more effort, they could come to terms. They were able to keep proposals moving through various iterations; make it clear when a proposal was up for discussion (but then also when it was up for decision); and clarify the context as well as the content of any proposal.

MANAGING DECISION RULES

Most of us are all too well aware of the hesitancy with which most groups approach even the simplest decision. One wonders how anything ever gets decided. A few meeting masters had stopped to wonder why this so-called decision avoidance psychosis is present in the first place. Chapter 10 examines the answer.

To be taken, decisions need to simultaneously satisfy several different and contradictory rules. These will be detailed a bit later. But by way of anticipation, note that the breadth as well as the depth of preference must be taken into account. Furthermore, the views of those who might implement the decisions, of the relevant experts, and of those in power all need to be sampled and factored into the final decision. Gaps here, or failure to manage at this particular point, are one of the most frequent causes of decision avoidance. After all, decisions allocate goods and values in the system, so there is a natural reluctance to proceed anyway, unless one is the clear winner. But even being a clear winner on issue Number 1 raises the specter of hostility emerging on issue Number 2, so one is careful.

The meeting masters had learned the decision rules. They had learned a simple truth to enunciate, but one hard to apply—namely, that if three or more rules are satisfied on a given proposal, the likelihood of adoption and forward movement is high. If it is two or fewer, the likelihood of adoption or forward movement is low.

It is the need to satisfy others that, when the extensive rule (voting) is applied, often causes people to say things such as, "I'm not ready to vote yet." Discussion has occurred; how ready can one really be? Readiness in this context means that the speaker vaguely or distinctly is unsatisfied with her or his knowledge about where people stand vis-à-vis the other rules and thus has discomfort in moving ahead. Meeting masters blended decision rules to create legitimacy. That blend, verbalized to the group, permitted action.

MANAGING DECISION AND CHOICE

As indicated, decisions and choices allocate goods and values of the system. There are winners and losers. Some people get what they want, and others get "the shaft." It turns out that specific steps aid the process of achieving closure, and these are detailed in Chapter 11. These steps form a process called *decision crystallization*. The meeting masters had figured these out and applied them.

When these steps are combined with an invocation of decision rules, it explains something that has long been a mystery to me. Others and myself made simple suggestions for action such as, "Let's go to McDonald's." These brought down a din of dissent, leaving us with our hands over our heads and with pencils, books, and insults flying in our direction. Meeting masters, on the other hand, often suggested something very complex, a solution to an issue of great sophistication, and seemingly with the ease of a knife going through butter. The group would comment as follows: "Great idea," "Sounds fine to me," "Let's go with it."

Why, then, could meeting masters advance difficult proposals for controversial issues with regular success, whereas the more mundane of us could barely get excused to go to the rest room without a cacophony of complaint? The answer lies precisely in the management of the decision point and our ability to invoke the steps in decision crystallization linked with decision rules—the vocalized action (crystallization) and legitimization (decision rules). Mastering these skills puts one well on the way to becoming a meeting master.

MANAGING POSITIONS AND ROLES

Chapter 12 examines how meeting masters managed positions and roles. It has already been suggested that they were not always the chairperson, although often they were. There was a significant minority of cases in which, although they were a chairperson in some other group, in the particular group that I happened to observe them in, they were simply a member participant (or one might say fully a member participant). In any event, they understood several truths.

First, there are things that one needs to know about being a chair, simple concrete job descriptions, as it were. There is a parallel set of requirements for the member and the staffer. Similarly, there are role requisites parallel to job descriptions, or a leader and follower, and other roles that one might play. They had very large position and role repertoire. So for starters, meeting masters knew a lot about the things that had to happen. This knowledge did not simply come to them fully formed one evening; rather, they worked hard at its acquisition.

Second, meeting masters were not trapped by role or position stereotypes. They felt flexible. As a chairperson, they sometimes took the role of leader and sometimes the role of follower. Sometimes, they played intellectual roles, sometimes interpersonal roles. Because the roles ultimately have far more power than the positions, they were able to, in effect, lead from the second position.

They did all these things while not being chair and simply handled themselves in a way that did not threaten the chair. Basically as they entered any group, they took a look at their role repertoire and created a role ensemble, or group outfit, for that particular group. This ensemble also changed as the group changed, so they were fleet of foot—adaptable and adjustable—and, in effect, kept doing what was needed.

MANAGING TASKS AND FUNCTIONS

Chapter 13 looks at the attention that must be given to meeting tasks and goal achievement. Meeting masters were goal oriented. But they did not forget process. They were not exclusively goal oriented. Balancing both is what is needed.

MANAGING VALUE CONFLICT

Participants and others come to a meeting with "in particular" and "in general" dispositions (Katz, Gutek, Kahn, & Barton, 1975). In particular refers to the specific preferences—the attitudes we hold on a specific issue or about specific instances. In general refers to the larger values in which the in particular preferences are embedded. All meeting issues operate in this two-level fashion, and meeting masters need to recognize and respond to the appropriate level.

But it is even more complex. Participants usually come with sets of values pairs, each member conflicting with the other. An item, for example, about what to do with a $50,000 surplus involves some values about equality (across-the-board raise) and some about achievement (merit raise). Each of us is somewhat committed to both equality and achievement (although the balance differs) and thus is in conflict over the specific decision. The issue is not only about raises in particular but also about raises in general and how social goods should be allocated. Chapter 14 looks at how meeting masters were aware of and sensitive to these conflicts.

MANAGING EVALUATION

Chapter 15 looks at how evaluation is the source of improvement. Without it, we do not know what to work on. Meeting masters looked at both process and outcome, and supported the nonthreatening use of evaluations for both.

The Skills: Application Issues

Part III explores the issue of "TQM." I use it here to mean "Total Quality Meetings." It suggests in some detail the specific things that meeting masters actually did. New meeting masters should just remember it will take a little time and that there is a developmental process that one goes through as one becomes better at these kinds of tasks. It is well worth it, though. More experienced readers should consider the great likelihood that they too can learn something here. One can always improve.

By this time, you are probably thinking that you cannot remember all these details. Let me share a couple of observations that might help. First, the participants with whom I worked told me that the payoff for planning meetings was in the range of 4 or 5 to 1. That is, for every hour spent planning, 4 to 5 were saved downstream, much of it through lack of rework. So the effort is worth it.

The second observation is that learning anything new involves an apparently complex front end—think of a cookbook or any of the *Dummies* books. They are full of specific detail, but once you grasp the ideas—and it does not take long—all this will become second nature to you.

Strategic Perspective on Meetings: The Negative Culture of Meetings

Part IV looks at the "context" of meetings. They are negatively enmeshed in our individualistic culture. We need to understand that hostile culture as we go about making changes. I collect cartoons and sayings about meetings—some of the cartoons are in this book. Meeting humor is invariably directed at exposing the ineptitude of the committee.

For example, consider the following typical canard: A camel is a horse assembled by a committee. Wow, what *are* they saying? We have low expectations of meetings, which produce low accomplishments, which in turn further lower expectations. You get the picture. We cannot address the whole of negative culture. But as the meeting masters showed, "local" changes of high value can be made, and made well.

Meeting and Decision Leadership in Social Settings

Part V—totally new in this edition—deals with decisions and meetings in an expanded array of social settings. Family meetings, civic meetings, governing board meetings, and community meetings all need attention and work. Crucial decisions in these kinds of meetings are vital to the overall health of our social fabric.

PART I

Paradigm Shift:
The Self-Fulfilling Prophecy

"First of all, this meeting never happened."

*P*aradigm—that is a word one hears a lot these days. What it really means is the model of thought that one has about some aspect of one's life. Paradigms are the engine behind the self-fulfilling prophecy. We all know about that. It is a four-step process.

First, you believe something is true that is neither true nor false. Second, you take action in concert with that belief. If, for example, you believe that meetings are awful, then you will not take much action to make them better. The third step is that the "feared result" occurs. The meeting *is* awful—even worse than you could have imagined. Finally, there is the "gotcha" phase, in which believers take a perverse sense of satisfaction in their presumed, initial correctness.

Paradigm Shift

If paradigm refers to the thought model, then paradigm shift calls our attention to a change in that model. This is what the meeting masters seem to have experienced. They went through a kind of metamorphosis or transformation. One person told me that it really was a kind of "eureka." The person suddenly realized that meetings were not sinkholes but organizational processes—a kind of "policy machinery" that turns problems, information, perspectives, and commitments into solutions and programs. Could meetings work? Yes, they could!

This different view of meetings is composed of a number of elements—principles, I call them—that mesh together to create a modern model of meetings. This approach regards meetings as productive, fun, and a part of work; it does not regard them, as the office poster puts it, as a practical alternative to work.

Part I outlines these key principles and shows how they drive a commitment to high-quality decisions.

This book can tell you how to do a better—really, a much better—job of meeting and decision management. But you will need to do work; part of it is learning and employing the new material. The other part is the "unlearning curve"—divesting of the older unproductive, but familiar, approaches. Good luck!

1

Principle Driven

The Seven Imperatives

The meeting masters I observed in my study had principles and lived by them. That is why I call them imperatives. They saw meetings as coopera- tive and not competitive endeavors. Meetings were places where information, skills, activities, and perspectives flowed in together and were processed.

Their view was also characterized by a healthy respect for preparation. As in any process that required thought, the meeting masters did not expect meeting participants to simply come up with ideas on the spur of the moment. The "ground" or meeting period was first prepared through pre-meetings and then fertilized with ideas. The principles were also characterized by a symmetry of participation—there was no one-way communication; everyone contributed and helped to draw out ideas from other participants. Seven overall principles capture the actual operationalization of these points of view.

The Orchestra Principle

Meeting masters saw their meetings as if they were orchestra performances. The hall had been prepared, the pieces selected, and some rehearsal accom- plished. Everyone there was an expert, trying to do his or her best. The job of the chairperson was to facilitate, to help, to conduct the committee orchestra. A humorous illustration of an orchestra poorly run might drive home the differences in this perspective.

You enter the orchestra hall and pick up the program. It is blank—there is no set of pieces for the evening on the program. The orchestra is about to begin when the maestro strides out. He says, "Ladies and gentlemen, you'll notice there are no pieces on the program. The reason for that is that we didn't know what you'd want to hear until you got here, and we wanted to leave room for openness and audience participation. Therefore, if you'll shout out the pieces you want to hear we'll do our best to play them."

Someone shouts out, "Beethoven's Ninth is my favorite."

The maestro replies, "That's really too bad. We don't happen to have a chorus handy. Gosh, if we'd known you wanted Beethoven's Ninth, we would have brought our chorus along."

"But I didn't know you were going to ask me my opinion, so how could I have asked you until now?"

The maestro replied again. "We can't be responsible for everything. Next time, let us know in advance."

More pieces are shouted out, until finally, after about an hour and a half of chaotic activity the maestro announces, "Ladies and gentlemen, thank you. We have the pieces that you want to hear that we can play. However, we do have a problem. Given that it is now about 10 o'clock, I've been informed that the oboist needs to leave to catch a plane to get to her next performance. Therefore, we've asked the oboist to play all the oboe notes right now. Then, as you hear the piece, you yourself can insert them back in where they belong. Thanks for your cooperation."

This sounds ridiculous. It is absurd even to contemplate listening to all of the oboe notes in a bunch and then assigning them to the right places in the piece of music. Yet who among us has not experienced a situation in which someone in a meeting gets up and says, "I've got to dash. Let me tell you what I think about all of the points right now"? The meeting masters recognized that there is a flow, pace, and an interaction in meetings—it is not simply everyone dumping his or her notes into a bin and stirring. The orchestra metaphor allows us to see instantly the interaction, the preparation, and the ongoing contribution that all members make, even those who play only a few notes.

The Three-Characters Principle

Most of our meetings are organized on the basis of the people who attend. That is, the content flows out person by person and department by department, usually starting with the most prestigious person and proceeding down, participant by participant, until the business of the lowest participant has been either dealt with or, more likely, put off. The meeting masters discovered that it is better to organize your meetings by the character of the items—their content and nature—than by the people who attend. They discovered that there are only three things you do in meetings:

1. Announce events and decisions.

2. Decide among options.

3. Brainstorm for future items.

These are the only three characteristics an item can acquire. Happily, it can only take on one at a time. For this reason, it is important to organize the meetings so that all items of the same character are dealt with at the same time. That means that all announcements are dealt with during the announcements section. A decision section follows, and all decision items are dealt with there. Finally, there is a brainstorming section in which items are explored and discussed but not decided.

At a typical board of directors meeting, this may mean that the treasurer appears three times on the agenda: once for some announcement items, again for some decision items, and yet again for some discussion items. This system is appropriate because otherwise meetings get out of sync, and participants forget sometimes why they are there and begin voting on the announcements. A *Second City* comedy skit illustrates this very problem.

> The comedian was asked the question, "Do fish think?" He replied, "I had a goldfish, which I fed every day at noon. Then my schedule changed, and I fed him at 1:00, but he was still coming at noon. My schedule changed again, and I fed him at 2:00, but he had only gotten to 12:15. He got more and more behind, until he starved to death. So my answer is, yes, fish think . . . but not fast enough."[1]

Something similar happens at meetings. Consider the following example. You are throwing a potluck dinner party at your house. Normally at a potluck, everybody brings a dish. But suppose you did not know what anyone was bringing and you decided to serve the dishes in order of the guests' arrival. Or you decided to serve the dish of the most powerful person first, followed by the dish brought by the second most powerful person, and so on. Or you decided to start with the dish brought by everyone whose last name began with *A*, followed by *B*, followed by *C*, and so forth, down to the main dish brought by Mr. and Mrs. Zeno.

Any of these options sounds ridiculous, not to mention the other problems caused by the ranking of who was the most powerful. Food has to be organized in an appealing and sensible sequence. For example, there must be before-dinner snacks followed by a lighter course, followed by a heavier course, followed by salad, and so on.

The notions of sequence, of ascending and descending order, of blending and simultaneity are all present with respect to issues in meetings. The only difference is that we do not pay attention, so meetings are catch-as-catch-can. Meeting masters pay a lot of attention, and as a result they create a sense of flow within the items that capture the commitment of those in attendance.

A sense of accomplishment is also built or constructed throughout the meeting. In that easier items are taken before more difficult items, there is a sense of progress throughout the meeting as well as a sense of sequence (this is discussed in more detail in the section on the agenda bell). One does not necessarily feel accomplishment in getting through a dinner—unless your dinners tend to be disasters. When tasks are to be completed, accomplishment is an important component, and the three-characters principle can help.

The Role Principle

Many times when presenting this material before corporate, government, and nonprofit groups, people will come up to me during the coffee break and look around in a somewhat guilty fashion before speaking. Then, in a hushed voice, they address me.

"Doctor?" they'll say.

"Yes?" I'll reply. (I know, of course, what they're going to say because this happens so frequently. The first clue is the use of the word "doctor." I don't go by doctor; I save that for the MDs. I go by something a little more acceptable, such as "Your Grace," or "Excellency.")"I know why things go wrong in meetings."

"Why?" I ask.

They look around even more furtively, as if they were about to slip me a nuclear secret, and say, "Mental illness."

"Really?" I say, feigning shock and surprise, "Tell me more."

"Yes," they reply. "The people in my group are crazy. You're a meeting doctor. Can't you get rid of them? Or surgically remove them? Anything! They make my life miserable!"

Indeed, meeting misery is a common disease. Its symptoms often include physical itchiness, the feeling of falling asleep, the inability to keep one's eyelids open, followed by that feeling of drifting off into actual sleep as the chin sinks and the head drifts forward. And then sometimes mercifully and sometimes not, one experiences the jerky recovery, often in response to one's name being uttered by the chairperson. Sometimes the jerk is so pronounced that coffee is spilled.

Often the suddenly awakened, in an attempt to keep others from knowing they were dozing (though it is futile; everyone knows they have dozed off) start participating in the moment of awakening. Unfortunately, they usually begin that participation as a continuation of the discourse that was occurring when they dozed off. Most groups will have moved on, and the "dozers" insert an opinion or view of a previous topic in the middle of the new one, compounding their embarrassment. This is called "lagged participation."

In the minds of many, the personalities of the other members of the group are the primary flaw, and the remedy to the situation seems to require personality excision or, failing that, removal of the entire person, personality and all.

Changing the other people in the meeting, instead of looking at one's own behavior, is the most popular thing participants think about doing. The paradox occurs when one interviews all members of a meeting and discovers that everyone blames everyone else. Each person sees the others as rancid with bad habits. If everyone's fantasies about member removal could be gratified simultaneously, the room would suddenly be vacant. The reason is that everyone wants everyone else to change, and no one really wants to look too carefully at his or her own behavior. But a couple of points may make it easier.

First, Erving Goffman (1959), in his historic book, *The Presentation of Self in Everyday Life,* picked up on Shakespeare's dictum "all the world's a stage, and we are merely players." Goffman argued that life is a drama. We play roles within that drama.

The meeting masters sensed this truth and acted on it. They realized it was far easier to change *their own* behavior than the behavior of others. And because the concept of *role* implies interaction, then changing the behavior of one of the actors is likely, after a short period of time, to change the behavior of other actors. Thus, the meeting masters paradoxically sought to change others by changing themselves, thereby changing the relationship. Their understanding of the role principle and its operation was one of the great clues to their success.

The No New Business Principle

New business is one of the great enemies of the contemporary meeting, for a simple reason. Nobody knows anything about new business, so it gives the freest possible license for all manner of discussion.

Consider the following episode in a recent meeting. Participants were invited to bring up items, and one of the participants suggested a somewhat complicated concern that, among other requirements, needed an attorney's view. Because the item had not been brought up in advance, however, there was no attorney present. The sensible course of action would have been to table in this case or to take the item independently to an attorney and then come back with the attorney's view. But that was not what happened.

After the proposer had finished, another meeting participant said, "Well, I always wanted to be an attorney and if I had been one, I would have sued. . . ." Someone else said, "My wife is an attorney and what she does in these kinds of cases is. . ." Neither of these views, of course, was worth anything at all. The participants still had to talk to the attorney. But the participants took up 15 to 20 minutes as they stimulated other semirelevant or irrelevant comments.

New business does not have a place in the meeting itself. It can be brought up a little bit ahead of time so that it can be configured into the total meeting agenda in an appropriate place and so that the information and people needed can be packaged together. To make matters worse, new business often drives out old business, as members of a meeting, in an attempt to find out exactly what the item is, take up much more time than was originally intended. Thus, new business often compresses the items that were actually on the agenda—and for which people have already prepared—into a tiny fraction of their original space.

The No More Reports Principle

Many meetings—I actually think a majority of them—are simply oral newsletters. The meeting begins and a chairperson says, "Jane, may we begin with a report from your department?" "Certainly," Jane replies, and around the table we go, listening to "helpful" updates. In the typical scenario of this type, individuals are not encouraged to surface problems that others at the meeting might actually be able to help them with; surfacing a problem makes you look foolish, as if you cannot handle the job you have. Hence, covering up seems to be the method of choice.

The reporting system tends not to identify topics that could benefit from mutual discussion; rather, it seems instead to focus on making the reporter look good. Because everyone knows the real focus of this reporting system, other participants place a premium on exposing or otherwise making life difficult for the reporter. Instead of cooperative, the game is competitive, or as mentioned earlier, at its worst, in the gotcha phase. The meeting masters eliminated this type of eventuality by restructuring the meeting so there was a focus on items to be announced, those to be decided, and those to be discussed (the three-characters principle) rather than reports to be "given."

The other problem with reports is that you may not actually have a report to give. But it is considered bad form to not give a report at a meeting where reports are being given. You are awfully tempted to make something up. This temptation leads to what we conventionally call "lying."

The Proactivity Principle

In the expertly run meetings, there was always time to discuss items relating to the future. This uses the proactivity principle. The meeting masters took the position that most groups learn about items much too late in the decision cycle. This causes frustration, lack of ability to affect the issue, and a sense of "rubber-stamp-osity." Sometimes, when asked to rubber-stamp items, groups would balk and refuse to act on trivial or semitrivial items, just to cause trouble and send a message.

The meeting masters shared with me their view that the real motivation for people to arrive at and participate in meetings is the excitement of *psychic income*[2] and the real reward of having an impact on issues. The ability to have that happen, however, is not automatic. It must be crafted, set up, orchestrated, and designed.

The High-Quality Decisions Principle

The meeting masters' meetings were excellent not only because decisions got made but also because they were of high quality. In many instances, the quality of the output was assessed using some kind of formal measurement system (an example is discussed in Chapter 15).

But the process, too, showed evidence of quality. With participation, one had a sense that a variety of views were heard, disassembled, and reassembled in combination with the views of others to construct a decision that advanced the interests of all of the stakeholders. That seemed to be the bottom line of what participants meant by a *high-quality decision*. Those affected, including those who were not necessarily sitting *at* the table, were ahead. There was a press toward optimization, and that made all the difference.

The paradox of action lies in our approach to it and our avoidance of it. On the one hand, we seek to decide—there is a satisfaction in coming to closure, and everyone knows that decisions really do have to be made, resources allocated, staff hired, and programs initiated and terminated. But the other side of that truth is that the psychological finality of decisions causes us to draw back. We do not want to make participants feel bad. And, perhaps more important, we do not want to experience the tension that occurs when winners smirk at us, and losers give us that hang-dog look. It is vital to realize that the emotional and psychological consequences of decision making are seriously problematic, and need to be dealt with if decision making is to go forward.

It is not only the "politics" of "interests," of me getting mine, or you getting yours (or me not getting mine and acting as a spoiler, keeping you from getting yours as well). But also the emotional costs of interacting with the winners or the losers, or both. Decisions made may have unplanned effects that could hurt us. So one can see value in delay. Sometimes premature action is undertaken to satisfy our urge for closure. This kind of activity—the "fire-aim-ready" approach[3]—is often unsatisfactory shortly thereafter, and one knows, even when participating in it, that it is not really the way to go.

The other side of that—the "closure-avoidance-psychosis" approach—creates squeals of pain whenever someone says, "Let's decide." (Decision making is complex with a number of decision rules having to be satisfied. We will talk about this in Chapter 10; but complex or not, action does have to be taken at various points.)

How sweet it is then, when participants in a meeting can feel that not only were decisions made, but that these decisions were reasonably good. Not only was the process open and equitable, but the result was not simply the lowest common denominator. It is something that can really be seen and felt to make sense, even to the losers and even to those who disagree.

Readers have all had similar experiences, but no doubt they have been few and far between. On the other hand, if one had the opportunity to work with a meeting master, such results would be the order of the day several times a day. The issue here is that decisions need to be made, on the one hand, and their toxic effects managed, on the other hand. Decision making is like chemotherapy: it helps you but you have to manage the down side or participants (and meetings and committees) will die from it.

Conclusion

Thinking about meetings using a different paradigm makes one act and approach meetings differently. The meeting masters were able to start from a different point of view. I do not know if they started thinking differently and then acted differently, or if they just did things differently and then gradually their views changed. From my point of view, it does not matter much.

One can use the principles in this chapter as a jumping-off place and wrap the techniques (to follow in subsequent chapters) around these principles. Or one could suspend judgment, try the techniques, and then revisit the principles, and perhaps modify them on the basis of one's own personal experience. Unity between thought and action, whether thought comes first and is immediately followed by action, or action comes first and is immediately followed by the reorganization of one's paradigms, is less important than the beginning of forward movement.

Notes

1   I heard this comedy skit on a record in the 1960s.
2   Psychic income is the emotional reward that comes from completing a task well.

PART II

Managing for Meeting Success

"I was just going to say, 'Well, I don't make the rules.' But, of course, I __do__ make the rules."

Whenever one hears that someone does something well, the word *natural* often appears. Beth is a natural athlete. Roger is a natural musician. Sam and Sheila are natural leaders. Very little could be further from the truth.

There may well be—are—natural affinities or talents, but any talent needs to be honed, practiced, and developed. On inspection, that was not what stood out among the meeting masters. What stood out was that they had taken all the things that we complain about in meetings and flipped them over, in effect, by asking questions: Given this complaint, what can be done to make it right? What can be done to deal with it? What can be done to make it not bothersome?

The meeting masters established procedures and practices that together created excellent meetings. Skills and competencies, not natural ability, made the difference. Chapters 2 through 15 discuss the practices or techniques these masters considered crucial.

Each chapter examines in detail one technique to which the meeting masters paid some attention or often great attention. It was their configuration of skills and activities in each of these areas that allowed them to orchestrate excellent meetings. Excellent meetings did not occur by chance or luck or by the odd confluence of the talented group. Excellence is never an accident. Rather, excellent meetings were constructed, built painstakingly and carefully by attention to the myriad of subparts or elements that made up the total.

Part II contains the recipe to make a good meeting "stew." As with all recipes, though, it is important to keep a couple of things in mind. First, when you are preparing the recipe for the first time, it is perhaps best to follow it closely. As one becomes a bit more experienced, however, one will want to add one's own twist and spin. This is fine.

Second, different cultures will make some parts of the recipe tougher to implement than other parts. It is important to do what you can when you can. Do not wait for the perfect time. Do not let the "best" be the enemy of the better, or the good. Begin now with what is possible. In time, more will be possible.

The purpose of writing this volume has been to provide new meeting techniques that increase the efficiency and effectiveness of meetings and help aim meetings toward their central good of creating high-quality decisions. It should be reemphasized that *just having people get along better* is good, but not sufficient. Following the techniques outlined here—employing them, adapting them, and implementing them—will indeed help people get along better but not because it is a central goal. Rather, that becomes a by-product.

People get along better because they feel that the particular group they are in is effective and efficient—in other words, they have the good feelings that come from task accomplishment or task success. It is this point that I would like to stress as the bottom line. People feel good when they get work done.

We all know this truism in our own lives—we feel good when we accomplish things—from cutting the grass to doing the taxes to whatever. Those days that we often feel the best personally are those days when a lot of things that need to happen do happen. Those days that we feel most troubled are those in which we seem to have a lot of activity but very little task accomplishment. These latter days are often referred to as days in which "I didn't get a thing done; I spent it all in meetings."

The application of these techniques generates task accomplishment. It is part of a total quality management scenario, and it improves the machinery of decision making that has been all too long completely ignored within the American corporation and the American system of higher education—in fact, universally. Somehow we felt that decisions were made automatically, that they just happened or "popped out." I hope readers will see that very little pops out. Meeting masters—individuals who are very skilled at this task—spend a lot of time thinking about and orchestrating their groups. It is worth it.

Readers might feel this is a lot of stuff to master. In one sense it is. But as is true in any set of instructions, the instructions tend to be elaborate and detailed, and can at times be overwhelming. It really is not all that complicated. After a little while, one will become very familiar with these rules, and they will become, as a song from *My Fair Lady* suggests, second nature to us—like breathing. We do a lot of things this way, such as driving or playing a sport. We do not think about the rules—they've faded—and we just do it. The exciting challenge to you readers is to become meeting masters yourselves.

2

Managing Agenda Organization

One of the amazing things about going to a meeting organized by an expert is that a number of things have already happened before you have begun (the orchestra principle), but they were unobtrusive. As a participant, you think, "Boy, this was a terrific meeting; I wonder what was so different about it?"

I am again reminded of going to a dinner party where the host and hostess were receiving, visiting, chatting, and yet the entire day may have been spent in preparation so that all was in readiness when you arrived. The focus was on you, the guest. In marketing terms, one might say that from a dinner host's or hostess' point of view the guest is the customer, and that from the meeting master's point of view in the case of the meeting, the participant is the customer. The meeting masters did a number of things that I have summarized as fraction rules—they are easy to follow and all that is really required is to, well, do them.

The Rule of Halves

The rule of halves is an agenda preparation and organizing rule. From the end of the previous meeting until halfway to the next meeting, the meeting organizer asks meeting participants to send in items for consideration at the upcoming meeting. The meeting organizer also culls the environment for other sources of agenda items and at the halfway point begins to organize the upcoming meeting.

Assume, for example, that we are talking about a weekly meeting that occurs Friday morning. At the end of the Friday morning meeting, the chairperson or meeting master would ask for additional materials for the upcoming meeting next Friday and suggest that agenda items would be welcome up until about 9:00 on Wednesday morning. This process may require a little participant training in that most of us as participants are not used to submitting items until just before the meeting. In this case, however, the goal is to get the information and necessary participants that each item requires to the meeting so that maximum use can be made at the gathering point.

At the halfway point (in our example case, around 9:00 or 10:00 Wednesday morning) the meeting organizer reviews the candidate items. Three procedures occur: *sifting, disaggregating,* and *sorting.*

Sifting is the process of considering each item and assessing whether it is truly an item for the meeting. Many participants suggest items for meeting agendas that really should not be there—because they are one-on-one items and need to be handled individually, or it may be that unbeknownst to the suggester, the item has already been decided or is now moot for organizational reasons, or the information and necessary participants cannot be garnered in time for the upcoming meeting. It must be placed on the tickler list and held for a future meeting when the relevant information and necessary participants are available. This process of sifting actually removes approximately 20 to 25% of the candidate items. Thus, there is already a potential increase in efficiency of the meeting.

The savings in the meeting is even greater than it first appears, however. Often, a great deal of time is consumed when an item is brought up and the proposer is told, "That item has already been decided," and the proposer says, "Who decided that? Why? Why wasn't I informed?" and so forth. This creates a negative ambiance as well as costing time in the meeting, and there is really nothing that can be done about it at that point anyway. It is much better for the chairperson to share that privately with the proposer and deal with the issue one-on-one.

Disaggregating is a process of looking at items and breaking them into appropriate pieces. Participants often propose items in a big bundle, such as "the Smith Project needs to be handled." A typical chairperson would simply place the *Smith Project* on the agenda, and place *Jim Smith* beside it. Nobody has the foggiest idea as to what the Smith Project refers, or if they do, they lack the details. In this context, the meeting master would check with the proposer and find out what the actual issues are with respect to the Smith Project and would disaggregate them into their parts.

Sorting involves identifying each item or component with one of three phrases: announcement item, decision item, and discussion item. As previously mentioned under the three-characters principle, those are the only three things that happen in meetings. This assignment means that the meeting master knows exactly what the meeting needs to hear, decide, or think through about a particular item; because these designations are placed on the agenda, everyone else understands as well. So instead of having some big item such as the Smith Project, which requires a lot of disaggregation *in* the meeting, the disaggregation occurs *prior to* the meeting.

There might be some announcement components, there might be some parts to be decided, and there might be still other parts that, at this stage, require discussion only. Such focusing allows the meeting participants to really target their efforts and energies on accomplishing the necessary task—not tasks that are ancillary to the main purpose.

The Rule of Sixths

As the chairperson is putting together the agenda, she or he will skim over it after the initial work-up has been completed, with an eye for the rule of sixths. This rule suggests that about one sixth of the items should address the past, about four sixths should address the present, and about one sixth should address the future.

Items Addressing the Past. Some of the items will address the past because they have not been completed. They have been held over for further discussion, further thought, and additional information. Most meetings will have some items addressing this category. The meeting masters, however, suggested that if these items go above one sixth, the group is experiencing *closure avoidance psychosis* and requires special attention and help. If all of the items—one third to one half—are left over, then closure is obviously not being achieved. At that point, the chairperson or participant can address the group with this concern and invite the group to think through how a greater degree of decision making can be achieved.

Here-and-Now Items. About four sixths of the items should address the here and now. Those are the current items that need attention.

The Future: Addressing Blue-Sky Items. The fun part, though, often turns out to be the blue-sky items from the last one sixth. Items addressing the future, the so-called blue-sky items, are items that individuals in the group and the meeting chairperson know are coming up. Instead of waiting until discussion of the item is urgent, the meeting masters made a practice of scheduling those kinds of items in advance.

This simple procedure has many advantages. For one, it allows participants a sense of creativity, of really having an effect on an issue. We have all had the experience of making a suggestion about a meeting item and being told, "Well, it's really too late for us to do that now; you should have mentioned this before." "But," you reply, "it wasn't on the agenda before. I didn't know anything about it. "Well, it's still too late. The contract has to go in later today. We just wanted to see if there were any 'last-minute' thoughts that anybody had."

This is the quintessential rubber-stamp item—the decision has in effect already been made. It is being "run by" or "cleared" with the group to see if there are any unbelievable explosions, but basically it is a done deal and a downer for the group. With such an item, there is really no point in discussing it. And what a shame, what a loss! Not only are good ideas not included, but people feel devalued and demoralized as well. The solution is simple. All one has to do is include it ahead of time, in the "items for the future" category.

Another advantage of the rule of sixths is that it releases emotional pressure. In this respect, it is very important to include controversial items. To some, this is counterintuitive or, at least, "counterpractice." The more controversial the item, the less likely it is to be listed for discussion until it absolutely must be handled. Unfortunately under this scenario, pressure builds up until finally, discussion and decision must occur in a framework of anger and exasperation. But discussing items ahead of the decision curve allows for a release of feeling into relatively benign non-decision space.

Scheduling items of a controversial nature is so important that it has a sub-rule of its own: the *two-meeting rule.* When applied, the two-meeting rule says that the most controversial items must be discussed first, with no decision at one meeting and must be decided at a subsequent meeting. (The first *must* is an absolute must; decision is not made when discussion is promised. The second *must* is a conditional must; we hope for, plan for, expect, and encourage decision, but we do not force it. It is in this sense that the *must* is a conditional one.)

The point of this exercise is to let participants express their emotions. Such expression will often occur in a burst or peak, and then there will be a cooling-off period. Whatever percentage of cooling off there is, it is an advantage to group decision making. Problems of decision making within the heat of emotion are almost always likely to ensure poor quality decisions. Why? Among the reasons are the following: participants are encouraged to be more sure than they really are about their positions; they feel trapped in their corner; information and time to explore information are limited; the pressure to make a decision is high; and under conditions of anger, participants are less likely to compromise.

The rule of sixths, therefore, allows for the release of emotion, allows participants to prepare themselves psychologically for the items coming up, and encourages creativity and the development of good ideas. As I have observed the rule of sixths in operation, I have often been surprised at the extent to which the controversial item, when discussed a second time, becomes so much less controversial than I had thought. Ventilation and giving participants time to process items of concern does help.

The Rule of Three Fourths

The rule of three fourths is the mail-out rule. At this point, the packet for the upcoming meeting is sent to those who are scheduled to attend. The packet includes three general pieces of information (attention to each will be paid in Chapter 4, "Managing Meeting Text: The Writing Rules"). The first is the agenda, which includes some useful detail. The second is the minutes, if minutes are taken. The third piece includes reports.

The purpose of the rule of three fourths, however, is not to discuss the content of the packet. That will come later. Rather, it is to discuss the process of thinking and the preparation for thinking. Almost any topic improves if one has a chance to think about it, and the rule of three fourths is designed to provide that opportunity.

Many times at meetings, we do not have the foggiest idea what is up until we actually arrive and the agenda and reports are passed out. It is not uncommon for participants to study a fairly complex document of several pages in length, single-spaced, with someone putting on the pressure, asking, "Well, what do you think?" A typical response at that juncture is for someone to say "I think there's a typographical error on page 2." Everyone then looks at the typographical error and several participants nod sagely. There is often a brief discussion of the typographical error—where did it come from, what does it mean, what clerical person can be blamed? This process usually takes several minutes, and by then someone has found a second clerical error.

I am sure readers find this example to contain the shock of recognition. Why is this so? Why do participants so typically engage in this kind of behavior? The answer is simple. The meeting participants are presented with a complex document and are simply unable to read fast enough, think fast enough, compare options fast enough, and say anything sensible. Yet they are being pressed to look good—and wish to look good. Finding a typographical error or grammatical error is a way to appear knowledgeable while desperately seeking comprehension.

Of all the rules that the meeting masters have suggested, this one creates the most difficulty. The first reason is that it creates administrative strictures—participants do have to get meeting material out. That it might be easier to do so in a planned way rather than to create chaos in the secretarial pool moments before the meeting as they frantically seek to assemble all of the necessary ingredients seems to escape the mind of most critics.

The second reason why the rule creates difficulty is familiarity. "These are people we know. We don't need to do these things for people we know." This comment assumes that the essential elements in meetings are interpersonal rather than intellectual. Of course everyone knows everyone else, but one would not use the fact that the members of the string quartet know each other as a reason why they do not have to practice a new piece before it is performed.

Much time in meetings is wasted as participants engage in a kind of verbal thinking. They cannot just sit and think quietly for a few minutes. They feel they must interact, but they do not have anything to interact about. The rule of three fourths suggests that participants be given the material ahead of time. This allows them to prepare and also acts as an outward boundary check on the chairperson's organizing processes. The three-fourths point seems, on the average, to be about close enough so that participants will be attentive to the material but have not received it so early that they will set it aside.

Rule of Two Thirds

All meetings are divided into three parts: the "get-go," the heavy work, and the decompression. Meeting flow is psychologically fixed by the amount of time that is set aside for the meeting, within standard acceptable limits. Generally, 3 hours is the limit. Were a meeting to be 3 hours, the get-go part would involve the first one sixth to one third, the heavy work part would certainly be in the middle third, and decompression would begin at the two-thirds point, or at the end of the 2nd hour or beginning of the 3rd hour.

If the meeting is only an hour, 20-minute segments become the relevant thirds. In the last third of most meetings, participants shift from using both of their brain hemispheres to one. They allocated the other, unused hemisphere to questions—Will the meeting finish on time? What's for lunch? Are the kids at home trashing the house? Hence the last third of most meetings is a time when most participants are mentally closing down the current situation, although not entirely, and opening themselves up to considerations of what lies ahead. It is, therefore, a suboptimal time to take up the key items.

Given this structure of thirds, it becomes possible to use it to organize our agenda in more detail. Although the specifics of agenda construction will be taken up in the next chapter, it is important here to note that the first third of the meeting contains the announcement items and easy-decision items, the middle third contains harder-decision items and the hardest-decision items, and the last third of the meeting contains those items that are up for discussion but not for decision. This last third may also include items scheduled under the rule of sixths, in that it is almost universally true that items addressing the future are not decisional in nature. Rather than simply letting the items fall where they may, the meeting master tries to orchestrate the flow of time so that there is a sense of flow and ascending and descending "controversiality."

Conclusion

These preparation rules allow the meeting master—and any reader—to use meeting structure effectively and helpfully. Nothing shared here violates anyone's conventions, takes away anyone's rights, or assumes unusual power to any particular person. Rather, they become procedural items that suggest, in sum, that the items for the meeting be gathered in advance; shaken down and organized; identified with respect to their decisional, brainstorming, or announcement character; and ordered on the agenda in an optimal way. It may not seem significant, but it makes a tremendous difference.

3

Managing Agenda Design

The Rule of the Agenda Bell

The rule of two thirds discussed in the previous chapter gives the overall pattern for the organization of meeting content. The meeting masters, however, were more specific than that. This specificity is contained in the rule of the agenda bell. Because of its popularity and power, it has a chapter of its own. The chapter begins with the specific ways that items can be scheduled within a meeting.

A Typical Meeting

A typical meeting might be graphed as a curve, plotting activity over time. If the meeting begins late, the curve itself will not begin until maybe 10% into the meeting. It will then rise slowly, as trivialities and pleasantries are exchanged and business is avoided assiduously. Often, this behavior is justified as a period of (a) getting to know people, (b) waiting for the latecomers to arrive, and (c) being open and responsive to issues that meeting participants may bring. Whatever the reason or justification given, things do not start on time and drag on for perhaps another 15 or 20% of the time available. At that point, some issues begin to be discussed and the activity curve begins to rise sharply.

In the typical meeting, the curve reaches its peak at about the 90% point. There has been enthusiastic avoidance of a difficult topic until close to the end, when somebody bites the bullet and the issue finally spills out. Because of its difficult nature, however, there is a lot of discussion and participants become very heated. The meeting continues actively past the announced ending time and into a time reserved, in that same room, for the next meeting.

At the scheduled time, some participants—usually those who arrived on time and were forced to wait—excuse themselves and indicate they have to leave to go to another meeting. (After all, they had planned their day around the announced times.) Participants of the next meeting begin to drift into the room. They also are interested in the issue under discussion and, amazingly, begin to participate.

At about 130% of the original meeting time, the chair will call for a vote. Participants of the original meeting, however, have only a fraction of their cadre present, and even though it is supplemented by voters from the next meeting, it somehow seems unclear what to do. A vote is nonetheless taken, although results are completely clouded.

The Agenda Bell

There is a way to do things better. It is described in the rule of the agenda bell and is illustrated in Figure 3.1.

Notice that there are seven categories of items on the agenda, and all agendas almost always contain these seven categories (except in the case of special meetings and other exceptions).

Category 1 is always the approval of the minutes. It happens at the beginning of the meeting and is done quickly As I will suggest when we get to the rule of

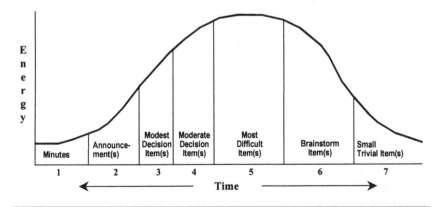

Figure 3.1   Rules—The Agenda Bell

minutes (Chapter 4), practices of using the minutes as a newsletter or as the general reporting document for the meeting or the committee is often a source of trouble and difficulty on the one hand, and vastly extends the amount of time needed for their review and approval on the other.

Category 2 is the announcements. These are short, straightforward, and factual and should not occupy more than 10% of the total meeting space. If they do occupy more than 10%, select the more important to announce and put the rest on an announcement sheet. It should be noted that some of what are often considered announcements are really brainstorming items. Announcements should not stimulate any questions except, "Could you repeat that?"

Items for decision, however, need to be tiered in terms of increasing toughness. The agenda organizer goes back to the rule of halves and divides the decision items into three piles. The first pile consists of the easy decision issues. This set is Category 3 and represents the items that need action but have little controversy and low "fatefulness," and can be handled relatively quickly. There may be several of these, and they can be listed as 3a, 3b, and so on to 3x. If so listed, they should be in ascending order of difficulty, as judged by the person who is putting the agenda together.

Category 4 represents moderately tough decision issues. These also can be enumerated from 4a to 4x but again, in a staircase model with 4c being more difficult than 4a, 4a being more difficult than 3x, and so on.

Category 5 is located in the middle of the meeting, beginning about 1/3 of the way through the meeting and ending about 2/3 of the way through. It represents the most difficult issues up for decision that day. These issues may not be the most difficult ever, but they are the most difficult in the batch or group that is being considered at that time. The reason for locating these most difficult items or issues here becomes pretty obvious, but it deserves restatement.

First, late arrivers will have arrived. Second, early leavers will not yet have gone (they usually stay until about the seventh inning). Third, psychological energy and attention is at its highest. Fourth, physical energy and attention is at its highest. These are group-level resources that can be brought to bear to assist in the decision-making process. Instead of waiting until the bitter end, when most have left and others are fatigued, this process is one that locates the toughest items with the greatest group resources to deal with them.

Decision making, of course, has the toxic effects I mentioned and tears at the fabric of group cohesion. It is the reason that the decision making should be more or less completed, if possible, by approximately the two-thirds point (recall the rule of two thirds). Then we can move from Category 5, which is the toughest, to Category 6, the discussion of items. Category 6, as with 3, 4, and 5, includes items with varying levels of difficulty or complexity. These can be enumerated as 6a, 6b, and so on.

The main virtue of these items is that they are for brainstorming only. This is where noodling around occurs. This is where ideas can be shared, where creativity can be regularly expressed. Very often, although not always, it is this part of the agenda in which items from the rule of sixths are located.

The function of Category 6 is severalfold. First, it allows for some decompression while interaction within the group continues. It is similar to walking around the track once after completing a hotly contested race. Second, as just noted, because these items are somewhat future-oriented, it is possible to actually re-craft them, make suggestions, and make a difference. We are seeking to end the meeting on a more pleasant note, both emotionally and "interactionally."

If there are some hard feelings based on the decisions made in Categories 3, 4, and 5, there is a chance for feathers to be smoothed and feelings to be mellowed a bit. When interaction around "nondecisional" items takes place, it allows the meeting to wrap up on a positive note, if at all possible. That is much to be desired, both because of the short-term benefits (the next meeting the participants go into) and because of the long-term benefits (how they feel when they open the meeting notice for your next meeting).

Some individuals have told me they feel that they must have a new business item somewhere in their agenda. If that is true for you, then at the end of Category 6 is an excellent place to put it. You can actually use it as a way to begin the operation of the rule of halves—that is, as a way to begin to get items for the next meeting. If there is time (and there may well be time under this more efficient and effective agenda-structuring technique), one may be able to spend a few minutes just getting some initial thoughts out. That is not something I recommend, however.

There has been a careful structure developed here, designed to end on a positive note. Why not leave it at that, rather than introduce the potential discord of new discussion around topics about which participants know nothing? That adds a jarring element right at the end of the meeting. Better to get the items noted and use them as a basis for future meeting discussion. The last item—a small "trivial" item—is used to complete the closure process; it can be a thank you, for example or simply "adjournment." They can be fleshed out later.

Conclusion

The rule of the agenda bell is one of the most powerful tools for meeting organization. It works best if it can be linked with the rule of halves and the rule of three fourths and there can be more careful, thorough, and thoughtful consideration of the agenda itself. If that is not possible, if there is an emergency meeting or a "quickie" pickup meeting, then one can still seek to use the rule of the agenda bell on the spot.

When those kinds of emergencies occur, start the meeting with a couple of easy items that allow the participants to get into the group harness again. Then tackle the tough item. Spend a few moments on discussion and pleasantries at the end. That one might have a pickup meeting does not necessarily mean that one cannot apply some of these techniques.

4

Managing Meeting Text

The Writing Rules

The fraction rules and the rule of the agenda bell dealt with some aspects of preparing for meetings. Other aspects, however, are important and dovetail with those already discussed. Specifically, it is important to look at each of the three written documents that are used regularly in meetings and see whether there are ways that they can be tailored to improve acceptance and comprehension, and generate interest. These documents are the *agenda* itself, the *minutes,* and any *reports* that are to be used or worked with in the meeting.

The documents that we usually see in meetings are appalling. Agendas are confusing, and minutes are written like detailed versions of soap opera scripts (He said, and then she said, and then—you're not going to believe this—he said, etc.). Companies, agencies, and bureaus that spend thousands of dollars to communicate with external constituents treat their internal customers in a manner that is close to disdain. It is important that these three document types use formats that increase readability and clarity, generate interest, and actually become useful pieces of paper.

The Agenda

Let us suppose that we wrote menus for restaurants in the way that we write agendas. There would be the following three words on the entire menu:

Meat

Vegetables

Drinks

On reading such a menu, the patron would immediately call the waiter over and say, "Waiter, I can't order just meat. Can you fill me in a little bit?" And the waiter would reply, "Why, sure. We have beef, we have lamb, we have pork. Whaddaya want?" You, the patron, look balefully at the waiter and ask, "Well, what *kind* of beef?"

What you want is the *dish,* and it is important that agendas be written with dish-specific clarity. An item such as meat on an agenda would be the "Smith Project." As noted earlier, the Smith Project tells no one anything about it— about what is to happen or what is hoped to happen, about what is needed and why, or anything of that sort. It simply lays out a broad topic—the Smith Project. Not only is the *content* missing, but the *context* is missing as well. Context refers to the kind of processing that is expected. Are we brainstorming it, are we hearing about it, are we deciding it? That is the "context of consideration." So, we need to have a directional word after the item—announce, decide, or brainstorm. That kind of item omits the two crucial things individuals need to think about in considering the item, yet it is probably the most common way of writing agenda items.

Let us assume that we write more exact items. Then after the agenda item, now dish-specific, we pick up another tip from the restaurant menu. Prepare a brief one-sentence description of what the item contains. Instead of the Smith Project, the item now becomes something like this:

Van purchase agreement. Bill Smith. (Decision)

It is recommended that the company purchase three vans at $20,000 each.

Please see Attachment A.

Now we are talking about something that allows for comprehension as it hits our in-box. The improved agenda format, therefore, contains a dish-specific description of the item, a longer description in a sentence underneath it, and the name of the individual responsible for it. In addition, the character of activity (announcement item, decision item, discussion item) is put after the name in parentheses so that people can understand the context of consideration as well as its substance.

One point needs to be added—time. On our meeting menu, on the right-hand side, instead of price, I suggest a running clock. This allows the agenda preparer to signal the importance or lesser importance indirectly, through the use of time clocks. This process creates a situation in which "equity for issues" can be maintained. After all, most of us recognize that all issues are not of equal importance, yet somehow the "square agenda"—that agenda where all items are listed as if they were of equal importance because there is no other signal attached to them—treats them as if they were. This would be similar to a restaurant menu having several dishes listed but with no price. A piece of apple pie might be $24.95 and prime rib, $5.15.

The importance of the agenda is that everyone can learn from it and use it. It is a document that truly tells the participants in the meeting what is coming up. Our menu metaphor is designed to create the set of expectations. Obviously, individuals will create agendas tailored to their own company specifications and using their own backgrounds and habits. The imperatives of dish specificity, context of consideration (announcement, action, or decision identification), and a rough time order, however, are essential. Consider the sample agenda given in Appendix A for guidance.

Minutes

Some groups take minutes and some do not. It almost always becomes the source of problems either way.

If no minutes are taken, the problem becomes recalling exactly what was decided and who was supposed to do what about which of the items. The answers to these questions are always recalled differently by the participants (and there are always some people who were not at the meeting saying, "Well I heard . . . "). That makes *this* meeting become *the last meeting all over again.* This "rework" is very costly; there is delay and redundancy. No wonder people hate meetings.

If minutes are taken, the problem of who takes them and what they are to be like almost always surfaces. No one likes to take minutes, and for this reason, the task is roughly the same as taking out the garbage at home. Not infrequently, the lowest-status person in the group gets saddled with the task. Interest in the minutes takes a 180-degree turn, however, when they are handed out.

At that point, everyone looks to see exactly how they, personally, are reflected. Backs arch, tempers flair, and the poor devil who was coerced into taking the minutes is now flagellated for inaccuracy and blamed for a poor job. One does not need a lot of imagination to consider the feelings of the minute taker.

Most of us have never learned how to write or take minutes. Hence, minutes vary from the cursory "bullet variety" to the long "court-reporter variety." In the bullet variety, short, snappy actions are recorded and no more. Some of these minutes end up being less than a third of a page. Consider the following example:

> The meeting was called to order at 1:10 p.m. After discussion, it was moved and
> seconded that the new budget be approved. The meeting adjourned at 4:15 p.m.

These minutes are tantalizing. Obviously, something happened during all
that time, but we will never know what. We do not know who was present, we
know nothing about the nature of the discussion, and we do not know the
specifics of decision. In fact, as minutes, they are a waste of time. The antidote
to "under-discussion," however, is not "over-discussion." Some people that take
the court-reporter minutes begin as follows:

> The meeting of the budget committee was called to order at 1:10 p.m. Jim and
> George chatted about last night's basketball game as they sat down. Sheila had not
> yet joined us, although she came in a few minutes. Sid was late, so we waited for
> him, and while we were waiting, we discussed . . .

These minutes will go on for five or six pages. Although the information
about what happened may actually be there, it is difficult to find and it will be
missed by most readers. Therefore, these minutes are really not any more useful than the bullet variety.

There are some helpful guidelines for minutes, and I would like to share with
you what the meeting masters do.

CONTENT MINUTES

One thing that meeting masters do is take content rather than court-
reporter or bullet minutes. With content minutes, each heading in the agenda
has a corresponding heading in the minutes. In this way, it is easy to leaf back
and forth and see exactly where a particular item of interest in the agenda was
dealt with and was reported in the minutes.

The minute taker writes a summative reflection of the item in one or two
paragraphs, no more. A summative reflection involves listening to the discussion and then providing a summary in which the main points are covered. The
tilt and spin of the discussion is reflected but names are not mentioned.
Consider the following example:

> The van purchase agreement was discussed. Some people were in favor of pur-
> chasing vans, as the finance committee had suggested. Others, however, felt that a
> mixed system of van purchase and car-mileage reimbursement might really be a
> better way to go until we had a fuller sense of automobile usage. Still others pre-
> ferred the car-reimbursement policy only, on the grounds that they had purchased
> special vehicles with this policy in mind. At the very least, it was suggested, they

should be given the option of continuing to receive reimbursement or a decent period of time to decide whether to sell their vehicle or retain it.

IT WAS DECIDED TO ADOPT A MODIFIED VAN PURCHASE AGREEMENT PROPOSAL, IN WHICH ONE VAN WOULD BE PURCHASED AND ASSIGNED TO THE MARKETING GROUP. OTHERS WOULD CONTINUE TO RECEIVE REIMBURSEMENT, AND THE POLICY WOULD BE REVIEWED AFTER 3 MONTHS. ANYONE IN THE MARKETING GROUP WHO HAD PURCHASED A SPECIAL VEHICLE WITH THE IDEA OF REIMBURSEMENT AVAILABILITY IS INVITED TO SIT DOWN WITH TED TO DISCUSS SALE, LEASEBACK, OR OTHER ARRANGEMENTS THAT MIGHT BE HELPFUL AT THIS TIME.

After the summative reflection paragraph, the writer skips a line and, in capital letters and in a box, writes the decision or action. This is where names are named, times are timed, and follow-up is outlined specifically. I will have more to say about other utilities of this process later, but from the minutes point of view, it summarizes and reflects the discussion and outlines the main point.

The text of minutes should try to avoid identifying particular people by position, and should instead reflect only the positions. In addition, the discussion is organized and presented in a logical sequence. Discussion itself may not actually occur in this way. Discussion in meetings—especially fruitful, exciting discussion—often sparks from one person to another and bounces back and forth around a topic in an elliptic and dynamic manner. It does not have the linear box structure that is reflected in the previous example. To reflect this in a blow-by-blow description, however, actually diminishes the vitality when it is written down.

The meeting masters found content style of minutes to be most useful. It gave a good bit of information yet avoided rehashing or replaying "last week's game." Losers, or individuals who found themselves reported as taking unflattering positions or making questionable statements and allegations, often claimed that they did not really say what they were reported to have said. (Most often they did, but that is beside the point.) Their wish to save face and to appear wise in retrospect created a problematic discussion in which they tried to claim that what was unflattering was actually inaccurate. Because the best defense is a good offense, they were often successful in adjusting the minutes. Negativity, as illustrated in the previous examples, can be avoided much of the time through the use of minutes that approach the meeting in a "content-based" way. The minutes should get the meeting off to a good start—quickly, easily, and accurately. The contents-minutes system stands a good chance of accomplishing this goal.

RECORDING

There is another positive element, however, that is available in this minutes system that can be used to help the group process move along. A good number of meeting masters were actually recorders—they themselves volunteered to take the minutes because of their ability to use the "minutes" as a way to help groups really understand decisions they were making. They listened to the discussion, but before they wrote it down, they provided a mini-summary of the discussion and action for the record. They said something such as, "For the record, then, these are the positions I understand are present at the moment. X favors this, Y favors that, and Z isn't sure. And if I understand the decision that we've just made, it's as follows: We have decided to adopt the position of X, modified in the following ways . . . "

By providing an oral summative reflection in the meeting itself, the recorder performed a very useful task for the group. Vocalizing the decision is even more useful because many times meeting participants do not really know what they have decided until somebody says, "We've decided, then, to have Chinese food." Vocalization of the decision becomes extremely critical.

Many times participants say "Oh no, that wasn't my understanding at all." These are the kinds of discussions that often occur in the next meeting, when somebody reads the decision in the minutes and says, "No, that wasn't my understanding. I had the following understanding . . . " Recording or repeating back actions and decisions made often prevents misunderstandings and time wasted at future meetings. As we shall see in Chapter 16, summarizing the activities of the group and vocalizing the actual decision become crucial in decision facilitation (as opposed to meeting facilitation). Appendix A also contains sample minutes.

Reports

The third major piece of written documentation that affects meetings is the package of reports and attachments that often goes out with the agenda. Frequently one receives in the mail a "fat packet" of materials. This packet often is something that is set aside and not looked at until it is too late. The basic paradox with which we must cope is as follows: More is less; less is more. The more we send the less the participants will read. The less we send, the more they will read. Customizing material to the readers so that there is enough information in a limited quantity of paper is the key to success.

The problem with the fat packet is that it over-informs—it provides so much information for individuals that they hesitate to get into it and are sometimes unable to figure out what they need to do with it. Frequently when they come to the meeting, they will be embarrassed to admit that they have not read the material, so they will either make excuses about not having received or *seen* the material (of course, they did not see it; they did not open it!) or invent or construct various forays involving new business. This allows them to divert the attention of the group effectively from something about which they know nothing to something about which (a) they do know something and (b) nobody else knows anything.

This creates the best of all possible worlds for them, involving as it does (a) their own failure to accept responsibility for lack of preparation, (b) their ability to expound on topics with which they are familiar and thoughtful, and (c) their cleverly putting other people at the meeting at an intellectual disadvantage. Two fundamental parts to the *rule of reports* need to be mastered—the executive summary technique and the options-memo technique.

THE EXECUTIVE SUMMARY TECHNIQUE

In the executive summary technique, the full report is not sent out, except by request. Rather, as part of the ongoing organizational style of report preparation, the first page of any report is an executive summary that highlights the crucial elements. This summary is sent out with a note of explanation that people can (a) call to get more information regarding the full report, (b) come a half hour early to look up some detail with which they would like to familiarize themselves, or (c) familiarize themselves in depth with the one-page executive summary they are holding in their hand. Most people will choose the last, and as we shall see in a minute, that has a particular structure that I shall recommend.

The point for now, however, is to try to present people with an appealing packet, one that is not too fat but contains some of the essential ingredients. What is paradoxical is that *less* often ends up being *more* because people actually pay attention to the material rather than setting it aside. Many organizations spend large sums in external marketing—they have materials and pamphlets artfully designed to entice the external customer. When it comes to the internal customer, however, they care less and are satisfied with almost any old thing. The executive summary is a step in the right direction.

THE OPTIONS-MEMO TECHNIQUE

Consider the following scenario: A subcommittee of a larger committee has been working. They are ready to come back to the main group with their recommendations. The chairperson gets up and says, "Thank you for your attention. We have looked into the problem of X. We think its essential elements are X-1, X-2, X-3, X-4, X-5, and X-6. Our recommendation to deal with these concerns is as follows . . . (The recommendation is then stated.) Are there any questions? Or does anyone have a different view?"

The problem, of course, for the rest of the group is how to proceed. Many will have questions and varying views. There are a number of negative effects operating already within the group. First, the chairperson has gotten up and indicated that the problem is X and the solution is Y. The first question that comes to the minds within the group is, "Is the chairperson right?" But if someone asks, "Are you correct?" it is often interpreted as a hostile question.

Then too, nobody is quite sure whether the option presented is the only option or about what other options the group might have considered. So group participants wish to ask. If somebody says, however, "Excuse me, but did you think also of P and Q as alternatives to Y?" the issue is expanded. If the subcommittee members did actually think of those alternatives and rejected them, they are likely to put the questioner down, throwing the question back as evidence of the questioner's lack of understanding and even stupidity (because recipients of questions believe they are under attack and the best defense is a good offense).

If, on the other hand, the chairperson has not thought about a particular option and it seems plausible and reasonable, the chairperson is likely to try to brazen it out or bluff it out, usually through lying. "Yes, we thought of that, but it didn't seem to be much of a factor at this juncture" (because when we are embarrassed in public, we hate to admit it). Consider the following example from childhood. You are a kid and in the kitchen with your hand in the cookie jar. In comes mom. "Johnny, what are you doing?" What do you say? What do we all say? "I'm not doing anything."

In short, questioners feel that they have to "take on" the reporter-proposer because of the structure of the way the report was given: Here is the problem, here is the solution, any questions? It is not terribly inviting and tends to pit the knowledgeable subcommittee chairperson against the somewhat naive but still interested and committed group members. This process tends to be inhospitable toward interaction and discussion and invites the very kind of rubber-stamping and *Groupthink* that later generates lack of commitment and even sabotage. We have all seen situations in which everyone in the room has agreed to a particular proposal, sometimes with a good deal of enthusiasm, only to trash it the minute the proposer leaves the room or the minute the meeting is over and three or four of the other participants (those who were not reporting) head out for coffee.

Fake agreement is not the only possible problem. The larger group may decide to "redo" the report, thus infuriating the proposing group. That is problematic not only because of the alienating element but also because the larger group has failed to take advantage of what the proposing group already knows. In either case we "achieve" a decision of poor to ghastly quality.

Avoiding this particular problem is not that difficult, but it requires a small amount of explanation as to what generates the problem in the first place. Psychologically, the proposing group feels that the proposal is "the best it can ever be." The subcommittee members have worked on it and made it into what they believe is an optimal set of suggestions. On the other hand, the receiving group believes the proposal is "the worst it can be" because the receiving group's members are going to make it better. This gulf is considerable, and bridging it requires both structure and skill.

The two-step model of presentation—here is the problem, here is our recommendation—creates great difficulty for the group, although it may not seem initially that this difficulty would be present. From the point of view of individuals sitting in the chair hearing the report, they have to decide whether to challenge the recommendation or not. Questions such as, "Did you think of this option?" or "Did you consider that possibility?" are often perceived as an attack on the recommendation. Sometimes the tone of questioners also conveys this notion of attack. To give the appearance of competence, the proposer may have overstated or overclaimed the certainty with which the proposal is in fact offered. The more aggressive questioning tone comes from an attempt to break through the shell of that certainty.

The proposer or recipient of questions often perceives an aggressive questioning tone as hostile, and the proposer seeks to put down questioners. A dialogue ensues, and the proposer often says something such as, "Well, we spent a lot of time studying this, and if you'd like to do it again, be my guest." This response sidesteps questioners' concerns (and uses force and repartee to put questioners in their place).

Naturally, no one is going to ask another question after that exchange, and everyone agrees. That everyone "agrees," however, does not mean that they "really" agree. They just decided that it is not worth the interpersonal trouble of potential exposure to withering criticism for a few points in a meeting. This kind of exchange—or lack of exchange, really—results in the *Abilene Paradox,* or Groupthink (which will be discussed later).

How can the options-memo technique help us avoid these difficulties? It allows the presenter to appear competent and thorough, but it also gives the group the opportunity to discuss any options available to the group. The challenge is to frame the issue such that the good work of the proposer can be recognized while at the same time the appropriate level of discussion can be engendered with respect to the policies under consideration. Both of these goals can be handled by the addition of a simple middle part to the actual report, hence the name "the rule of reports." This rule applies both to oral and written versions.

The approach is simple. The first part is the same as we are used to—the statement of the problem. The second part is a statement of the options available in the situation under consideration. When we speak with a doctor, a mechanic, or a plumber, we expect something such as the following:

"Ms. Jones, here's the problem that you're facing." (Step 1)

"Ms. Jones, you may wish to be aware that under these conditions the following options are available to you: *a, b, c, d,* and *e.*" (Step 2)

And finally the last part: "Ms. Jones, my recommendation is that we opt for *c* for the following reasons." (Step 3)

The addition of options in the report sequence serves a number of useful functions. First, all groups and all listeners want to know what kinds of options were considered before coming to a recommendation. It is a simple, natural question that does not imply a challenge to the competence of the proposer. Rather, it simply provides information to the hearer about the range of possibilities from which a choice was drawn. Much discussion in groups that appears to challenge presenters is really around this issue. What were the options that you considered, and why did you pick the one you picked?

A second function that the options provision provides is one of "pump priming." Many times, individuals sitting in a group are not really sure where or how to cut into an issue for discussion. Options, because they are a kind of question, give participants a place to begin. For meetings, it serves the same function that discussion questions serve for students—professors provide them because the field of discussion of some text or story is so unbelievably wide that students often are unsure of where to begin.

A third function is that options allow the "level" of the discussion to be established. Frequently, some minor detail that the questioner feels certain about is used as an opening gambit. The discussion then becomes embroiled in this tiny point, with the bigger, more important elements set aside. That "malfocus" on the detail with the "big questions" left hanging is a sure way to achieve low-quality decisions.

A fourth function is that options identify two important but different roles for the proposer. One role, represented by the provision of options, is that of substantive expert. Somebody has looked into an issue and has pulled together a range of alternatives. When a physician or a plumber provides you with a set of options concerning a particular medical or plumbing problem that you have, you expect the individual to be relatively neutral about providing that information. Although there is no question that individuals can skew the options, it is also true that the up-front professional will say something like the following: "Here are the kinds of medical procedures you can have," "Here are the kinds of remedies for your plumbing problem," or "Here are the kinds of insurance policies I have available."

Recommendations, however, shift the role of the presenter from *expert* to *judge*. At this point, the individual proclivities and wisdom of the physician, plumber, insurance person, or proposer in a meeting come into play. It is important for a group to distinguish between arguing about the facts (the options) and arguing about the judgments (the recommendations). These discussions are different. In many cases, they become hopelessly entangled and unclear. Differing with individuals about their preferences (judgment) is quite different from differing with them about the available options (options). The rule of reports seeks to clarify and focus this discussion.

One issue remains to be discussed—options ethics. Individuals can certainly skew the choice field by not giving a fair presentation of options. Ethical meeting behavior requires that all of the options be presented in a fair and straightforward manner. Group members quickly find out about and tag those individuals who do not present a full and fair range of options. Those individuals may find themselves unaccountably losing influence and continually under challenge. But avoiding challenge is not the main reason for presenting all the options—it is the ethical thing to do. It also helps to achieve high-quality decisions.

Presenting a report in the right way is part of achieving high-quality decisions. The other part is helping the larger group know what to discuss. Generally, meeting masters worked with the subgroup to get the report in the "options-memo" format. Then they worked with the larger group to have a discussion of the report with the following four questions in mind:

1. Is the recommendation *logical*, given the evidence presented or other evidence that might be relevant?

2. Does the recommendation embody good *judgment* given the political climate in which we are now working? (Good judgment means knowing when to act and when not to act, and understanding the political implications of either acting or not acting.)

3. Are there any *problems* or *errors* in the report or the recommendations? (We do not start with this question because it looks to the proposers as if we are picking on them and causes resistance. Some problems or errors will come out indirectly through discussing the previous two questions. We do not wish to avoid direct scrutiny of the document, but we prefer not to lead with it either.)

4. Based on our discussions resulting from the three questions above, is there anything we can do to improve the decision? (This is the *CQI question*. CQI means continuous quality improvement. Time and process having passed, the larger group and the proposing group can now work together to craft an improved decision.)

Conclusion

The task of managing meeting text requires that individual meeting planners pay attention to the written configuration of the agenda, the minutes, and the reports. All too often, individuals wait until participants come into the meeting to figure out what to do, which is the rough equivalent to waiting until guests come for dinner to decide what to serve. In the absence of well-crafted agendas, minutes, and reports, the likelihood of misunderstandings, confusion, and general chaos when the meeting actually does get together is very high.

Reports should be configured specifically in the three-step process that was just discussed; however, the process can also be used to frame oral presentations. The writing rules are important not only because they shape behavior at the actual meeting but also because they provide leverage for the meeting planner. Meeting text can be done ahead of time—one can give thought and experiment with different configurations of the agenda and to different ways of writing the minutes, to some extent, outside the actual pressure of the minute-by-minute meeting. The preparation described in this chapter does not ensure high-quality results. It does, however, take an important step in that direction.

5

Managing Participant Trust

The Integrity Rules

A meeting process is a "deal" between the participants of the meeting and those who have called the meeting. The general form of the deal is that participants expect to be treated well, to be involved, and to use their time productively. They hope to accomplish something. On the meeting caller's side, there is the expectation that the collectivity will act in a responsible way to assist in the development of high-quality decisions. Despite our ability to articulate this deal, it is almost never kept.

One reason for this problem is that the agenda—which embodies the meeting-specific instance of the deal—is not followed. Participants then feel betrayed and used. Preventing that development calls for agenda integrity. Similarly, meeting participants expect their time to be respected appropriately, which calls for temporal integrity. Each of these rules is part of trust development. Trust requires that participants be treated well and that commitments to them be kept.

The Rule(s) of Agenda Integrity

There are two integrity rules:

1. Deal with all the items on the agenda.

2. Do not deal with any items not on the agenda.

An excellent meeting requires work by the participants. For example, consider how you felt as a high school student when a teacher suddenly announced on Thursday that there was to be a quick quiz on Friday. You canceled some plans with friends, roped your parents into helping you, and went in there ready for bear. Suddenly, the teacher said, "Well, I've decided to postpone the quiz." The surge of anger that you felt at that point is pretty similar to what meeting participants feel when they prepare for a meeting and then are sidetracked.

Here is another example. Suppose you go into a theater ready to relax and enjoy a light, romantic comedy. The paper announced a light, romantic comedy was showing; you bought tickets for a light, romantic comedy. Suddenly as the film flicks on, you realize that it is not the comedy at all—it is a suspense thriller. Not only has your serenity and expectation been shattered, but you are also being forced to deal with very different content from what you expected.

One could even reverse that scenario. Suppose you did go to see a suspense thriller and suddenly, a light, romantic comedy pops on the screen. Again, a sense of betrayal. You rush out to the popcorn person, complaining about the switch, and the person replies with a shrug, "Hey! Nothing I can do about it. The people who came early wanted the switch." You would say to yourself, and perhaps to that person, "But it's irrelevant whether they wanted to switch or not—announcements were made, plans were arranged, tickets were sold! That's what counts."

These examples contain both elements of the rule of agenda integrity. When people have prepared by reading, they expect to go over that material when they get to the meeting. We should honor that expectation. That others may not have done so is really not relevant and no excuse. Indeed, it is important that the original agenda be adhered to if the group norm or group pattern of preparation is to be developed.

Similarly it is important not to talk about items not on the agenda. They become "new business" and have a number of the toxic effects that were described in Chapter 1. Sometimes meeting participants will introduce new items as ringers so that they can appear to have something to discuss when they have not prepared for the old items. To retain integrity and to create the proper respect for the effort that participants have put into preparation outside the meeting, we must try to uphold the rule of agenda integrity as much as possible.

The Rule(s) of Temporal Integrity

Closely allied to the rule of agenda integrity is the rule of temporal integrity. Temporal integrity has three parts:

1. Start on time.

2. End on time.

3. Keep a rough time order interior to the meeting.

Implicitly there is a fourth point: Do not jerk those participants around who have prepared in order to accommodate the schedule of those who have not prepared.

The first part of the rule of temporal integrity is to start on time. Few things are more irritating than to be one of the two or three individuals, in a meeting of six, who have arrived at the appointed hour—you have adjusted your schedule so that you could be there. The chairperson says, "Well, let's wait a few minutes so that everyone can assemble." Often, a "few minutes" becomes 10 to 15. Somehow, courtesy to the discourteous seems to be accepted in this situation, and it is a practice that we should question and stop. It is fundamentally unacceptable.

For one thing, those who have arrived on time will become—as in the case of agenda integrity—angrier and angrier. Angry folks are not the kind of people that you want to participate in your meeting. So the meeting begins on a bad footing. Second, the small banter and discussion that occurs as the meeting is waiting for the tardy often continues into the meeting itself and gets the meeting off to a poor decision-making start.

There is an old story about a man running down the street who knocks down another man. The perpetrator stops momentarily to help his victim up. The victim asks, "Where are you going in such a hurry?" The perpetrator responds, "I've got to get to my psychiatrist. If I'm not there on time, she starts without me." In a humorous way, that story says it all.

Meetings need to begin regardless of whether everyone is there or not. The agenda system, beginning as it does with a review of some well-written and comprehensible minutes and a few announcements, can allow the meeting to begin without necessarily getting into the meat of the meeting. Herein lies an important observation about meeting norms: The process must begin promptly even though the most difficult items do not come up right away, because "beginning" is defined by the process, not by the importance of the items. Individuals who are late need to enter an ongoing process. Otherwise, they will think to themselves, "Whew! Thank God I'm not late!"

One might ask, "What do we do with people who are late? How do we bring them up to speed?" There are a number of ways to achieve this goal. What should *not* happen is that the entire process stop and be repeated for the late-comers. In fact, we are going to follow a rule of "what is done is done."

Consider other situations in which this rule applies. Most symphonies announce that they will not seat people until the orchestra stops between movements of the first piece, so if you arrived during the first movement, you have to wait outside. Reflect on how odd it would be for an orchestra conductor to look around as people were entering and say, "Oh, ladies and gentlemen, excuse me. We have a number of latecomers. We're going to go back to the opening of the piece and start again so they can be with us." That is exactly what we do in meetings.

Or suppose we are sitting in the stands of a major university football game and 10,000 to 15,000 people have yet to get in, but 85,000 to 90,000 are already there. Would it not be strange for the coach to come out and say, "Ladies and gentlemen, there's about 10,000 people who haven't come in yet, so why don't you have another beer, and we'll start in a few minutes." It would not happen.

When the latecomers enter, then, they need to be brought up to speed. As the chairperson, you might say, "Jim, Ted, glad you were able to join us. I'll brief you with what we've done at the break." Or "Jim, Ted, glad you were able to join us. Sheila, you're sitting next to them, perhaps you could just take a second, one-on-one, to let them know where we're at on the agenda." Sheila will then lean over and point to the place on the meeting agenda so that Jim and Ted know the meeting items that have already been completed and those that are still upcoming.

Obviously one has to approach the implementation of the rule of temporal integrity with good sense. One does not make fun of people who are late. One also does not completely refuse to take a moment to bring them up to speed. It needs to be applied flexibly and with good judgment. It is still the case that the underlying pattern that we seek to implement here is one that says, "We are going to start on time, and if you are late, you are going to lose the opportunity for influence, and we are not going to stop the whole train just so that you can get on."

Ending on time is the second part of the rule of temporal integrity, because many meetings do not stop on time, but often run a bit over. Somehow when a chairperson says, "Well, I hope you all can stay for a few more minutes so that we can wrap this stuff up," the request is uttered in a tone that suggests that the chairperson feels that this is a reasonable request and that members are somehow inflexible if they do not accede. Yet in today's highly integrated, complex society, most of us schedule our days. If a meeting is supposed to go from 12:00 to 1:15, it is fairly likely that we have something else scheduled at 1:30. That may have been planned with travel time in mind as well, so it is not a matter of flexibility or goodwill as to whether one can stay—it has to do with the interlocking of everyone's schedule.

To get out on time, therefore, it is necessary first, to start on time. Second, as the meeting process unfolds, one is watching the clock (more on that later) and making adjustments throughout. There is no reason to punish those individuals who schedule well.

It is obviously true that there will be times when a few more minutes can make all the difference, and here again, one has to approach the implementation of this rule with flexibility and good sense. Nonetheless, things need to wrap up close to the appointed hour with only an additional minute or so. If content is still present, then the chairperson and others will have noticed how the flow is going and have made arrangements to meet again, to switch the order of content, to summarize, to ask for comments to be written, and so on.

Starting on time and ending on time are the two anchor points to the third rule of temporal integrity—keep a rough time order interior to the meeting. Time order means allocating times, sensibly and appropriately, in some relationship to the importance of the items on the agenda. This point has been covered before during the discussion of the actual writing of the agenda, when it was suggested that times be placed next to each item so that participants would have a sense of what is happening. With that already present, gentle but insistent enforcement on keeping to those times is the sensible way to go.

Each of these three rules supports the fourth implicit rule, which is making the time and effort that participants spend to prepare for and come to meetings a good investment. It has to pay off for them, not necessarily as a win or loss situation but as a situation about which participants can later say, "That was a good meeting." This phrase refers not only to the integrity rules but to the process of the meeting as well as the output and outcomes of the decisions. As those in total quality management would say, however, it is very difficult to have *little q*—good output—without *Big Q*—a total quality process (see Chapter 21). In the same way, it is very difficult to have high-quality decisions emanating from a crummy process.

Conclusion

Creating a structure that pays off for the participants is part of what meeting masters need to do. There is no point in beginning a meeting with people who are angry with you because they have been kept waiting for 10 to 15 minutes, and whose anger was increased by your dealing with topics with which they are unprepared, having spent some time outside the meeting preparing for the announced agenda. The magical secret of the integrity rules is trust—that it is part of the process of mobilizing commitment within the meeting participants toward high-quality decisions.

6

Managing Pre-meeting and Post-meeting Tasks

Meeting masters need to deal effectively with *before* and *after* management of a meeting. On the one hand, they understand that the meeting is at the end of a process of development (we called that the orchestra principle) and that much of what happens in a meeting depends on what goes on before the meeting begins. On the other hand, meetings as crystallizing points in a decision-making process have elements within them that require follow-up. Thus, meeting masters pay attention, before and after, to three key areas of management: preparation, follow-up, and results.

Managing Preparation

Preparing for the meeting requires attention and thought. Perhaps a good example would be that of a dinner party. Hostess and host give some thought to who to invite, what to serve, how to arrange seating, what kinds of decorations to prepare, and so on. Each element interacts to some extent with the other.

Certain foods are chosen because certain guests will appreciate them. Other foods are avoided because other guests cannot tolerate them. When the guests arrive, all is ready. The table has been set, initial preparations have begun, and the focus has shifted to sustaining a pleasant and exciting interaction among those who have been invited. Accomplished entertainers know that everything needs to blend together well to achieve a successful and enjoyable experience. No subpart of the experience should leap into undue prominence. For example, if the host disappears completely to cook, the menu selection was not good, in that the host's contribution to the interactional field was very necessary.

What we take for granted in the dinner party scenario has not become a part of general meeting norms. Often, we simply reverse everything in meetings that we assume to be needed in preparation for a dinner party. Since little planning has been done or forethought given, preparations are last minute, materials handed out only at the meeting, and the meeting's content is sometimes a surprise to everyone, even to the person who called it.

Certain preparation elements for meetings that should exist have already been mentioned. For example, the rule of halves deals with soliciting items in advance from potential attendees; the rule of three fourths involves getting material out to participants in time for them to get a chance to think about it. In the case of the rule of halves, all items suggested will not be included in a particular meeting, and thus a running list or tickler list of potential items needs to be maintained by the meeting planner or chairperson. This list can be a source of items in and of itself as time moves along.

With respect to the actual selection of items, as to their designation as action, discussion, or announcement items, it is important to have some interaction with participants on a one-on-one basis outside the meeting. A phone call to Sally will have to clarify exactly what she had in mind by the agenda item she submitted—"We've got to deal with the Jones matter." *Deal with* is often used by meeting participants in discussing the need for some kind of action, but it is not sufficient in agenda construction because we do not know whether an announcement is suggested, discussion with decision to be made later is required, or Sally really means that a decision needs to be made today.

Consistent with the rule of three fourths is the package of writing rules (discussed in Chapter 4) that provide guidance as to how the actual package sent out under the rule of three fourths is to be assembled. As mentioned, the agenda is part of the package and is similar to a menu—a menu of informative topics. Contained within the agenda is a summary of the information needed to think through an issue, at least in a preliminary way.

As in the case of the dinner party, meeting preparers should not ignore the physical facility. It should be organized and ready for the participants. Endless time is spent in many companies shuffling around the building trying to find a place to meet, or discovering that due to some glitch, the room has been double-booked. Occasionally these difficulties will occur, but it is imperative that all efforts be made to avoid them. When something such as this happens, the meeting begins on a sour note, consumes unnecessary time, and creates an ambiance of incompetence that can spread from the initial annoyance about the site to the actual topics themselves.

The last aspect of preparation management involves learning about preferences, orientations, and dispositions of potential attendees, and making a link between appropriate meeting members in advance of the meeting. As one is securing information for the rule of halves, for example, one is in contact with meeting members around agenda-specific items. Through that channel, additional information often comes—information about the depth of feeling participants have about an item that they have suggested, or some other potential item. Alternatively, there might be a hint or tip of a suggested solution. The meeting planner absorbs all of this information and knits together, in advance, meeting-specific strategies to handle the likely issues that come up.

For example, one might say to Sally, "You know Jim was mentioning that he feels pretty strongly about this as well. You might want to just touch base with him informally to share views before our big meeting Friday morning." This allows strong feelings to be exchanged in a neutral, nonpublic setting (one-on-one), and individual participants can get a really good feel for the others' opinions before they actually have to sit down and negotiate some difference.

Or perhaps a pre-meeting between two individuals is not necessary—the chairperson might sit down next to Sally and say, "You know, Sally, I've heard that there are a lot of feelings about this particular issue. Perhaps it would be helpful if we could just chat about it ahead of time. That would give me a better idea of where you're coming from in advance." In this way, the chairperson provides some needed information to Sally about how others may feel with respect to her area of concern. But it also allows the chairperson to test out informally exactly how Sally feels on a number of the issue's subparts before moving into the public setting.

Preparation management, therefore, involves managing or orchestrating the information and people who will be at the meeting, in combination with setting, so that when the meeting actually occurs, a lot of work has already been done. In discussing this with a number of non-masters, they often comment, "Well, you do so much damn work before the meeting, you may as well not have the meeting at all." But, as we all know, good preparation is essential for any event, whether it is a dinner party, an orchestra performance, a football game, or a business meeting. Preparation makes the event more rewarding and more enjoyable, not less. It is also important to keep in mind that much of the preparation is woven into our daily interaction with our colleagues. A chat with Sally, for example, can be inserted into a spot when you and Sally are having coffee anyway. In a sense, meeting preparation allows us to leverage the interaction that we already have with colleagues and turn it to more advantage. The advantage, however, is not a personal one; it is a meeting advantage aimed at helping achieve high-quality decisions.

Managing Follow-Up

Meetings are crystallized points in a decision-making process, just as football games are crystallized points in a football program and orchestra performances are crystallized points in a symphonic season. They have many activities that need to be done beforehand. But they also have many activities that need to be done afterward, and indeed, meeting follow-up and managing meeting follow-up blends into managing meeting preparation. They are both part of the nonmeeting or inter-meeting period.

Immediately after the meeting, a certain debriefing is needed. This can be done alone or together with others in an informal chat. Debriefing looks at the strengths and weaknesses of a particular meeting and tries to analyze what went right and what went wrong. Debriefing is a concept that replaces complaining. Simply sharing negative effect—"Boy that meeting really stank!"—does not help to understand what was wrong and what one might do in the intermediary period to improve things so that the next one does not really stink also.

Sometimes debriefing requires managing the personal feelings of participants who played specific roles or had specific things happen to them in meetings. For example, participants who made particularly good points or handled themselves in particularly outstanding ways would probably appreciate a compliment. The next time one sees that person, a compliment can be paid. Perhaps more urgent is someone who took a beating in the meeting. Despite your best attempts to prepare things in advance, Sally's view simply did not prevail and she was roundly defeated. Touching base with Sally after the meeting and indicating your support for her (as opposed to her particular proposal) would most likely be appreciated. Such a conversation may actually reveal additional information that was not available before or that Sally was unable to articulate during the meeting.

There are also specific mechanical details. The minutes need to be written and sent out. If meeting managers are doing that themselves, that job needs to be handled right away. If someone else is doing it, a bit of follow-up is needed to ensure that the minutes task is accomplished.

Sometimes there is specific follow-up that is needed for the next meeting— some kind of information needs to be gathered or an additional person needs to be consulted. Part of managing follow-up, then, deals with the specific actions that need to be taken for the next meeting. They may be taken by the individual meeting manager or by others. If it is action to be taken by others, then the meeting manager needs to touch base with them and encourage them to proceed.

Managing follow-up deals with all of those items that stem directly from the meeting but also loop back to the next meeting. One talks with participants in a debriefing mode to understand how the next meeting can be made better. One follows up with minutes and with specific actions so that the next meeting can have the kinds of information and participants it needs to be effective.

Managing Results

Results are a kind of follow-up. They differ in that they refer to actions to be taken by others as a result of the meeting process. Decisions made in a meeting often require actions not only by those at the meeting, but also by people not at the meeting. An important part of the meeting master's talent is seeing to it that those actions are taken.

Obviously, people who participated in the decision need to do their part and follow up on things they agreed to accomplish. But the fact of the matter is that being human as we are, we forget. (Or sometimes we *want to forget!*) People not at the meeting need to be informed of what is needed from them. Many of the announcements in the announcement section of the agenda reflect the successful implementation of committee decisions. (If, on the other hand, the implementation was not a success, then the item becomes either a decision item for fresh action or a discussion item for exploration.)

Conclusion

Managing before and after is an important part of meeting management. All too often, meeting managers wait until the meeting begins and then try to do all the preparation in the booming, buzzing confusion of the meeting itself. Through the dinner party example, I sought to illustrate the importance of preparation. Preparation refers to that period of time leading up to the meeting itself. But then after the meeting, follow-up—the rough equivalent of "watching the game films"—allows individuals to understand what happened and what needs to be done next, and identifies those who are responsible for implementing the decisions made at the meeting itself.

7

Managing Rehearsals, Performances, and Audiences

The concept of preparation discussed in Chapter 6 began to touch on the *rehearsal-performance split*. Rehearsals are the preparation phase of the meeting. The performance is the actual meeting itself. It is not a complicated concept but one that is quite important—critical, really. It can involve one-on-one rehearsal, the so-called *sectional rehearsal*, or *subcommittee rehearsal*. But first, a word about the importance of rehearsal.

The Importance of Rehearsal

Public settings are those where we hope to do the very best that we can. They involve what Goffman (1959) calls "performances." A performance setting is one in which we are evaluated and in which we do not have a second chance to go over, improve, or redo. Performances can be in front of strangers or they can be in front of family members. Many of us will recall those embarrassing moments when our parents said at some holiday gathering, "Why don't you play your new piece on the piano for us?" Suddenly, there was that sick feeling in the pit of our stomach as we recognized we had moved from informal to formal, from rehearsal to performance.

Most of us understand the need for practice before performance. This is true of cooks, athletes, and musicians. Yet in meetings, we often do not have the opportunity to rehearse. In the meeting setting, rehearsal essentially refers to two components (each of which will be picked up in subsequent chapters) with respect to their management in the meeting itself—*affectual* or *emotional rehearsal* and *idea* or *proposal rehearsal.*

Affectual rehearsal refers to the provision of an opportunity to experience how particular decisions, actions, and points of view feel to us and how we feel about them. It involves provisional, recallable sharing of feelings but in a private or semiprivate domain that does not require us to be committed to those feelings. In rehearsal, one can try again or withdraw without appearing to be foolish or stupid.

In a parallel vein, rehearsal also involves playing with ideas that are combination sequences and packages to see how they fit and what might fit better with what other kinds of ideas, but in a setting that does not require commitment.

In both affectual and idea rehearsal, the practice component involves seeing how particular approaches feel and seem. In reconfiguring them so one can make the best possible case or have the most optimum package of ideas in a meeting, sharing feelings (for example) is often difficult to do unless one has had a chance to work them through oneself. Sharing ideas, similarly, can often leave us tongue-tied in public. Rehearsal allows us to go through these in advance of a meeting.

Managing the One-on-One

Rehearsal occurs in several ways, but the one-on-one, already suggested in the previous chapter with respect to Sally's proposal, is a good example. Either the meeting master or the meeting participant takes the occasion to touch base with another participant in the meeting to try out an idea or a feeling. Meeting masters made much use of this technique. They stopped by participants' offices or gave them a call and touched base with them on particular items coming up for the next meeting. This technique was helpful not only because it allowed meeting participants to think through in advance what might be coming up and see what ideas and feelings might be relevant, but also because it simply brought those items to the forefront of consciousness. We all have a range of skills, abilities, and dispositions that we do not use all the time.

Suppose, for example, somebody was a good chess player but had not played in many years. Suddenly in a meeting, a participant turns to that individual and says, "Sid, you used to play chess. I brought a board along. Let's play." Sid is trapped. Yes, he was a good chess player and probably still is. But he has not had a chance to practice his chess in a long time, and here he is in public in front of others, being evaluated in this surprise mode.

Time after time, situations such as this occur in meetings. Sid may not need a lot of time to recall those chess skills, but doing so in public, under the scrutiny of time and the potentially critical eyes of others, is not the time to do it. Consider the advantages—to Sid and everyone—if the chairperson had called Sid a week or so in advance and said, "Sid, I have a feeling that we may get to a chess game at this upcoming meeting. Since you used to be pretty good and have that reputation, I have a feeling that participants may look to you for a little guidance here. I just thought I'd let you know so you could give it a little thought." Thus forewarned, Sid can recall his chess skills and be a bit prepared when that event comes to pass.

Managing the Sectionals

Anyone who has played in a complex team event, such as an orchestra or sports team, knows that those individuals who perform the same functions frequently get together for rehearsal even before the overall concert rehearsal, dress rehearsal, or team practice. Members of the brass section, the woodwinds, the strings, the goal-line defense, the infield, the outfield, and so forth all get together and go over their parts. Similarly, meeting masters involve those participants with similar functions in short, sectional pre-meetings that allow them to prepare for a presentation, a discussion, or whatever. The whole point here is that participants who are going to be "on" in meetings need to have a chance to go over their area of expertise.

Managing the Subcommittee Rehearsal

Subcommittees are simply a more formal version of a sectional. They arise when specific assignments have been made for a group of meeting participants requiring actual work outside of the meeting itself. Meeting masters work hard to encourage subcommittee activity so that participants can build upon the work of the subcommittee, and so that the subcommittee does not do its work in the general meeting itself.

The Dress Rehearsal

Sometimes what meeting masters did was to create a situation in which the actual meeting was a dress rehearsal. A dress rehearsal is semipublic or quasi-public. It has many of the features of a full meeting, but it does not have the full public, final elements of it.

One meeting master had a small pre-meeting a half an hour before the meeting actually began. The purpose of the pre-meeting was to run through the agenda, bring committee members up-to-date on items, and at 7:30 the full board would meet. Almost everyone attended the beginning session, and it was extremely helpful. It was very similar to tuning up in an orchestra or throwing some pass patterns before the game.

Pulling It Together

The production of high-quality decisions through effective meetings involves managing a number of large and small details. The rehearsal element may seem insignificant, but it is really quite important. Meeting masters were able to get a lot of work done within a rehearsal mode, work that "set up" or "prepped" the subgroup for effective and efficient performance during the more full-scale meeting. Meeting masters used not only one-on-one but also sectional and subcommittee activities to accomplish this purpose. In addition, they used the dress-rehearsal vehicle for the entire meeting itself.

The whole purpose of rehearsal is to bring to the front of consciousness skills, perspectives, and ideas that participants have and to allow them to freshen their own minds or explore their own minds with respect to these elements. What the meeting masters were anxious to avoid was any sense of trapping or capturing participants unaware in a meeting. In that meeting masters were themselves aware that many of us do not know how we are going to feel about something until we have had a chance to chew on it a bit, the informal setting allowed this to happen without a great deal of personal peril. Thus, it becomes a very important vehicle for moving ahead.

These techniques are especially useful in decision making in the same context as they are in music and in sports. That is, in those areas of great difficulties, or in the meeting context of controversiality, a simple passage or play does not require much rehearsal—one can go right into it. A complex play or a complex passage requires a going-over.

The same thing is true with decisions. The simple, easy matters do not require a great deal of rehearsal, if any at all. The very difficult, the very complex issues, those that might be an Item 5 in the agenda bell, often benefit greatly from a bit of rehearsal. Hence, the most specific use of the rehearsal mode is in a situation in which there is great difficulty and complexity and in which participants need a more relaxed setting to work out their ideas, feelings, and proposals.

The Performance

One of the most important points the meeting masters recognize is that a meeting is a public performance. Public performance means that there are audiences of which the participant is *taking account*. It is a defined situation in which taking account tends to mean that actors (chairperson, meeting participant, staffer) believe their performance is being evaluated, assessed, and measured against some kind of standard. The public nature of meetings can create stress, which I will comment on in the next chapter. The point here is to keep in mind the nature of the audiences and to both manage the public meeting setting and create some nonpublic meeting settings where a certain amount of helpful prework can be conducted.

Who Are the Audiences?

The public nature of meetings involves at least four different audiences that might operate simultaneously and that indeed might conflict with each other.

The first audience is what many of us usually think of when we think of audiences. Sometimes in meetings there are observers—the regents of the University of Michigan have a special gallery where observers sit. Many board meetings have organizational employees sitting in for one reason or another as observers. Meetings of governmental bodies are often public in nature and may have time for open comment from the floor. Chairpersons and meeting participants need to be aware that some of the comments that they and others may make are really intended to "play to the galleries" or address the other people present in the room. Attention must therefore be paid to recognizing that what is said publicly may not always be what is meant privately.

The second audience is the other participants. All of us prefer to look good in front of others. None of us enjoy looking the fool or being caught unprepared. That there is a "script" (material that may have been sent out earlier) for a meeting means that once the meeting has been declared to have begun, the participants' mental condition shifts. Suddenly, the casualness of the *informal* setting has switched to a *formal* (and evaluative) performance.

We have all been in situations in which meeting participants have assembled before the actual meeting was declared to have begun. There is frequently informal chatting, sharing, and exchange, sometimes around the topic of the meeting. Indeed, sometimes it is very spirited. When the meeting starts, though, discussion ends.

I was in a situation not too long ago in which this very point was illustrated—spirited discussion on a complex issue had begun informally. Others joined in as they arrived. Quality points were being made and exchanged on both sides, and I had a good feeling about how the meeting was going to go, until the chairperson said, "Well, since the discussion seems to have started so well, let's formally begin." It was as if somebody had dropped a lead weight on the group. Discussion stopped.

The chairperson said, "Well, why don't we just continue? Does anyone have anything to say?" No one had anything to say—it was the difference between night and day. The meeting stumbled and failed to resolve anything.

Bizarrely but appropriately, almost at the moment the chairperson said, "Well, we haven't really accomplished what I had hoped we would accomplish today, but we've at least started. Let's adjourn, and we'll meet again next week to continue the discussion." The word *adjourn* almost acted as a signal for the discussion, which had been so animated at the pre-declaration point, to resume almost instantaneously.

Indeed, one of the members addressing another said, "Jim, you had a point that I was interested in pursuing . . . " Paradoxically, the meeting that was supposed to discuss the material was a complete flop; the pre- and post-meeting discussions that were supposed to be an informal social exchange were the real meeting.

This happens because nobody wants to play the fool; nobody wants to take the risk of summarizing. The pre- and post-meeting discussions were informal. Evaluations, though perhaps made, were not addressed directly. Everyone felt relaxed, unthreatened, and unstressed. In that context, the points of view and bases of negotiation that subsequently became the formal bases for solving the problem came out beautifully.

The difference appears to be audience, but it is not the presence of other participants that seems to make the difference—it is the insertion of the evaluation component. That is what audience really means. We have all observed phenomena of a similar kind, such as the tennis volley that you were performing fantastically until someone says, "Well, I think we've warmed up enough; let's begin." Your first serve goes into the net, followed by the second.

Another example we have observed is the golfer who, on the practice green, putts phenomenally, dropping 20- and 25-footers, one right after the other. On the first real hole, the ball circles the cup and then shoots out on the other side. Before we go on to discuss the third and fourth audiences, let's look at some techniques for dealing with the first two.

DISTINGUISHING COMMENTS

How does one deal with the presence of these two audiences? In the first case, the meeting masters distinguished between comments for the galleries and actual expressions of preference, and they were reasonably skilled at making this distinction. Sometimes they were so skilled that even the participant was unaware of what had happened. In part, that was because participants do not always recognize when they are playing to the galleries and because the meeting masters were skillful at validating the point made to those galleries and reframing the question so that participants could avoid being trapped by a "public" comment they did not really intend to be constraining or limiting. The problem for participants, in public, is that it is hard to float ideas without becoming overcommitted to them.

For example, a chairperson might say, "Well, Jim, I think that's a very excellent point and certainly one that your constituents will be very happy to hear you articulate. [That is validation without agreement.] But taking the perspective of the national community . . . " What the meeting master has done here is to introduce another, larger, possibly transcendent basis for the member to use in taking a somewhat different position from the one that the member has just articulated. The skill is in not assuming that members (in articulating a particular view, with an eye toward the gallery) meant exactly what they said in words.

Meeting masters understand that words only recognize the surface level of a meeting, and because the meeting masters could regularly enter the meeting flow and grasp several levels of communication, they were able to help members articulate what they had in mind. They avoided creating situations in which members were trapped in positions that they had only vaguely articulated and about which they had only recently thought. In the dynamic and give-and-take of a public session, it is often the case that individuals who are trying a concept experimentally through vocalizing it find themselves, with bewildering speed, committed to a position that they did not even believe.

Public sessions are easily able to engender this kind of fraudulent commitment, in which trapping and encapsulating people in unfortunate positions exists in reality and always as a threat. In meetings where meeting masters were present, this threat was lessened in that the meeting master, either as a chair person or as a member, refused to put people on hooks but, rather, regularly took people *off* hooks. The freedom thus created and the empowerment thus engendered creates and supports good discussion.

"OKAYNESS"

With respect to the meetings in which the other participants are the audience, the chairpersons used a number of techniques to create a climate of okayness for sharing views. One technique was *overstatement*. The meeting master might take a more bizarre position than anyone else, thus freeing the discussion from the arbitrariness of self-imposed, narrow limits.

A second technique is what I call *preliminarity*, in which the chairperson announced ahead of time that the views to be expressed shortly would be considered preliminary. The fear, therefore, of encapsulation and capture in an unwanted view was removed. Often, this technique was linked with a third technique—the *round robin*. A meeting master might say, "Since this issue is extremely controversial, why don't we all go around in a preliminary fashion and share our beginning thoughts. It will be understood that these are just our beginning thoughts, and we'll obviously want to modify them after hearing what others say. So we'll take the occasion to get everybody's views on the table so that each of us can know where all the others are coming from, and that will allow us to springboard into the discussion."

The round-robin technique not only can be linked with preliminarity but allows everyone to know where everyone else stands before the discussion really begins. It also prevents the unfortunate occurrence in which silent members suddenly blurt out, far into the discussion, that they have always disagreed and will never agree, and this is a terrible plan, and so forth. A tremendous amount of discussion water has gone under the meeting bridge by the time these individuals let everyone know where they stand.

An early declaration of concern would have allowed those persons' particular dispositions to be taken into account in the ensuing discussion. Thus, it could have become a creative force in the discussion rather than a negative, point-stopping, heart-thudding, gut-wrenching "blurt-out." (A blurt-out is exactly that—quiet members or otherwise reclusive members, who everyone thought were actually deceased, suddenly and amazingly come to life and blurt out a depth or well of feeling. Apparently they have been bottling it all up when some releaser was activated, some trigger pulled, and out everything comes.)

A part of the round-robin technique is *brainstorming*. In brainstorming, no criticism is allowed; thus, one can share the most weird and strange ideas about what the problem is and how it ought to be handled. This is an extremely useful methodology in that one does not have to get into the position of premature defense, and often the weird ideas, although (sometimes) not useful in themselves, are amazingly helpful in triggering the ideas of others.

Other Audiences

There are two other audiences: the internal, personal audience and the minutes or posterity.

To a certain extent, one's own self is an audience. One's comments and vocalizations are frequently self-censored, and indeed, we are often instructed to do just that—"think before you speak," or "loose lips sink ships." The old war axiom suggests that wisdom is best associated with rectitude in public performances. The general approval of the strong, silent type is further evidence of this orientation.

On the other side, who wants to be associated with somebody who "runs on at the mouth"? One might think of *the self as audience* as a phraseology to describe this phenomenon. Not only are there participatory strictures, but the idea of wanting to do and say the right thing based on one's own value system becomes a factor as well.

Meeting masters handled this disposition in a number of ways, but central to them all was the recognition that, for many individuals, the self was an important audience, even when unarticulated. Meeting masters provided validation phrases, such as "somebody with your experience" or "it's appropriate for someone such as yourself." These phrases were, in a way, substantively empty. What does "someone with your experience" really mean?

It obviously does not mean the person is right or wrong in that many times people with equal amounts of experience have differing views on the same points. Rather, it recognizes the validity of the *background* of speakers and the legitimacy of their participatory suggestions. At the same time, the meeting master is not trapped into having to agree with a point made as the answer to the question for which the meeting was called to discuss. If the situation had been clear to begin with, you would not be having the meeting.

The second technique that meeting masters used was recognition of unarticulated, yet operating, conflict and complexity. They might say, "Janet, I know you recognize the complexity of the situation given your experience, and you've articulated one side of it. What might other sides be, from your point of view?" Now here is an amazing intervention. The individual has just expressed a particular view. One possible response, which one sees in many meetings, is "Surely you don't mean that. How can you take that view?" In other words, the group is off and running.

Speakers, who may have had an uncertain view of their commitment to the view they expressed to begin with, are now trapped. By recognizing or, rather, assuming that the speakers' vocalizations were more than likely the result of a contest of values within themselves and that current expression was at the moment the winner (but possibly not a clear or decisive winner), the chairperson invites speakers to articulate that other side. This not only gives information to other participants in the group, but it also creates equality of vocalizations. This point needs a bit of discussion.

In public venues, what is vocalized—or what the media tells us—is often what we think is true. Thus, a balanced discussion needs to have balanced vocalizations. All points have to be discussed. If only one side of a point is spoken about, a snowball effect can occur.

It may seem true that there is only one point of view being expressed. That is the surface structure of preference, however. The deeper structure of preference may be more nuanced and multilayered, with much uncertainty. The greater the uncertainty, the greater the danger of being trapped into positions of which you do not really approve.

Here, then, is the dilemma for the internal audience. As complexity increases, especially value conflict, one needs to have a full discussion—a real, back-and-forth, honest-to-goodness exchange of views and ideas—to understand the full implications of a variety of positions. Yet that very discussion is likely to create premature crystallization.

What made the meeting master's meetings so terrific were the discussions. Using the variety of techniques mentioned here, the meeting masters helped participants feel okay about sharing their views. Meeting masters built toward a resolution by adding pieces from a range of participants.

The last audience is posterity or the record. When meeting participants say something such as, "I'd like the minutes to show . . . " or "For the record," they are thinking of this future audience, those who will read about the organization downstream. The meeting masters again proceeded with a beginning gambit involving their ability to avoid entrapment.

When individuals say, "for the record," the meeting masters almost invariably agreed, "Yes, that's good," but they might also say something such as, "For the moment, I think that's a good point. Let's see how the discussion comes out and whether you wish to continue it." In other words, meeting masters allow individuals the validity of the emphasis that the individuals wish to place on their point, while at the same time inviting them to be open to such adjustment as might be appropriate as the discussion proceeded.

The meeting masters managed the discussion with an eye toward the audiences that individuals might have in mind when they are making certain points. The core of their technique, in this situation, involved lowering the threat of premature commitment and entrapment, balancing vocalizations, and asserting the complexity that was already recognized in the deep structure of the issue itself, but perhaps had not been articulated, even by the speaker. The meeting masters empowered and inspirited the individuals in the meeting, exposing for them the truth about themselves, namely that their views were a lot more sensible, legitimate, and valid (though never necessarily correct) than they had thought. It was perhaps these interactions that left the individuals exiting the meeting feeling so positive.

They were positive about the meeting because, at root, they were positive about themselves. The meeting masters created a setting in which individuals could experience a larger, richer self, but one that they in some sense as members or chairpersons had not even fully recognized. Meeting masters were almost always able to create an exciting experience, and in more than a few instances that I have observed personally, the lowly meeting became a transformational experience.

The Meeting Is at the End

One thing about meetings is that, as with most performances, they come at the end of a period of rehearsal. The minute that one captures the essence of this insight (that the meeting is at the end of a process of development and discussion), it creates the necessity of recognizing rehearsal. Meeting masters created multiple opportunities for rehearsals: practice sessions, spot meetings, and off-the-record sessions. The inner meeting time, even if it was a weekly staff meeting, was not a time when nothing happened. It was a time when practice happened.

What meeting masters did varied in formality. The most formal was the assignment of the subcommittee. Although subcommittees have their own internal dynamics and thus follow the rules of meetings that I have been discussing in respect to the larger group, they represent an informal collectivity. Thus, the full group becomes *they* and the subcommittee becomes *us*.

Us is always informal when juxtaposed to *them*, and discussions such as, "We think thus-and-so, but *they* will never accept it," begin to permeate the dialogue. Meeting masters exploited this "we-osity" in some instances by assigning opponents to the same subcommittee. Some of the opposition was almost invariably melted by the "we-ness" created in and through subcommittee functioning.

Another technique for rehearsals was the use of the task force. The difference between a subcommittee and a task force is that one is processing material *into* the committee (subcommittee), whereas the other typically processes things *out* of the committee (the task force). The task force takes as its point of departure the decisions that have already been made. It is a military term referring to a group that has the authority and the resources needed to carry out tasks.

Many task forces are, of course, more correctly titled "task farces." Meeting masters use them as implementation juggernauts. When a decision had been made that required some kind of implementation activity, a task force was often appointed. They need not even cycle back, except to report that the job had been done; however, they might cycle back if resources proved insufficient or if unforeseen difficulties in implementation arose.

Meeting masters never appointed task forces without what appeared to be at the time enough authority to move ahead. Such activity not only was gratifying to the members, but also gave them a certain amount of means flexibility once ends had been determined in a larger group. It was not exactly rehearsal, which one tends to think of as coming before a performance. Rather, it was post-performance course corrections.

Meeting masters also used a variety of one-on-one meetings and small group meetings for "thinking-around" activities so that there was a bit of mastication of the issues before the actual deep discussion occurred. These rehearsals served two functions. One was the improvement on the members' conceptual and idea processing as they had a chance to get together ahead of time and briefly discuss items. The other function was that it provided a great deal of intelligence about where the truly difficult, truly problematic points were for the meeting master. Rehearsals provided to the meeting masters information about where they should put their energy.

In this sense, rehearsals helped implement the *80/20 rule,* which suggests that out of 100 things that one has to do, 80 are of lesser importance although they should be done at some point, and 20 are absolutely crucial if goals are to be achieved. The most efficient, most successful individuals in any walk of life are able to identify the 20, or so-called "vital few." Meeting masters knew which items were crucial because members of the committee, and others, told them which ones were crucial. They represent the conductor who walks into a dress rehearsal with a lot of knowledge about which sections are strong, or the coach who goes into final practice knowing which plays run extremely well and which plays are problematic. Information and practice, then, are two main gains from rehearsal.

The use of rehearsal sectionals or special teams meant that the meeting master had to do more work. Often, a meeting master popped in, entered the flow briefly to drop a few points, and ebbed out. Or the meeting master met briefly with somebody to facilitate a sectional session. Sometimes there were meetings with all of the subcommittee and task force chairs separate from the whole meeting itself. These submeetings actually gave the meeting master a chance for enhanced influence. The sequestered setting, low-key style, and tendency to act offstage rather than onstage all suggested that the strictures that kept the meeting master from actually participating substantively were removed (although meeting masters were able to participate substantively in their own interrogative way).

Conclusion

Managing rehearsal and performance involves understanding first that the meeting, when declared, is a public setting. There are perils in that declaration, and there are a variety of techniques that one can use to "de-perilize" the public meeting and create greater openness for exchange of ideas.

8

Managing Emotional Elements of Meetings

Part of what has to be managed in a meeting has to do with the feelings, the affect, and the emotions of people. Meetings are a combination of ideas and feelings, and both are needed in all phases of the meeting process. Meeting masters were expert at coupling and decoupling affect and emotion from ideas—coupling in some cases to inspire motivation and commitment, decoupling in others to remove hurt and embarrassment while keeping a temper within the meeting that was fun, enjoyable, and positive.

Recognizing the Signs of Affect

Meeting masters seemed able to recognize how people expressed their feelings, and they were able to rate participants as to their modalities of expressing feeling. They could tell that when Jim said, "I feel strongly," he really did not care a whole lot, whereas when Sheila said, "It's my opinion," it was understood that she cared very deeply. It was not only the vocalization that meeting masters paid attention to—beyond the actual words used, it was the tone, the expression, and the body language that were all read and noted.

Masters could sense when a participant was bursting at the seams to make a comment. In one meeting I observed Sid was very eager to get into the discussion. Awareness of Sid's tension led a meeting master to turn slowly around and say, "Sid, I sense that you'd like to get into this part of the discussion." *Sense* was exactly the right word, and in the episode I have in mind, the meeting master was looking down toward the end of the table at a completely different part of the meeting interaction. Yet some message alerted the meeting master to the urgency that Sid felt.

It really is not all that mysterious, as they have shared with me. Basically they used prior knowledge of issues and preferences that they have compiled on each meeting participant and what one meeting master called the "instantaneous scan." I thought that the meeting master had not noticed Sid, but I was wrong. She later told me that she makes it a practice, analogous to a driver looking in a rear-view mirror, to scan the room every ten seconds or so—scan, attend, scan, attend. Minute differences of behavior—tilt, attitude, expression—are noted and linked with the issues under discussion as well as correlated with the preference schedules and interest schedules that are already known to exist. As one meeting master said, "I never have to intuit everything; people always tell me more than I ever need to know."

Kinds of Affect in Meetings

One can describe the kinds of affect in meetings in a variety of ways. One way is to think of positive and negative affect. Positive affect has a validating theme to it. It creates enjoyment and fun. It is the spark that provides the little push, the excitement that invites and draws others in. Negative affect can be a bit depressing. The person who says, "It'll never work," casts a pall across the meeting. Even the most positive individual has trouble within that kind of context. In meetings, as with individual persons, different kinds of evidence suggest that a positive outlook is linked to positive results. Meeting masters, therefore, seem to allocate their energies in two broad areas.

Nagativism Control

The first of these was in preventing negative or hostile affect from dominating and seeping out into the meeting itself and characterizing the meeting or meeting series. The second was going beyond the prevention of the negative and adding the positive.

Releasing Negative Affect

A number of sources of negative affect in meetings can play a destructive, corrosive role in not only the intergroup bond but also in actually achieving decisions in a timely fashion. Hostility control, negativism control, ventilation, stress reduction, and feeling processing are among the most important ways to control these problems.

HOSTILITY CONTROL

Some people, for whatever reason, are in the habit of making *ad hominem* attacks. They seek to invalidate points by creating questions about or hostility toward the character of the speaker. Not infrequently they justify their activity with a preface such as, "I'm just telling it like it is," or "Let me be perfectly honest," or "It's important to get this material out on the table." Meeting masters usually played a laid-back role. Their grasp of the breadth and depth of the process was so complete that they needed to intervene only at selected points. But there is another side of the meeting master as well: one that protected the weak and kept the strong under control. Nowhere did the image of a coiled snake waiting to strike, and then striking, appear more quickly or more startlingly than when hostility expressed itself. The apparently laconic masters thrust themselves into action and grabbed the insult, sometimes in midair.

The tactics used were as intuitive as they were imaginative. As an insult was being formulated or during the actual formulation, one meeting master said, "Whoa! Hey Hank! We're getting a little bit hot under the collar here, aren't we?" That kind of comment from an important person was roughly equivalent to hitting a javelin thrower in the stomach just as the javelin was drawn back and ready to be thrown. It reminded me of a scene from the movie *Raiders of the Lost Ark* (Lucas, Spielberg, & Kasden, 1981), in which an apparent martial arts expert begins to go through his motions, including sword twists and knife throwing, only to have his opponent whip out a pistol and shoot him! This example is a direct chastisement of one individual by another. Although rare, it usually occurred as the meeting master protected and shielded the meeting participant from psychological harm administered at the hands of another.

Sometimes diversion was used, in which the hostile person was sidetracked. In a second case, the discussion was getting hot and we could almost sense a personal attack was about to be launched. The meeting master awkwardly spilled a large cup of coffee onto the table by brushing against it. Naturally the meeting process stopped, participants helped clean up, and the moment passed. I was never sure but felt that it *had* to be deliberate.

Masters of meetings are also masters of timing. They have called for breaks, they have told jokes, they have broken the negative theme, and they have been extremely active when hostility and personal attacks were issued.

Hostility is not always the problem. Sometimes it is just negativism. The devil's advocate—that hardy perennial—is one frequently in need of an important amount of management. "I don't want to be the devil's advocate" is a preliminary phrase to "It'll never work; we've tried it before; it wasn't invented here," and so on.

In another book, I spoke of the role of the "angel's advocate"—a phrase I invented to refer to those individuals who look to the good side, to the positive side, rather than the negative side when concepts and ideas, especially new ones, are expressed (Tropman & Morningstar, 1989). It is a telling point that although we have a well-accepted, well-understood phrase for sharing negative views (the devil's advocate), we have no phrase at all for expressing positive views. The meeting masters created a situation in which they sought to balance the negativism of the devil's advocate by either sharing positive ideas themselves, or more typically, inviting someone else to share them.

Sometimes, in groups in which there were known devil's advocates, the meeting master began by saying something such as, "Well, there are certainly going to be problems, and we'll get to those in a bit with this proposal. Why don't we start out looking at the positives? How could we make it work? And let's get those out so that we have a pretty good sense of the up side of the thing, and then we'll look at some of the difficulties." The entire climate is changed by that ordering. If one starts discussion of a proposal with the problems, somehow the positives are thought of as having to overcome the difficulties decisively.

The inversion I just mentioned creates an ambiance in which the positives are laid out and the negatives are now operating at a disadvantage. That is an important point to remember in that positive and negative points are really not equally balanced: What I have called "the power of the negative" suggests that it takes fewer negative points to derail a new proposal than positive points to put it over. Hence, most of the meetings that we go to routinely, unfortunately, and unfairly undermine the new proposal because they fail to pass muster in the face of considerable negativism. Basically what the meeting masters tried to do in the face of negativism was change the order, blunt it, balance it with positive comments, and in a variety of statements by themselves, allow it to be present but not let it dominate the discussion.

A couple of points about hostility and negativism need to be made. Hostility is directed toward persons primarily and, secondarily, toward proposals. Negativism is often directed toward proposals, but it may spin off to persons. In both cases, it was more the nature of expression and the feelings it contained rather than the actual point that needed to be managed. Frequently underneath a hostile comment there is a good point about the proposal in question.

Meeting masters sought to unpack the affect from the idea and present the idea itself, often as validation for the speaker, while at the same time whopping them upside the head. The amazing combination of chastisement and praise, occurring virtually simultaneously, was often enough to create a face-saving scenario for the perpetrator, and it also modeled face-saving behavior. In other words, what the meeting master wants to do is intervene pleasantly, diplomatically, and directly but in a way that does not replicate the behavior that is objectionable.

VENTILATION

Before the meeting begins, and even as the meeting is going on, feelings build up. They need to be released. Sometimes these feelings are not angry or hostile. Indeed, hostility and negativism are often the result of unventilated buildup within the meeting situation.

Given the rehearsal elements, the meeting master always knows a little bit more than others about the position of others. I also noticed that the meeting master came a few minutes early and chatted with individuals as they came into the meeting. A lot of information about how people felt that day, as opposed to how people felt on the issue, was uncovered. It reinforced the notion that the meeting masters were exceptionally well informed, not only about longer-term strategic matters and people's feelings about them, but also about the day-to-day and almost minute-by-minute changes in the particular coloration and composition of individuals.

Exactly how were feelings ventilated? The most direct way was often the statement, "You seem to be uptight [or not in agreement, upset, or whatever word seemed appropriate at the time] about what we're discussing. Is there something that you'd like to share at this point?" This kind of recognition was often welcome. So frequently we as individuals feel hesitant about sharing our own feelings on our own legitimacy as it were, but we are more than willing to share once others say, "You seem to be upset about this."

The round-robin technique is useful not only for getting ideas out but for getting feelings out as well. Sometimes meeting masters used a phrase that almost directly referenced the feeling level of the group by saying something such as, "Let me take your temperature here" or "Let's take our temperature here," "Are we ready for a break?" "Are we ready for more work?" These kinds of phrases allowed feelings to be expressed without fear of difficulty or "devalidation."

Meeting masters seem to recognize that an essential difference between feelings and ideas is that feelings cannot be right or wrong as ideas can be. One can have a certain feeling, such as anger or envy, and it may be an unproductive feeling. It may be troubling. But it is not right or wrong. All too often, we get involved in arguments about the correctness of feelings. Feelings are valid and need to be accepted and processed. Sometimes ventilation is enough, but sometimes feeling processing is needed.

REDUCING STRESS

Without reviewing a lot of literature on stress at this point, it is important to note that group stress can spiral almost as if it was contagious. One individual feels stress, another feels stress, they in turn, sharing anxiously, cause stress in a third, and so it goes until the whole group is incapacitated with affect. Under stress, people tend to revert to earlier learned behavior. We back up on the learning curve.

In group decision-making situations, it seems that the conservative response is most likely. When stressed with a combination of time, anxiety, finances, and so on, blame becomes rampant, hostility may increase, and nobody wants to devote the time needed to have an innovative type of discussion and consideration. Hence, "doing what we did yesterday (or yesteryear)" is very common under these kinds of situations. "Affectually" (meaning, feeling-wise), people know that it may not really be the way to go, but they are tired, they are pressed, and they want to get out. They do not want to go through the kind of discussion that new ideas will require, especially if the climate is negative. Stress reduction, therefore, is an important part of managing negative affect.

One way stress can be reduced involves planning—getting items on the group's agenda earlier than usual. If you are aware of which items and situations are likely to be stressful, advance scheduling can relieve pressure. Some of the rules already mentioned—the rule of sixths and the two-meeting rule—are also especially helpful. In addition, taking appropriate breaks and even doing exercises in the meeting can be helpful.

THE PROCESSING OF FEELINGS

Sometimes it is necessary to talk about feelings themselves. This activity is often called processing of feelings. When it is necessary to process a feeling in a group, one is required to understand the bases of that feeling to the extent possible. Sometimes processing occurs in the meeting; if it is a single person, it is best done privately.

Meeting masters frequently promised attention at a later private meeting— "We don't have time to really get into the underlying ideas and feelings here, but if you would have a few minutes after the meeting, or tomorrow, or whenever it is convenient, it might be useful to help me better understand where you're coming from." The phrase "coming from" is a synonym for "let's understand the bases of these feelings." The phrase "after the meeting or tomorrow" is a synonym or signal for moving from the public arena, where I understand that you will be less able to share, to the private arena, where trust is higher and we can explore with greater accuracy and less fear of public embarrassment.

Building In Good Feelings

Handling negative feelings is only half of the affect management task. The other half is creating a positive climate, and there are a number of ways a positive climate is reinforced.

FUN

It became clear that the meeting masters built in times to have fun. This sometimes involved dinners, celebratory occasions, and even parties. Food occasionally was served after the meeting ended. It is important to create a situation in which the social and "affiliative" needs of individuals can be met but in a subsetting separate from the meeting itself. Thus, confusion of roles and confusion of processes is avoided.

POSITIVE DEMEANOR

It is important for meeting participants and chairpersons to show a positive demeanor. The chairperson who comes in and says, "Well, here we are again, another 2 hours about to be wasted" is certainly giving a negative message. On the other hand, a chairperson and participants who are positive and upbeat, who acknowledge the difficulties and complexities of issues, but who also are expressing hopes for successful outcomes, are giving and modeling a positive message. There is a bit of the self-fulfilling prophecy here, and for this reason it is very important to invoke whatever power the self-fulfilling prophecy has.

SHOWCASING

One of the things that creates good feelings in a group is the showcasing of group activities. Sometimes this means reporting back on a particularly successful enterprise that was discussed in the group. Sometimes it may mean a visit to a site where something is going on that was originally developed in the group. The general imperative behind showcasing is to allow groups as a whole and members within groups to take gratification out of the things they have done well. All too often this does not happen.

Showcasing is especially important in that, as we will find out under the rule of decision audit and autopsy, we are going to look not only at both the positives and how they were accomplished but also at the negatives and how they were produced. Ongoing showcasing sets a positive climate that allows for and creates the psychological and social-psychological conditions that permit the acceptance of critical feedback, absorbing that feedback, using the feedback to improve, and moving on.

Individuals are showcased, as well. Here, care is taken not to overdo the showcasing of one person. Over the course of 2 to 3 months, one should try to work it out so that everybody has a chance at a little praise and receives a few compliments.

EMPOWERMENT

Positive affect is built within the group through the concept and the actualization of empowerment. Kanter (1983) talks about the importance of empowerment in her book *The Change Masters*. Part of the reason that people do not speak up is that they feel "unempowered." They feel no one will listen. As correct or incorrect as this may be, if they feel it to be so, there is probably some validity to it, and it activates the self-fulfilling prophecy—they feel no one listens to them, so they do not speak up. So no one listens to them because they are not saying anything, and they can now conclude that they were right that no one listened to them in the first place.

Whether anyone would have listened were they to have spoken up is a bit too theoretical a consideration for most of us. Empowerment occurs through inviting people to participate in the meeting process. To create the conditions that allow for that participation (or assist in the creation of those conditions) and to let the individuals themselves experience the validation of participation, it is important to recognize, too, that people do not have to feel empowered throughout the entire part of their lives. All that we are really concerned about is whether they feel empowered within this particular meeting or meeting series.

EQUALITY AND EQUITY

One thing that creates good feelings and is a positive force within a meeting context is the creation of equality and equity. The trick is the following guideline: *equality for persons, equity for issues.* Participants should be treated equally. Issues should be treated in accordance with their importance (using times on the agenda as a signal). Everybody should be given a chance to participate. This rule applies to the powerful in the group as well as the less powerful, those with great prestige as well as those with less prestige, women as well as men, and so on.

That some of these groups may self-exclude based on prior experiences in other meetings only suggests that the high-quality meeting that leads to a high-quality decision has to be the kind of experience that can modify the climate. Thus, that experience can overcome other experiences and become one setting where participation can be fun and psychically rewarding. Keeping track of who participates, controlling the "overparticipator," facilitating the "underparticipator"—all these are ways in which equality of participation is maintained. It will go a long way toward creating an exciting, positive, feel-good climate in your group or meeting.

CREATIVITY

One of the things that meeting participants like to experience and that gives them great psychic income is a chance to see their own ideas put into practice. This point also was discussed previously but it needs to be stressed again because now is the time to recognize that creativity is partly intellectual and partly affectional. It is partly an idea and partly a feeling around and about an idea. Positive group climate creates the possibility and enhances the probability of creative ideas and approaches being expressed.

So much of the creative begins with the weird, the zany, and the truly bizarre that a non-threatening climate must be maintained to give creativity a chance. A positive climate is really what is required. We all know how we feel when somebody comes in and says, "Boy have I got a great idea!" and everyone looks down. That person's idea is not going anywhere; the idea could have been a cancer cure. But we will never hear another thing from that person. Creativity is the central part of psychic income. Positive psychic income is what really drives attendance.

Emotional Intelligence

In the past several years, there has been a lot of work on the idea of "EQ", the "Emotion Quotient," or emotional intelligence. Basically, the concept of the EQ involves both intrapersonal awareness (knowing how you feel) and interpersonal awareness (knowing how others feel). It is a surprising fact that may people do not know what they themselves are feeling ("I am NOT angry!" he shouts.) and have little understanding about how their behavior affects others. People who have deficits in both of these areas are truly in the department of the deeply clueless. Yet they show up at meetings "spewing participation" on a regular basis. And even if they have a deficit in just one, they are dangerous participants.

Meeting masters were consummately aware of their own feelings, and those of others. Because they knew how they were feeling, it was much easier for them to keep their own affect under control. They never got suckered into contests with meeting participants. Because they understood how others were feeling, they were able to intervene at just the right moment, in just the right way. Because they understood how what they did impacted others, they were able to do just what was needed, no more, and no less.

Exactly the right amount of intervention was a key here. They never overdid it or "under-did" it. It is like detergent in your washing machine—too little or too much creates problems.

Conclusion

Basically people come to meetings, participate in them, and contribute to them for the most selfish of reasons—they feel good when they do it. Many of the problems encountered in meetings are a direct result of people feeling forced to be there (for any one of a variety of reasons), and they leave with a negative sense of what has happened. The simple truth is that we do what makes us feel good, and this has to be "operationalized" and then realized within a meeting context.

What makes people feel good? The absence of feeling bad—that is why negative affect must be handled. But not feeling bad is insufficient. There has to be a positive climate. Feeling good is what is needed, and that is much more than absence of just not feeling bad. Running a successful meeting, as the meeting masters did, involves positive, active steps—a lot of them—that showcase, that reward, that validate, that create laughter. Out of this array of efforts comes a positive emotional climate that is one of many necessary conditions for high-quality decisions.

9

Managing the Flow of Ideas and Proposals

Dealing With Difficulties in Idea Processing

Although emotion and affect have roles to play in idea-processing difficulties, they are not the principal cause. You do not get good decisions by dealing with feelings alone. There are meeting managers—not master meeting managers—who make the mistake of too much "process" (dealing with feelings) and thereby sacrifice accomplishment. Ideas and the way ideas are handled and brought to a conclusion (a decision) are vitally important.

A major difficulty in many meetings is that a logical, necessary, and appropriate order for coming to decisions is not followed in processing the types of information needed to arrive at the decision. Meeting masters learned some simple rules to follow. Let us begin by thinking about the kinds of difficulties that might arise.

Chapter 20 discusses in detail several examples of poor results of idea processing (e.g., Groupthink, the Abilene Paradox, Folly, the Garbage Can Model of Organizational Choice, and the Boiled Frog). Part of the reason they occur comes from something called *poorly structured problems.*

Poorly Structured Problems

There are two aspects to poor problem structuring. One of them has to do with the location in the meeting sequence, and the other has to do with the way in which the problem itself is approached.

In the first case, an item is placed on the agenda in the decision category without proper brainstorming. The reason brainstorming is at the end of the meeting is to allow a "decision-free" space where options can be developed free of the immediate press of decision. Premature scheduling of an item for decision will, paradoxically, cause delay in the actual decision itself. Meeting masters were alert to the complexity of problems, and kept an item in the brainstorming section until there were about three reasonable options. Two options have a tendency to divide the meeting participants, four options are like two, and by five options, members start grouping. While it will not always work, three seems close to ideal.

In the second case, it needs to be "guided" through an intellectual process. Most discussions of ideas begin with a problem. Even at this early stage, the problems are often structured in such a way that the group does not really know how to approach them. A number of years ago, Rittel and Webber (1973) developed an analysis of "wicked problems." Two of the criteria they mentioned are particularly destructive in a meeting (or group) setting: wicked problems have no stopping rule, and when discussing wicked problems, there is no right to be wrong.

First, if problems are formulated in such a way as the famous question, "When did you stop beating your wife?" it will be impossible to have a discussion, because there is nothing to discuss. One of the jobs that the meeting leader can do for participants is to phrase the discussion of the problem in such a way that it is very possible to take a variety of points of view without intellectual self-incrimination.

Second, the problem has to be set up in such a way that the participants can find some way to stop discussing. Most problems can be discussed endlessly. Under the rule of temporal integrity, time blocks were suggested as a way to create a natural stopping point. Taking that approach, meeting participants tried to fit the discussion within the time available rather than creating the time to fit the discussion.

Something other than time occasionally will be useful and necessary. One might wish to suggest some dollar or time parameters. For example, "Whatever we do has to happen within the next 2 months." The creation of parameters allows participants to focus much more usefully on the issue before them. Creating the structure that moves the problem from a wicked problem status to a manageable problem status is often a major, if not the major, characteristic skill of a meeting master.

The Management of Ideas

Idea management needs to follow a logical process. Jay (1976) suggests a system made up of the following five steps:

1. State the problem.

2. State the evidence.

3. Argue about what the evidence proves.

4. Decide.

5. Implement.

Similarly, Janis and Mann (1977) suggest proceeding with the following:

1. Identify the need or problem.

2. Generate alternatives.

3. Identify gains and losses to self and others.

4. Assess overall pros and cons.

5. Commit to action (decision).

6. Proceed to implement.

You can develop your own system. The key in any of these approaches is to move through some kind of problem-solving model. Almost any approach has the same overall elements.

The Problem-Solving Model

A good problem-solving model has six steps: problem specification, option generation, option reduction, selection or decision, implementation, and evaluation and recycle.

Problem Specification. The first step is some discussion of what the problem is, and that is why it is important to involve problem knowers. At this stage, one needs to avoid triteness, avoid indicating that the problem is just what it has always been, and create the conditions that allow for the open sharing of ideas and perspectives. It is sometimes good to chat with people ahead of time, one-on-one, to get their informal idea about what the problem may be. A chairperson can then begin a discussion with some degree of summary, in a way that does not identify anybody with any particular diagnosis.

In this way a range of ideas is put on the table, but nobody feels particularly attached to them, for good or ill. The use of a meeting aid is helpful here—a whiteboard or flipchart—to actually get the ideas or problems written down. Forcing us to write them forces us to be more concrete and more specific about exactly what we think, and allows others to visualize it by seeing it as well as hearing it. (Writing is God's way of showing us how sloppy our thinking really is!)

Option Generation. There is always a question about what alternatives might be available. Sometimes there are individuals within meetings who always argue for the most draconian, the most severe, or the most conservative, but high-quality decisions are best achieved if premature closure is avoided and a range of "might-be" ideas is outlined. The use of some kind of visualization technique, through whiteboard or flipchart, helps to get the details down.

Option Reduction. Then there is the selection of the relevant options. Sometimes what is involved is a combination of options. One of the great features about option listing is that it creates the possibility of doing a little combining, some from this option, some from that option. As was discussed earlier, option generation can be done outside of the meeting as well as inside. Wherever it is done, it is important not to overlook this step.

In a way, option reduction is the first step of the decision process. The broad generation of options in Step 2 leads to a lot of options, more of which than one can really deal. It is usually best to get down to between three and five options, and as I mentioned above, three is especially good. These initial steps are best handled in the brainstorming area.

Decision. The fourth step is decision or selection. I will discuss managing the decision point in Chapter 16, but for purposes here, let us just assume that we pick from among the reduced set of options, or combination of options, that seem sensible.

Implementation. This leads to implementation. Although the committee or meeting group as an entity rarely implements a decision, it always wants to know what has transpired after its decision, which is reasonable not only from the specific perspective of the decision in question but also as a kind of feed-back to how well the decision process is working.

Evaluation and Recycle. Finally there is the "look see" to assess how things are going and to ask if there are problems that need to be handled. Usually there are, and the cycle repeats again.

The Idea Flowchart

Ideas start out fairly abstract and, as discussion proceeds over weeks and months, often become more and more concrete. Not infrequently they leave the meeting place, are worked on by subcommittees or individuals, and then come back in a more concrete form. The discussion "boils down" the broad problem into smaller specifics. It is important in this process to seek to develop, especially for complex ideas, a flowchart in which one can see the more general and then less general developments that are going to be undertaken, and approximately when in the time frame they need to occur.

The flowchart is useful because one can begin by working back from a timely point. If a decision on X needs to be made by July 1st, where must we be in April, March, and so on, as we discuss this complex concept? This kind of record keeping helps keep groups on track. Furthermore, it also helps avoid constant back-and-forth movement.

Once a particular point of policy has been decided, it should be retained, unless there is overwhelming or massive evidence to the contrary. Otherwise, one is continually debating first principles and never gets into the level of detail necessary to make something work. Meeting participants have to keep on reminding themselves that certain decisions have already been made. Maybe they were not the ones that an individual favored the most, but to keep returning to it only causes aggravation and dysfunction within the idea-processing system of the meeting.

Destructive Opposition

One of the most difficult tasks in managing ideas is to avoid destructive opposition. This topic was dealt with in part when I discussed (in Chapter 8) the hostile devil's advocate kind of person. Here, though, I am not referring as much to the "affectual" or emotional side of criticism as to the intellectual side. Opposition is not always destructive, of course. It becomes that way if it blunts the creative spirit of the group. It is destructive because it diverts attention to securing the approbation of one particular person—the critic—rather than paying attention to the problem and the ideas available to solve the problem.

Devil's advocates are needed but, in this sense, they need to be kept in check as well. If such a situation develops, one might say something such as, "Terry, that's a good point; there probably are some problems with the proposal. What do you see as some of the good points?" (Of course, it is possible Terry will say, "There are no good points," but that kind of reply is rare in my observation.)

In General Versus Specific

Ideas discussed in meetings are made up of a central policy core and details on how that core is to be operationalized, such as a certain amount of dollars on X, or a certain amount of dollars on Y. Sometimes meetings get caught in an unhelpful oscillation between the general and the specific. At this point, it is beneficial to sever the relationship between the general and the specific. One could, for example, say to the participants, "It does seem that there are a number of us who are interested in supporting project Y. There are a number of details to be worked out, and I, for one will be happy to look into them and come back and share my findings with you. It would be helpful to know, however, whether we are in principle ready to go with this kind of support and at the point of taking that step."

In other words, the question asks the participants to allow the details to be worked out later, with their information and approval, and focuses their attention on the central matter at hand: the imperative of whether to move ahead. This technique is also useful when looking at documents. Individuals frequently become involved in editing documents before the committee's eyes. This is time-consuming and unnecessary. Phrases such as, "subject to the usual editing conventions" or "if anyone has any textual suggestions, I'll be happy to take them into account in the final draft—just give them to me by Tuesday next" are useful in helping the group to come to closure.

Conclusion

Ideas, as with feelings, need management. Management does not mean manipulation, covering up, or failure to disclose. Rather it means following some simple recipes that will help ensure the successful development of the discussion and help bring it to an appropriate and productive conclusion. In the handling of ideas, there are some well-accepted sequences: first the discussion of *this*, followed by a discussion of *that*.

Most of us do not really think very much about what these sequences are and follow them only at random. (But we know them because after an unsuccessful meeting, participants say, "We were all over the lot.") Maybe in some sense Cohen, March, and Olsen (1972) were right—decision making is like throwing stuff into a garbage can. But even if a garbage-can model of decision making has been our history, we are not condemned to its repetition. We can do better than a "random walk" through a decision process.

10

Managing Bases for Decisions in Meetings

The Decision Rules

Meetings are an information processing system, the output of which is a decision stream. The next two chapters focus on what may be the heart of the meeting process: how to get groups to come to decisions and to accomplish this task with due regard for the range of inputs, the complexities of the issues, and the press of time. I am not speaking of jamming something through the group. Indeed, if the tips and hints already suggested are followed, the group will be in a much better position than it has ever been to think through issues. But as the saying goes, "You can lead a horse to water but you can't make him drink."

In the meeting world, one can do all the kinds of preparation and development discussed in this book, but still not get the group to the decision point. Decision avoidance is so deep within us that special techniques and knowledge are needed to actually manage the decision point. What has been discussed up to now is the necessary but not sufficient condition for decision.

AUTHOR'S NOTE: This research was sponsored in part by the 3M Company's Meeting Management Institute, which deserves special mention and credit here for helping me pursue the idea of decision rules and developing them in some detail through intensive observation of decision-making groups.

Why Do We Avoid Decisions?

Decisions are avoided for several reasons. One reason is that they allocate goods and values in the system. Someone gets the cellular phone; someone else gets the pay phone. Someone gets the corner office; someone else gets a desk in the basement. Interests and goods and services, however, are only part of the difficulty.

Another reason decisions are avoided is interpersonal relations. We do not want to make people feel bad. We do not want to deal with the emotions of the losers, even if we think the allocation is the right one. And if we are losers, we hate to deal with the self-satisfaction of winners—even if they conceal it. A related point is that we often do not want to harm group cohesion by bringing up "issues," a problem that leads to Groupthink.

A third reason has to do with the way that the discussion process is managed. We fail to have enough good ideas and enough innovation and inventiveness to figure out ways to make the decision better. The highest-quality decision is the one in which all stakeholders gain (see Chapter 15), but getting to that decision is not easy. One must find the appropriate alternative first. Even if it is found, the group may reject it because at the decision point, the group pulls back. A number of useful techniques can help here. First, an understanding of decision rules is needed.

What Are Decision Rules?

Decision rules are those internalized norms that we bring to all groups that make a decision legitimate. To be successful in producing high-quality decisions, one must be aware of the concept of decision rules, the different decision rules that are present within the group, and the ways in which these decision rules might be managed to be helpful to the group in its decision-making task.

Cultures provide belief systems that make some things okay and other things not okay. In the Middle Ages, if a king said, "Do X," that was legitimate because the king was legitimate. If someone challenged the legitimacy of the king, as happened frequently, then the laws and rules that he promulgated would be similarly questioned. Even today, attorneys argue whether certain types of authority have jurisdiction in particular cases. These are legitimacy questions, and it is helpful to know that in all groups there is a range of decision rules that provide legitimacy when invoked.

A second point to consider is that there is more than one rule. There are actually several. To make matters worse, these decision rules conflict with each other in the sense that following one rule will not necessarily lead to the same result as following another rule. It is because a range of different interests needs to be taken into account in decision making that there is a range of rules. Most of the time, the group or group members are not conscious of the rules, except when they are violated. Let us outline the rules first; then we can talk about some of the conflicts.

The Five Decision Rules

Most groups operate with five decision rules—not because group members have agreed to the rules, but because the group members are part of the culture in which they live and they bring that culture with them to meetings. The five decision rules include the following:

1. The extensive decision rule

2. The intensive decision rule

3. The involvement decision rule

4. The expert decision rule

5. The power decision rule

THE EXTENSIVE DECISION RULE

A powerful decision rule—and one of the most powerful in Western culture, generally—is the rule of "one person-one vote," which I call the extensive decision rule. It seeks to assess the breadth of preference in any group. How many want to go to McDonald's for lunch? Hands go up, and the ayes have it. We have used this rule to make decisions for as far back as we can probably remember, as far back as kindergarten. Why is that rule not enough? It leaves other interests unattended.

THE INTENSIVE DECISION RULE

Within groups and within decisions, account needs to be taken of those who feel most strongly about particular items. That a majority, or even two thirds of the people, wishes to have lunch at McDonald's does not do very much for vegetarians, who may feel that there is nothing for them to eat. In fact, if you are a vegetarian, you would be a fool to call for a vote, because you would always lose. There just are not enough of you to make a difference.

Rather, you would prefer to articulate a different rule, one that says that the group really should account for your minority status and strong feelings about not being able to eat meat. You should not be forced, therefore, to eat meat. To some extent, all groups recognize this rule, and a lot of times discussion in groups is an attempt to see who feels strongly and how strongly. It is not an easy thing to measure, this strength of preference, and it sometimes requires work to tease it out. Nonetheless, groups are often unwilling to act decisively until they know what the distribution of intensity is within their particular decision domain.

THE INVOLVEMENT DECISION RULE

Most decisions involve some kind of implementation. Those who have or are likely to have responsibility for implementation get additional say in what the decision is to be. This rule is exemplified by the following formulation: The one who prepares dinner gets to pick dinner. In other words, the operative rule is neither what everyone would like nor how strongly some people feel (though those are taken into consideration), but rather the question of who does the work of cooking. In a company, firm, or government bureau, the ones at the table who have to carry out the decision often have more say than others.

THE EXPERT DECISION RULE

We all recognize that some people know more than others. Some issues have specific expertise allied to them—a medical or legal issue, for example. Other issues may have a range of technical and expert testimony that is needed before a decision can be reached. Typically, discussion in a group seeks to tease out or unpack which elements of the decision are subject to expert opinion and what the expert opinion is.

THE POWER DECISION RULE

This rule asks a single question: What do the boss or powerful people want? Groups are always interested in what influential people desire. This interest does not necessarily mean, as in a Groupthink case, that they will automatically go along with a particular view. Certainly experience with power teaches that if they are going to go against the boss or go against someone with influence, they would prefer to know ahead of time what the attitudes of those individuals are and what some of the specific substantive points in their thinking might be. This allows the group to account for the positions of people with influence when they make their own decision.

Each of these rules is present and operating in most groups. Although groups have norms about which ones they prefer, all were there and could be used, because they were brought in with them by participants themselves. It can be seen clearly that different results would be forthcoming if different rules were invoked consistently. What might occur by majority rule (or two-thirds majority if one prefers) might be different from a decision that would take minority and intensive interests into account, which might differ from a third decision that would take those who have to implement the decision into account. Any of these three might differ sharply from what the boss or experts might want.

How Do These Rules
Actually Operate in Meetings?

These rules operate in what might be called the deep structure of meetings. They are frequently not articulated, although they will occasionally surface in ways that can be seen. For example, someone might say, "Let's just vote then," and someone else will say, "I don't think we're ready to vote yet." What can "ready to vote yet" mean? You either vote or do not vote. The person often means that there has not been enough discussion.

But to what end is more discussion helpful? Persons may be speaking on behalf of themselves or for the group in saying, "We don't know enough about what the bosses want," or "what the experts think," or "what the implementers think," or "what those who feel most strongly think," and for this reason, voting is premature. Many groups do not vote at all; they have a "consensus" approach.

The point to keep in mind is that, in many cases, as group members are articulating different rules, the group, in effect, stalls. The conflicts between the rules become manifest in the conflicts between proposals or augment the conflicts between proposals. Somebody says, "Vote," and then somebody else says, "Voting wouldn't be fair." Then somebody else says, "How many votes does the boss get?" and so forth. One of the big reasons for nondecisions in groups is gridlock or, better yet, "rulelock."

Decision Rulelock

Decision rulelock occurs when the results that would be produced by the application of any one rule neutralize the results of the application of other rules, stalling the decision. Sometimes the power rule (What does the boss want?) comes into play and the group then discusses "The boss was going to do that all along"—an analysis that is actually untrue. The boss, on the other hand, said, "They talk and they talk and they talk and they talk, and nothing happens, so finally I had to make a decision. I'd prefer that it not be that way." Both fail to understand what is happening and wind up blaming the other.

The Confluence of Rules

More by luck than anything else, the reverse situation sometimes occurs, and there is a confluence of rules—two or three rules moving in the same general direction. Meeting masters often worked toward articulating the operative rules, and the following guideline seemed to emerge: When a candidate decision can meet and be shown to meet, three or more rules, the likelihood of a "go" is high. If it is under three, the likelihood of a "stall" is high.

What this observation means is for a group to feel okay about moving ahead with a particular decision there has to be a gut level satisfaction that enough of the rules are satisfied to make the decision defensible or legitimate. The difficulty is that individuals in the group are not always aware if a rule has been satisfied because of the deep-structure nature of the rules. Thus, leadership, in the use of decision rules by meeting participants and chairpersons, is extremely essential. To make matters more complex, ordinary language is used in articulating the presence of the rules.

Consider something like the following statement made in a meeting I was at not too long ago: "It seems like Bill's proposal looks good." The translation is, "Let's accept Bill's suggestion." Why? Consider the following reasons: "Most of us seem to be in favor of it" (Reason 1, the extensive rule is satisfied); "the boss doesn't care" (Reason 2, the power rule is satisfied); "the Office of General Counsel has given it the okay if that's what we want to do" (Reason 3, the expert rule is satisfied); and "although there are different points of view, none of them seems tremendously strong in opposition" (Reason 4, the intensive rule is inoperative).

This simple statement contains four of the rules, but one has to pay careful attention to see how they get articulated. Let us review their application. The phrase "most of us" invokes the extensive decision rule. "The boss does not care" means that the power rule has just gone to zero. "The Office of General Counsel has given it the okay" means that the expert rule has been addressed. That opposition is recognized, but its strength rated as only modest lets meeting participants know what the climate of intensity is in this particular case. Although the issue was extremely complex, I said to myself, "This is a go." Indeed, it was.

As this example demonstrates, the relevant decision rules need to be articulated—pointed out to the group and vocalized—for them to be seen as relevant.

They come at a particular point in the process of decision crystallization—exactly when this vocalization should occur is the subject of the next chapter. In any event, awareness of decision rules and a recognition of their need to be explicitly shared at the appropriate time is likely to be new material for most meeting participants, and will require a little thought.

What Should I Do?

I would like to suggest that readers not rush out and *do* anything right away with decision rules. Rather, take a few moments with this material, digest it, and then *observe* in a number of cases the actual decision process and see if you can spot the operation of the decision rules. Most people have a "Eureka!" reaction. They say, "Wow! Now I understand more about what's been going on and in ways that I didn't understand before." With respect to the decision rules, careful observation would be a good place to start. After one has seen several rules cancel each other out or form a confluence that leads to a decision, one is ready to manage or orchestrate the processes that are helpful to the groups in question.

Conclusion

It would seem that a pluralistic society would have pluralistic decision rules. A decision rule is a norm or value that makes a decision legitimate. Five of them have been identified in this chapter. I pointed out that they each conflict with the other—the application of one leading to decisions that would not occur if an alternative one had been applied. Groups spend a lot of time trying to figure out which decision rules are applicable and where the group stands on the variety of rules. Understanding that decision rules exist will be a major insight for most meeting participants, and as they begin to see how they are applied and not applied, a major force of leverage to assist groups in coming to decisions will be available.

11

Managing Decision and Choice

Decision and choice are the heart of the meeting, and we have already begun discussing it through the introduction of the material on decision rules. Everything we do in a meeting leads up to this point—the preparation, the organization, and the minutes of the previous meeting. Decision is the name of the meeting game. If it cannot be done effectively, efficiently, and within appropriate time frames, then all the previous material will not have been helpful.

As with a dinner party, one can go to extensive preparations and still have a flop. The preparations represent necessary but not sufficient conditions for a good time. There is the party itself and the processes of the party—décor, food, the conversation, and interaction of guests. So it is with meetings.

Managing decision and choice actually helps the group to achieve decisions, but does so in a way that is not heavy-handed or authoritarian and that has true regard for the feelings and ideas of those present. It is a very challenging and exciting task. The bad news is that it is a very complex package of tasks. The good news is that the complexity can be mastered and one can become adept at providing this assistance. It will be a source of immense organizational influence, but it, too, begins with the need to understand certain things about the concept of decision itself.

Decision Is a Collective Noun

We tend to use the word *decision* in our culture as if it referred to a specific thing. Take, for example, the phrase "Let's decide what to have for dinner tonight." Although we are referring to a single decision, there are really a large number of elements in the question. Among them are topics such as the food, the time, and who does the preparations.

Thus, it is helpful, if one is to understand the decision-assistance process, that a small vocabulary be developed. The question "What shall we have for dinner?" is a question about a *decision mosaic.* It has many smaller pieces within it that, when assembled, create the "decision." The decision is really built from a lot of smaller decisions. This larger picture is the decision mosaic. Learning about the decision mosaic creates the need for a new vocabulary.

The Decision Mosaic

Imagine a mosaic pattern built of interconnected stones—each of the stones can be thought of as a *decision element.* An element is the smallest piece of the mosaic—the stone—that cannot be broken down further. Something such as the meat for dinner or the time to eat in the example given before would be an element.

Decision crafting assembles the elements, one by one, in a certain order such that the entire mosaic can be pieced together. *Decision sculpting* looks at the total mosaic to determine whether, in the development of the total picture, something has been overlooked that should address the whole.

A *round of discussion* refers to going around the table or room once and allowing each person to speak at least once (and preferably only once), or allowing those who wish to speak the opportunity to speak.

The *end of a round* is that psychological moment in decision management that must be exploited by someone in the group or the moment will pass and its potential will be lost. Decision opportunities are like freeway exits. They only come every so often, and one must exit the round during the window of opportunity. If one misses that opportunity, one has to go on to the next exit. (As a practical matter, the group is actually waiting for something to happen at the end of a round. If nothing happens, the members go on to round two, usually repeating themselves so that round two is round one, again.) It is in the space just at the end of a round that the meetings masters went about their work.

That work—the work of putting all of these pieces together—is the process of decision crystallization. Decision processes are sort of like links of sausage. There is a plump part and a squeezed part. Decision crystallization is where the squeeze occurs.

Decision Crystallization

Helping a group crystallize a decision is very difficult. It requires all of the preparation that has been discussed before, but it also requires the ability to work in real time in the middle of a meeting maelstrom of competing viewpoints and perspectives and agreement and disagreement and still be able to help the group come out on top with a high-quality decision. It can be done, but it requires competence, not luck.

In a typical process of a successful decision crystallization, an item from the agenda has been introduced. Let us say it is a Category 4 item (recalling from the rule of the agenda bell that Category 4 is not the toughest but is moderately tough). Recognizing that what is actually written on the page may be more of a decision mosaic than a decision, the meeting master would seek to begin the discussion with the *determinative element*—that element in the decision mosaic that, when decided, tends to define the positions of all the others. For example, element *A* is such that *B*, *C*, and *D* depend upon it; element *B* does not influence *A*, but does influence *C* and *D*.

In the case of dinner, for example, depending on a variety of factors, it is most likely to be the main course or the meat dish. That typically requires the most effort to prepare, demanding time, choice of wine and vegetables, and so forth. Beginning with the determinative element is important because if one begins with lesser elements and then approaches the determinative element, one might then have to discuss the subsidiary elements again in light of the decision made on the determinative element. Once the determinative element has been decided, the meeting master proceeds through the second most determinative, the third most determinative, and so on.

Figure 11.1 illustrates this situation. (Some readers will recognize this situation as a Guttman Scale.) Choosing the order of the items is a skill that takes practice and honing of the intellect. When you can do this, the discussion proceeds smoothly, because there is less rework (starting with *B*, going to *C*, then to *A*, then discovering that *A* impacts *B* and *C*, doing *B* and *C* again in the light of *A*, etc.). Items fall in a dominance hierarchy. It helps to take the most important one (*A*) before the second most important one (*B*) and so on.

The chairperson, or person who is crystallizing, listens carefully. A lot is going on. Consider just a few things: (a) assessing which decision rules apply, (b) considering how substantive elements of the discussion might be harmonized, and (c) scanning for underparticipation. One is simultaneously recalling decision rules, and judging which ones apply as well as assessing the actual substantive content of the discussion and how it might be configured to make a decision. One is also assessing the process of participation itself and whether it is open and inclusive or whether certain individuals have been shut out or put down. This intellectual and affectual simultaneity makes the process of decision crystallization a difficult one indeed.

The process begins, as I suggested, at the end of a round of discussion. As noted, a round of discussion is that point in the group process in which everyone who wishes to make a point at that juncture has done so. Rounds of discussion are easy to recognize because someone might say something such as,

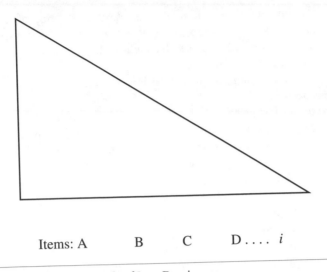

Items: A   B   C   D . . . . *i*

Figure 11.1   A Guttman Scale of Item Dominance

"Is there anything else? Does anyone else have another point on this?" and no one will volunteer. At this point, the process of decision crystallization is necessary. There are four stages through which decision crystallization passes, although as one observes it in practice, it seems like a single, fluid event.

The first stage is *summative reflection*—pulling together the key points made by the various individuals in a summary form. It should be emphasized that the discussion is usually disorderly with members saying a wide variety of things. The summative reflection organizes the "group view." At this point it is important for the crystallizer to say, "It seems like a good number of people are in favor of Elmer's proposal, whereas some favor Fred's proposal, and others feel that we should not move ahead at all at this juncture until Sid has had a chance to do some further checking." Summative reflection organizes and lays out, in fairly neutral terms, the views that have been discussed. Everyone can do a summary that favors one's own view; that's not the point of assisting in decision crystallization.

If summative reflection is stage one, stage two is the *action hypothesis*. At this point the decision crystallizer offers a suggestion for action. It is important that the suggestion be vocalized. Readers will see later that lack of vocalization is one of the causes of the Abilene Paradox. Somehow it is difficult for individuals in groups to understand what they might do without hearing it.

The third stage is *action legitimization*. This is the point at which the rules come in. It is not enough to suggest something; one has to give a reason why the suggestion makes sense. Here is where the decision rules come in. One needs to explain how this suggestion addresses issues of breadth of preference, depth of preference, implementation preference, expertise, and power. In actual discourse, this did not take as long as it might sound, and it appears very natural. An example follows shortly. It is at the end of this contribution that the moment of decision occurs.

Then the master moves to step four—*discussion refocus*. This is the act of pointing the group to the next element of discussion. If, say, one has just completed *A*, then the group needs to be guided to *B*. It will not necessarily go there at all.

Let me give a common example of this process. We are at a professional conference and in the lobby with colleagues. We are trying to decide where to eat. Everyone says essentially the same thing—"Anything is okay with me. It doesn't matter to me. You pick." So you say, "Let's have Chinese food." Suddenly the vocalization of a particular alternative crystallizes the latent preferences of others in the group, who say "No, no! I don't want to have that kind of food! Not on your life!"

I think we can see from this example that vocalization is essential. People need to hear the alternatives vocalized, and in hearing them, a reality is constructed. The important thing, of course, is not to become committed to that reality but to let it flow out for further review and discussion within the group itself.

The action hypothesis is followed, as I mentioned, by action legitimization. In the substantive suggestion, the phrasing is tentative, not authoritative or definitive, but it is definite enough to allow people to get the feel of a decision in the making. "It seems, therefore, that Bill's proposal is the one that we might want to consider going with." Legitimization provides the justification for the decision based on decision rules.

At this point, the decision rules are called into play again, although in ordinary language. One may say, "Most people seem to like Bill's proposal and the boss doesn't care." What groups apparently need is a *suggestion for action* plus a *reason for action*. A suggestion alone is often insufficient unless the reasons are so palpably clear that they do not need mention.

Two Possible Directions: Go or No Go

At this point, the group will move in one of two directions. One direction is affirmation. The decision crystallizer can see the nods and the facial gestures that indicate it is a go. On the other hand, participants may say, "No, wait a minute, I don't think that's what we ought to do at all." Participants who stumble into decision crystallization, in effect accidentally suggesting an action hypothesis, often become uptight and defensive at this point and either blame the group for disagreeing or become inappropriately defensive when group participants indicate they do not care about the particular option.

GO

Let us pick up on a positive scenario first. The action hypothesis has been stated, consisting of substantive and decision rule elements. Affirmations are given, and the last step in the process of decision crystallization is ready to be undertaken. This is step four, *discussion refocus.*

The decision crystallizer takes the next most determinative element and says, "Let's look at X, then," directing the discussion, which, agreement having been made, is now going to temporarily float directionless to an important new item. This process is repeated, element after element, until the decision mosaic has been built from small agreements about particular elements. At this point, the last step in the entire process occurs—decision sculpting.

NO GO

Suppose, however, that the negative scenario had manifested itself and one does not have agreement. This result is likely to be the more typical, especially as one begins to learn the process. At this point, one goes to round two, issue one. It is a second round of discussion, with a twist. One invites the group to look again at the alternatives available but asks the participants, in doing that, to hold back on the most popular alternatives from the last round. This holding back—to which most groups will agree—allows participants to think afresh and creatively, and the ensuing discussion seeks to uncover new approaches rather than simply restating the old ones just rejected.

Indeed, this twist makes the difference between a discussion that spins its wheels and a discussion that really progresses and builds. If participants are invited not to give up on, but hold back on, their initial preferences to see how the thing shakes out, the likelihood of a creative solution is greatly enhanced. After the second round of discussion, the process of crystallization occurs again. In this particular case, the action of the summary consists of material not only from round two but also from round one. Sometimes on complicated issues, two or three rounds of discussion are needed, and that is fine as long as there is a progressive sense to that discussion and wheel spinning is avoided.

Decision Sculpting

Once a decision has been built, decision sculpting begins. Decision sculpting involves stepping back, taking a look at the whole mosaic, and taking care of and accounting for all the interests. Sometimes in our attention to single items, we overlook the shape of the whole. That something has been overlooked is nobody's fault, and nobody deserves to be punished; now it is simply a matter of fixing it. Sometimes, if the decision is very complex, it is good to let it sit until the next meeting, view it as a preliminary construction, and then come back with a fresh look at the whole thing and proceed.

In the process of "decision building" you cannot always be sure of how the whole thing will look when you are done. Thus, reserve the right to look at the whole as a whole when you are done. That at-a-distance perspective might allow for something you missed in the building portion to be corrected now.

How Can I Learn This Technique?

The technique of decision crystallization is a complex one because it is handled in real time and one does not have much opportunity to prepare, to go over drafts, and so on. Thus, practice is the only answer to the question of how one learns this technique. One must practice in meetings. The first step is to outline, perhaps with pencil and paper, the key steps. One might even prepare a couple of index cards as an aid.

The second step is to discuss it with others. Discussion will help drive the points home to you. Also, it will assist in developing a sense of what objections participants might raise so that you will be better able to deal with them in your own thinking processes.

Third, one might wish to practice in meetings that are not high powered. One can even practice at home—a little role-playing and some pre-meeting exercises will help.

In a meeting, do not try to crystallize more than one issue unless you are the chairperson. Unless done expertly, it can be viewed as an attempt to "be big" or take over. The reason for this negative view (at least initially) is that we have been trained to expect the chairperson to do something, and if the chairperson does nothing, we do nothing; we just complain. As time goes on and individuals see the helpfulness of the technique, however, this view will lessen, but until that time, modest application will give you a developing experience on the one hand and avoid creating a lot of controversy on the other.

The Decision Array

The decision array involves doing the right thing, the right way, the first time. It is often unclear exactly what decision is. To use one example, company managers and meeting participants often have different, or at least conflicting, ideas about what is wanted when something is "up for decision." Sometimes company managers want the group to decide, but do not let the group know this, and the group thus hesitates. The company managers then make the decision, and the group complains that management wanted to do that all along.

Other times company managers want input and perspective, but reserve for themselves the right to decide, thus irritating the group—not because the group objects to that, but because they feel "suckered." Much angst in organizations—often called "responsibility without authority"— arises because company managers and others fail to clarify exactly who can do what about which items.

Generally items can be distributed in the following array:

- The decision has been made. We are discussing implementation.
- The decision will be made by management, but they would like your input. However, because other inputs will be sought, the final decision may not reflect all (or any) of what we discuss here. You have a voice, not a veto.
- The decision will be made by management, and management has other input already that will be reflected in the presentation to you. You're more or less last in the input line, and the decision will take into account (which may mean reject) what is said here. Management will explain its thinking to you, however.
- You—the group—can make the decision within parameters set by management. Management agrees not to micromanage. You—the group—can make the decision. It will really help if management's parameters or "decision opportunities" can be clarified before the meeting starts.

Conclusion

The process of decision crystallization is the core of the meeting process in the sense that decision is a core meeting goal. As suggested in this chapter, all of the preparation in the world cannot make the decisions pop out. They can assist and they can create the kinds of climates that will be helpful, but until groups become very experienced, they will often need help in the actual process of crystallization. The four-step process of decision crystallization—summative reflection, action hypothesis (including substantive suggestion and legitimization), and issue refocus, followed at the end by decision sculpting—provides a perspective on the deep structure of meetings and the way decisions are (or are not) made.

The outlining of the decision-process complexity suggests why decision-management assistance is needed. All too often, decisions occur by chance. Some elements of the process click and things work, but in today's competitive society we do not want to rely on luck. Luck will always be present, of course, but when there are things that we can do to improve the processes with which we work daily, it is fun and instructive to employ them in our own activities.

12

Managing Positions and Roles in Meetings

As already noted, Goffman (1959) emphasized the importance of roles in human behavior. His emphasis has special meaning for decision-making groups—one can view the decision-making group as a theater and can view us in the actual meeting itself as role players.

In the discussion of key principles, the role principle was mentioned. This principle suggests the idea that we tend, especially in American society, to blame individual participants for things that go wrong in meetings, to pick up on personality traits and argue that if that personality trait were different or that person were removed, everything would be okay. It should now be clear, however, that personality is present but much more as a marginal modifier than a dominant determiner of what happens in meetings. In particular, this chapter focuses on the roles that we play and the possibility of changing those roles, thus changing the behavior of others. We also have certain positions—especially chairperson and participant—and unfortunately, there is all too frequently a "position-role" rulelock. Let us begin by talking about the concept of positions and roles and then move into some consideration about their management.

Positions and Roles

Positions are official responsibilities to which one is appointed—the chairperson and the participant are two of the most popular positions. Roles, on the other hand, are kinds of behavior that one displays within a meeting context.

Box 12.1   **Positions and Roles in Meetings**

POSITIONS	ROLES
Chairperson, Member	Leader, Follower
	Task, Process
	Process, Task

The leader role and the follower role are two of the most common; task and process roles are also common. Roles are displayed in the box above. (I included *task* and *process* twice so no one would think that *leadership* is task and *followership* is process. One can lead and follow in each.)

Although one can be appointed to positions, roles are taken, earned, or given. One cannot be assigned roles in any official way.

What is important to recognize is that roles, apparently linked to particular positions, really should float freely and be exercised by all meeting participants. Hence, with respect to leadership, both chairpersons and meeting participants should exhibit the same behavior. With respect to followership, both chairpersons and members should exhibit it as well. Sometimes, it is important for a chairperson to let others take the lead in developing and pursuing a particular issue. The important point is to avoid assuming that participants are always followers and chairpersons are always leaders. There needs to be a diversity of position and role mixture.

The Chairperson: Requisites of Position Performance

To develop effective chairperson skills, it is important to understand what is expected of the position. What do people view as exemplary performance in a chairperson? What are the things that you, as a chairperson, might need to do to assist in the group's accomplishment of its goals?

CHECK OUT THE EXPECTATIONS

Perhaps the most important requisite of the chairperson position is to do a little work before one accepts it. First, one should seek to avoid simply being stuck with the chair position because one is handy. What that does is dump all of the problems onto you. If at all possible, talk with the sponsoring or appointing person or authority (and this might be an individual or a group) and find out what the hopes and expectations are. The essential questions to ask are these: What is expected of me? Will I have the resources to fulfill these expectations?

That individuals who appoint chairpersons (and groups that appoint chairpersons, as well) have expectations of accomplishment that simply cannot be met, or cannot be met with the resources that they are providing, apparently does not inhibit those individuals from making such appointments. Appointing a chairperson becomes a way of passing the buck. Most of you already know this to be true. The phrase "Let's appoint a committee" is a testimony to the inaction that is expected once the committee is appointed. People, however, tend not to think about chairpersons of committees and in what kind of a box they might have been put inadvertently.

NEGOTIATE APPROPRIATE EXPECTATIONS

The point of these meetings and explorations about the appointment to that position is to negotiate appropriate expectations and resources. One always should seek to avoid being put into a no-win situation. Because of the eagerness sometimes to pass the buck to a chairperson of a committee, it is not uncommon for appointed authorities and appointers to misrepresent the situation or to lie about what is expected. Probing here will pay great dividends.

Indeed, the bottom line is as follows: Avoid assuming a chair position in a situation in which expected results are impossible unless you can negotiate appropriate resources needed to accomplish the desired goals. This guideline will be useful whether one is being appointed to a committee that has a life over a year or one is simply asked to chair a particular meeting. Despite all the kind words, most people have results in mind, and the question of whether the structure allows those results to be accomplished or whether one is dead in the water before the swim meet begins is always important to ask.

PROVIDE WRITTEN MANDATE

For any group meeting (except a one-time meeting situation), it is imperative that the chairperson provides a written mandate to the participants. This mandate accomplishes a couple of purposes. The first purpose is that it provides for the transfer of intentions from the appointing authority through the chairperson to the participants. Time after time, participants do not know why they are gathered.

In the classic training film *Meetings, Bloody Meetings*[1]—starring the popular Monty Python actor John Cleese—the actor's character is on trial for criminal misuse of time, among other charges, and the judge asks him what the purpose of the meeting was. He replies, "It's the weekly meeting." "Why?" the judge asks. "We have it every week; we always have," Cleese replies.

In short, Cleese's character had no idea why they were meeting; it was just an organizational tradition that every week they met. Because he did not know, no one else knew. If you have a weekly staff meeting, for example, in which you are acting as the chair, then you should provide for the staff in attendance a statement of the purposes and goals for this kind of weekly gathering. One should never assume that everyone knows.

The second purpose is that such a mandate puts the chairperson's spin on the more general instruction. Individuals have a unique way of approaching things, a particular way that they prefer to handle things. One may as well share those views at the beginning. A written mandate clarifies, focuses, and centers the group's purpose and becomes the core value that informs the choice of agenda items, operating style, and so on.

BE A STATESPERSON, NOT A PARTISAN

One of the most difficult twists that chairpersons-to-be must consider is whether they can move away from the partisan role of a participant and become a statesperson. Chairpersons often think that because they are now the chairperson, they get their way. Nothing could be further from the truth. Indeed, one expects participants to have certain points of view that, within the bounds of good taste, they will push. Chairpersons, however, because they have additional authority, must hang back and not enter the fray as frequently or express an opinion too boldly.

The chairperson's job in this respect is similar to that of the orchestra conductor. Let us suppose that a chairperson had moved from position of first violin to orchestra conductor. The unfortunately typical chairperson conducts for a while, then jumps back into the violin section, fiddles around there, jumps back on the podium, and is thus very inconsistent. The chairperson does not provide orchestral leadership, and irritates the new first violinist.

"Statespersonship" involves a balanced view of the items under consideration and a balanced selection of repertoire—that same orchestra conductor should not, for example, choose only orchestral pieces that feature the violin. All the other sections would be upset, and the audience would be bored. Statespersonship involves not pushing for one's own point of view exclusively, but facilitating the entry of a range of viewpoints and persons into the discussion. If you are the chairperson and someone asks what your personal view is, you can say, "I have the tendency to Version A" (note the tentativeness and potential openness of the word *tendency*); "however, I can see merit in Versions B and C" (note that although an indication of one's tilt has been given, one is not excluding the validity and possibility of other views).

Why all this tiptoeing around? I used to work for a chairperson who said, "Let's discuss Tropman's proposal. I think it stinks. I just want you to know where I am coming from. But if anybody has anything to say, be my guest." Naturally, everybody played "Kick the Proposal" or "Kick Tropman." The thing that is very important in playing the chairperson's role and the reason why statespersonship is essential is *authoritative augmentation*, which suggests simply that what the chairperson says has more weight, carries more influence, and is more difficult to oppose than those things that other people say. Opinions from a chairperson are similar to fists of a boxer—they must be used judiciously and cautiously.

Even *Robert's Rules of Order* recognizes this necessity by providing that if someone chairing a meeting wishes to speak to a motion, they need to leave the chair. Statespersonship is a change of orientation that is required when one becomes a chair, although most do not do it.

USE THE INTERROGATIVE TECHNIQUE

Chairpersons should seek to use the interrogative technique. Simply stated, it means one asks questions rather than makes statements. Questions, paradoxically, are more powerful than statements. Questions allow the chairperson to guide the discussion down certain routes without necessarily raising a position.

A chairperson could say, for example, "Let's take the discussion in this direction." Others could say, "No! We don't want to!" When phrased as a question, however, such as, "How does the proposal under consideration deal with issues of this type?" the word *type* serves the same as *direction* mentioned a moment ago and moves the discussion in the desired direction. Because questions do not push, no one pushes back. Thus, questions do not raise opposition.

Questions also keep the dialogue open. All too frequently, discussions in meetings deteriorate to dialogue such as, "T'is!" "T'aint!" "T'is!" "T'aint!" "Shall we step outside?" Introducing questions such as, Why? How? In what manner? Could it be this way? or Might it be this way? accomplish the same purpose but through a dialogue that progresses rather than one that simply anticipates a winner and a loser.

FOLLOW THE RULES

Chairpersons are expected to establish rules and follow them within the meeting itself. In this volume, a number of rules for running effective meetings have been provided. They are great guidelines, but it is the chairperson's job to assert their operation in particular meetings, enforce them, and to also follow them. Thus, chairpersons unfortunately have a special responsibility to model good meeting behavior.

They must arrive on time or a bit early. They must end on time without fail. They must follow a rough time order interior for the meeting. They must intervene at key points and either move the discussion around or wrap a discussion up, using decision-crystallization processes. As the narrator in Cleese's sequel, *More Bloody Meetings*, says, "Protect the weak and keep the strong under control."

At one level, being a chairperson is not terribly difficult. It does not require magical knowledge, secret skills, or Promethean doggedness. It does, though, require that one master a few basic skills.

The Meeting Participant

Somebody once said, "What is there to learn about being a meeting participant? You simply show up and doze off until the meeting is over." Unfortunately, this attitude is all too prevalent with respect to participation: We will come, we will wait for somebody to tell us what to do, we will probably object to it once that person does tell us what to do, and then we will quit, complaining about the meeting in the hallways and restrooms afterward. Participants have a number of responsibilities, and although they are not earthshaking, if they are not carried out, a great deal of trouble can occur.

BE PREPARED

Participants have a responsibility to review and think about the material in advance. This responsibility mirrors and balances the responsibility of the meeting organizers and preparers to provide such material. It is an exchange relationship.

PARTICIPATE APPROPRIATELY

Members should challenge themselves with participating at about the same level that is the average participatory level for the meeting in question. We are all aware that some meetings are high-participation types, in which everybody is getting into the act. Other meetings are much lower and more tempered. One should seek to evaluate one's own behavior based on what the style is for the meeting in question and adjust one's own comfort level within that framework.

In my own case, for example, I tend to be a high-participatory type. In meetings in which the culture and style are more subdued, however, I try to cut back. This was true of meeting masters as well. Once you had the opportunity to see them in two or three different meetings, you noticed that they did not always manifest the same level of participation. There are a couple of reasons for this adjustment, each of which relates to a fundamental underlying fact:

Others notice how much you participate and adjust their view of your credibility as a result.

Overparticipators have a discount rate applied to them. The person who is always jumping in is recognized as somebody who is not giving others a chance and is thus punished by the group. Even though the ideas may be good, the group establishes a norm of acquiescence, and if one overparticipates, the ratio is lowered. On the other side, if one does not participate at all, one is thought of as being critical and hostile. It may be completely untrue; one may simply not be feeling well. But it is important to be aware of how groups think and try to fit your own style to theirs.

AID THE CHAIR

Most people seem to feel that it is the chair's responsibility to keep order in the meeting. When participants are acting inappropriately, they will complain later that the chair did not do anything. This blame is unfair, since keeping order in a meeting is a function of everybody in the meeting. Thus, on occasion, members can come to the aid of the chair.

One can occasionally say things such as, "Sid, I think you're being a little hard on Sally's proposal, at least from my point of view, and I think Sally feels a little bit bad about it. It may have some problems. I can see one or two myself, but I think we owe it to her and to all of us to have a balanced discussion." Sid, who had been pounding on Sally's proposal mercilessly for the past few minutes, is suddenly reined in by the comment.

But the chairperson did not do it—a member did it. When it is done, other members affirm support and the chairperson chimes in as well. Sid has been effectively boxed in. The chair is aided because the chair cannot exercise discipline all the time. It reverses the kind of student-teacher relationship that emerges with the teacher being the total custodian of order and the students completely taking no responsibility for the activity at all.

The scenario could be reversed, however, and the chairperson could suggest to Sid that perhaps he was being a little bit tough. At this point, the chairperson would very much appreciate a member saying, "Yes, I agree with that, and perhaps we could focus on some of the positives as well as the negatives." Few things are more troubling to a chairperson than to perform the intervention that, were it not performed, everyone would complain about and then find members averting their eyes and failing to provide support.

DON'T DUMP ON THE GROUP

Many members seem to feel that if they do not like a proposal, it is sufficient to say, "I don't like that." Unfortunately, simply stating the negative is insufficient.

What is really needed is something more assertive. *Dumping on the group* refers to the practice of expressing your feelings and then somehow expecting the group to find out the answer to the question "If John doesn't like this mileage proposal, what would he like?" The antidote to not dumping on the group is to provide a solution as well as a question when one is raising problems with a particular proposal.

Consider something such as the following: "I really don't like this mileage proposal, because I feel that it is not really enough money to make it worthwhile for me to use my own car. Twenty cents per mile is well below what others provide. However—and this may not be possible—at 27 cents a mile I would find myself in support." The virtue of this type of contribution is that it focuses the discussion on an alternative proposal rather than inviting the group to say, "How about 21 cents, John?" and so forth.

The difference may seem subtle, but meeting masters, as members, always try to offer ideas of their own, even if they are very tentative. In the example just given, the speaker recognized that the proposed higher amount might not be okay, but, it at least provided a focus for the discussion to move toward a strategic goal.

PROVIDE SUPPORT FOR OTHER PARTICIPANTS

The last point that a member should bear in mind is the obligation to occasionally provide support for other members. In a sense, this point was mentioned in the example of putting Sid in brackets because he was being too harsh on another member's proposal. But the point needs to be stressed explicitly—one needs to listen, to nod, to attend, and to validate (more on these points in the chapter on tasks and functions). Membership requires attention to the other members and to their interests and needs as well as your own.

Membership, then, is a vital active position. It is not simply sticking oneself in a chair and putting a zipper over one's lips. Individual members will find a lot of different ways to make their position their own, but it is important to keep in mind that there are many specific activities that are expected of a member.

The Leader

Leadership, of course, is a role. One cannot be appointed leader—one has to take that position or accept it as a gift from others. So much has been written about leadership and so many feelings and concerns and hopes become invested in the idea of leadership, that one almost forgets the central simplicity of leadership itself. In a nutshell, leadership involves taking risks that allow others to take risks. Leadership involves getting out in front of others in a way that allows them to move comfortably into the space behind you. Leadership involves risk taking, which at its best is not for personal gain.

The meeting masters were leaders who understood the necessity of putting oneself ahead, saying that sometimes-unpopular thing, vocalizing the difficult problem, and setting the strategic mission. It was not their exclusive mission. If you play the role of leader and risk proposing new directions for consideration or knotty problems that are important for us to address, and if you do so in ways that we recognize and understand are not simply your pet directions and hang-ups, we will in turn reward you with prestige. One is not a leader when one simply advances one's own agenda—that is, "boss-ship." Leadership involves not only creating possible futures but inviting others to join in creating those futures as well. Leadership, therefore, involves a vision of the future, risk, and a certain degree of selflessness.

Selflessness is central to the leadership concept. To get to a preferred future, many people have to be involved. One cannot chase someone into the future. For this reason, there are two aspects to leadership: outlining a possible future and creating (or helping to create) the conditions, the climate, and the excitement that allow people to climb on that bandwagon. Ultimately, those who climb on the bandwagon are the ones who have to put the package together.

There has to be, in the famous contemporary phrase, *buy-in*. This becomes crucial. That buy-in is needed does not mean that leaders do not have ideas. Rather, it means that they are able to build futures out of the pieces of ideas— their own and others'. They are able to see how some of those pieces may relate to an overall vision. It truly becomes something more than "my idea of where we should go is . . . "

It is hard to fool dogs, kids, and meeting membership. Meeting participants quickly figure out when your suggestion is strictly something you want to do or is something that you might have some interest in but you are open and willing to discuss it with others.

Because it is a role, leadership floats between and among positions. Often, of course, the chairperson takes leadership, but just as often, other participants take leadership. One can think of a meeting as a football game in which there are various positions, but there is also an overall assumption that individuals will take leadership as the game is in process. No one person in the football game is *the* leader. Yes, there is a quarterback, but the quarterback is equivalent to the chairperson. As the game unfolds, everybody has to pitch in. There is only so much a quarterback can do, and if the quarterback is not protected by the line, he is going to be sacked.

Not only does the football analogy suggest that there are many leaders, but it teaches us about the dynamic aspect of leadership. It can pass from person to person as the game unfolds. Thus it has a fluid, ever-changing quality to it. The opposition passes, the defense intercepts. Suddenly, all the defensive players become offensive players (in a manner of speaking, of course). The person who has intercepted the ball begins to run toward the goal, but without blocking there will never be a successful run. Almost as a single unit, the players begin to scan the field; some block right around the runner, others may dash ahead (taking leadership) to do preemptive blocking or position themselves downfield so that when the runner gets there, they will be available to run interference.

Teams with that kind of assignment—everyone has a position, but everyone also is supposed to help everyone else—are good metaphors for the meeting process. On the very best teams, *everybody* takes leadership. The baton passes from person to person, and the excitement that is created by the ability to take leadership is immense.

The Follower

Followership is the other side of leadership. It, too, is fluid, dynamic, and ever changing. If one takes leadership too much, one is seen as "hogging the ball." In general, one should seek to alternate between leadership and followership roles for several reasons. For one, it is very difficult to exercise leadership in every area and on every issue. Part of leadership is being able to feel comfortable about risk taking, but it is also knowing enough to be sensible and appropriate in a particular area. Thoracic surgeons take the lead in chest surgery, but they do not take the lead in other kinds of surgery.

A second reason is that in the very best meetings, everyone has a chance to lead and to follow. If one is always leading, then others must always be following, and a routine or rut develops. Followership involves stepping back and letting someone else move into the leadership role for a while. Meeting masters do, both in structure ("Jim, at the upcoming meeting will you take the lead in discussing this issue?") and in process ("Jim, as we're discussing this, I know that you have a lot of knowledge about this area. Could you get us going?").

Followership, then, is essential so that others can lead, and because without followers there are no leaders. Leaders need the support of followers. Nothing is more discouraging to a potential leader than seeking to develop a leadership intervention and finding that there are no followers.

Task and Process Roles

If the leader-follower role dyad is the most famous one, the task-process division comes in a close second. Task roles are those that keep the group on point.

Process roles are those that attend to issues of support, encouragement, and validation. Each of these roles is usually played many times by leaders and followers in the typical meeting—unless of course a participant is locked in one role or another.

Problematic Roles and Some Antidotes

There are a lot of roles we play in meetings that are not helpful. I am going to mention a few by way of illustration, and suggest, as well, some helpful roles.

NEGATIVE ROLES

- The Controller—one who is overly concerned about doing things "the right way," which is usually their way
- The Blamer—one who has the tendency to always find out—or seek to find out—"who is responsible" as opposed to looking at the problem and fixing it
- The Pleaser—one who always says, "Excellent point!" regardless of the content of what you say
- The "Distractor"—one who continually introduces sidebar items and distracts the group in other ways (being on a cell phone, for example)
- The Terminator—one who says, "Gotta go, gotta go—can we wrap this up?"
- The Ghost—one who can never remember being at the previous meeting and also can recall nothing they had agreed to or agreed to do
- The Whiner—one who is always complaining about the temperature, the chairs, the room, the agenda, and the world

ADDRESSING PROBLEMATIC ROLES

One way that the masters dealt with negative roles was to assign positive ones. Individuals do not necessarily want to take negative roles; they often just sort of "fall into" them. That means that there is opportunity for "rescripting"—providing something better. As a chair or member, leader or follower, you can yourself take on some of the roles below or ask others to do it.

- The Task Taker—one who stresses focus on tasks
- The Risk Taker—one who suggests the new and balances negative roles
- The Caretaker—one who cares for the fragile and provides support
- The Note Taker—one who records the conclusions
- The Decision Taker—one who suggests decision options
- The Undertaker—one who buries the dead, helps closure, and frees up the future

Conclusion

Positions and roles are important components of the meeting dynamic. Positions are things to which one can be appointed. Roles are played within the meeting context. With respect to the chairperson and the member, some specific kinds of expectations (one might think of this as a job description) loosely settle in each of these two areas.

It is helpful for people to know what they are to do when they take on a position in a committee or meeting. They can then do an inventory of themselves and their skills with respect to the tasks and see how good a fit there really is. Roles, on the other hand, are dynamic, fluid, and changing. Leadership involves risk taking and "futuring"; followership involves buttressing and supporting. Both are needed, and one should take care that one does not overdo one role as opposed to the other. It is important to stress that each position requires—indeed, demands—both roles. Otherwise, the meeting becomes a frozen structure and the real meeting is later, in the hallway.

Note

1 This film, originally released in 1976, and its sequel, *More Bloody Meetings*, originally released in 1984, are available through Video Arts. The script of the first film is based on "How to Run a Meeting" (Jay, 1976).

13

Managing Tasks
and Functions in Meetings

Throughout this book, I have talked about various activities that meeting participants and chairpersons undertake to make meetings better. In effect, I have been talking about tasks and functions. It seemed important to bring all of this material together in a short, focused discussion of task and function management. Tasks and functions are *metaduties* of the group—all groups have to pay attention to task management and functional management if they are to be successful, regardless of what the specifics are. An engineering group designing a fender has the same imperatives as a United Way allocating committee deciding on a budget, and as a brass player in an orchestra: Group members needs to be aware not only of their own part, but to pay attention to the whole as well—the car, the budget, and the performance.

Tasks refers to the job of keeping the group moving toward the goal (the goal task) on the one hand, and ensuring that appropriate process toward that goal has been maintained (process tasks) on the other hand. *Functions*, however, refers to the ongoing need to introduce a constant supply of ideas into the discussion (intellectual functions) and to pay attention to feelings and emotions (interpersonal functions).

Goal and Process Task Management

One requirement for every group is to move regularly and methodically toward their goal. In meeting groups, committees, and boards, this goal is simple—decision making. Decisions need to be made, and the group needs to move on to the next category of items to consider.

Members and chairpersons, leaders and followers, should continue to ask themselves, "Are we making progress toward our goal?" Part of the contribution of every participant should be to help the group move toward its goal. Decision crystallization is one example of a technique that can help in goal attainment. Evaluation, which will be discussed later, is a retrospective attempt to ask, "What decisions were made? How good were they?"

But the headlong rush toward goal attainment can, on occasion, develop into a preemptory process. Although nondecision is the most frequent kind of group outcome, there is a minority of cases in which premature decision occurs. Thus, attention to process is vital. *Process* refers to the discussion steps mentioned earlier (state the problem, present the evidence about the problem, argue about what the evidence means, decide, and act).

The two-meeting rule, in which an item is scheduled (first for discussion, but not decision, and then for decision), is an important process element. Process means not being too fast but not being too slow. Whereas an overemphasis on goal attainment can result in premature decision making, an overemphasis on process can result in no decision or decisions that are so late, so untimely, that they have no effect. All participants need to be sensitive to goal and process in meetings.

Intellectual and Interpersonal Function Management

Meeting groups, committees, and boards are driven by ideas on the one hand and by feelings on the other. Thus, as we step back from the meeting itself, we can see that a decision is really a set of ideas that has been put together in a package and approved for whatever the appropriate next step is (e.g., another group or implementation). Surrounding that idea are other ideas that have to be processed or fit together. So part of decision processing is idea processing.

It is also the processing of feelings and emotion. People have feelings about certain ideas. People get attached to them. People are more or less sensitive to disagreement, criticism, and attack.

Many times, excellent ideas are not advanced not because of their technical merit but because they were unable to secure enough emotional commitment from the participants of the meeting. Other times, absolutely rotten ideas go forward simply because people's emotions become involved in the discussion and they are prevented from saying things by either themselves or others because of these feelings, or they say things that they regret later.

INTELLECTUAL FUNCTIONS

Several techniques have been mentioned that deal with the area of intellectual or idea management. One of them is to become an idea champion, to take a leadership role with respect to a particular idea. To champion it or to be a champion means to advocate it and to push for it, to get the information that is needed about it, and to become its sponsor within the group. Especially for new ideas, a champion is often needed, because new ideas are excessively vulnerable.

In addition to the idea champion, roles of devil's advocate and angel's advocate can be used. Most of us have heard of the devil's advocate. That role is very appropriate, but it is best applied to established ideas rather than new ones. The reason for this suggestion is that, as the meeting masters knew well, new ideas are very vulnerable. New ideas, because they are new, often do not have all their "parts"—in other words, the champion may not be able to respond effectively to all questions simply because enough time and work has not been spent and done. Entrenched ideas, however, are often captured by the past, by tradition—"We all know that . . . "—and therefore appear to deserve careful scrutiny and deference.

New ideas, on the other hand, can benefit from the angel's advocate—one who is very supportive of an idea, sees reasons why the idea might work, and provides validation and encouragement. Angel's advocacy is especially appropriate when applied to new ideas.

Intellectual functions essentially relate to the development and encouragement of new ideas within the meeting framework on the one hand and questioning and testing of old ideas and the assumptions on which those old ideas are based on the other. Meeting masters do not overdo either the encouragement function or the questioning function. They are sensitive to the need for a balance. They probe continually for possible limitations with respect to existing assumptions while also being extremely sensitive to the need for creativity, innovation, invention, and new approaches.

Indeed, one of the exciting features of the meeting masters' meetings was that it was not "s-o-s-o" (same old, same old); rather, there was often an opportunity to deal with the developing, the new, and the innovative. Paradoxically, despite that it is common wisdom that people are frightened of the new, of change, of the different, I would say that the single most exciting theme within the meetings run by the meeting masters was the presence of innovation and creativity. Perhaps the difference is that the meeting masters allowed the participants of the meeting to be creative; hence, it was not somebody else's creativity but our own creativity that we had a chance to express. Although somebody else's change is often resisted, our own proposal for innovation often receives our wholehearted support.

INTERPERSONAL FUNCTIONS

Interpersonal functions have already been covered in some detail when I discussed the management of emotion and affect in Chapter 8. Only a brief recap is needed here to underscore the constancy of this pressure. Wherever people are present, feelings and emotions will be present, along with ideas and proposals. It is almost as if we have two parts of our brain to deal with these two elements. The meeting masters continually "dual-scanned" for (a) developing ideas and approaches and (b) developing affects and feelings.

All kinds of cues were used as indicators of developing feelings and emotions, the least of which were what people actually said. Because the meeting masters had already visited with, talked with, and knew something about the meeting participants (even in a new meeting group, they had taken time to touch base), they already had a feel, a sense, a perspective about where participants stood regarding their commitments and convictions. As the meeting developed, meeting masters were especially sensitive to nonverbal communication.

As I discussed this aspect of meeting management with the meeting masters, they almost universally said that nonverbal communication was "where it's at." They observed the frown, the grimace, the curled lip, the foot and pencil tapping. They observed participants who leaned back and in fact moved their chairs back to dissociate themselves from the proceedings, as opposed to participants who seemed to move forward and engage themselves with the very same proceedings.

The first technique meeting masters employed to manage interpersonal functions was *noticing*. Meeting masters noticed what was happening, and as a guide for us, we should be aware of the nonverbal communication that meeting participants are sharing with us. Indeed, participants may not even be aware that they are sharing their feelings with the group through these actions. The question, however, is what to do about that. It is one thing to notice, another thing to act.

To diffuse potential negative feelings, meeting masters used a second technique: *ventilation*. Rather than let participants who were clearly giving messages of anger and disaffection simply remain present and scare the rest of the participants, meeting masters "lanced the boil" of anger and asked the individuals something that allowed them to express themselves. (One master articulated a principle of "No festering!" though all had something like it.) For example: "Sheila, you seem to be disturbed. Perhaps I'm not sensing your feelings very accurately but I wonder if there's something on your mind that you'd like to tell us." Almost invariably once permission was given to share feelings by the chairperson (or by a participant, because as I mentioned, meeting masters were not always chairpersons), the participant in question got the feelings out.

There are several reasons why this is important. The affected participant is very likely to act on the basis of feelings rather than arguments. To the extent that feelings are present, information becomes irrelevant. Until those feelings are ventilated, shared, and dealt with, any kind of argument or evidence for the case is going to be more or less useless or ineffective.

We have all had the experience of trying to present "incontrovertible facts" about a particular plan to individuals who simply keep saying "I don't believe that," "It doesn't seem right," and so on. One often has the impulse under those conditions to strangle recalcitrant persons and wonders "what possible evidence could they want?" It is not a question of evidence. If somebody believes that the answer lies in the numbers, whereas somebody else believes that the answer lies in a gut feeling, then neither will be convinced by the perspectives or evidence of the other.

In fact, for the person who believes in gut feeling, the numbers are really not evidence at all. Nor is gut feeling evidence for the person who believes in numbers. Thus, one of the things that chairpersons and others can do to make meetings better is to ventilate feelings. Do not let them build up. Do not let them fester, as the person before mentioned. They affect not only the person but also others in the room as well. We are all too aware of issues on which Joel or Jane are very sensitive; we tend to bypass them, not address them directly for fear of unleashing a storm of emotion.

A third technique is *validation*—a process by which the validity of the feeling is recognized, whereas the validity of the result is put aside. One of the great secrets about the management of interpersonal functions is the great desire to have feelings rather than points validated. Hence, when someone speaks passionately about a particular point of view, one might think that what that person wants is agreement with that point of view.

For many years I thought this was true, but as I observed the meeting masters, they often said something such as, "Jane or Sid, I understand and I think we all do know how strongly you feel, and we all respect the depth of your feeling. Others, however, seem to take a different point of view." Time after time, the persons in question—Sid and Jane—seemed to be satisfied. That is because they got, in effect, half a loaf—recognition of the validity, the rightness, the appropriateness, and the strength of their feeling. Once this was done, they were often willing to set aside their commitment to a particular result.

Ventilation and validation are only a couple of the interpersonal management functions with which one needs to deal. Protecting the weak and keeping the strong under control is another kind of interpersonal management function that is needed desperately, and it was discussed in Chapter 12. Some of us—perhaps since first grade or earlier—have been vocal and unafraid of participating in collective situations. We are happy to share our view, and indeed, because others tend not to share theirs, we may participate more vigorously.

Others, though, also since the first grade, for whatever reasons, may be hesitant, shy, or unwilling to participate publicly. We know these individuals because they sit in our meetings. All too frequently they say nothing, and then, in the hallway debriefing, the more vocal among us complain that Sid and Jane never really said very much and we lament their lack of participation. Sid and Jane, meanwhile, now feeling okay about talking with each other, complain about the vigorous and overparticipative nature of the rest of us and how they never had a chance to get in.

It is pointless to argue about who is right here. What the meeting masters did instead was to invite Sid and Jane to join the discussion during the meeting. They addressed questions directly to them, as I have already mentioned, and sought to bring them into the loop.

There is yet another interpersonal function that is needed. One might refer to it as good taste. Basically one is sensitive to issues of gender and race. What is involved here is the direct confrontation of individuals in the group who make hostile or offensive comments. This is one of the few times when individuals are directly challenged and devalidated.

If someone made a comment such as, "Well, that's just what a woman would say," or "It's my experience that Jews, African Americans, Asian Americans, et cetera, take just that point of view," chairpersons and members who were masters suddenly became a blizzard of action, as occurred when hostile comments were made. Comments such as, "Jack, I don't think that those kinds of comments add to the discussion" shot like a bolt from an otherwise quiescent and amiable facilitator. Jack often sat stunned. A clear, unequivocal statement had been made to his face that such kinds of comments were outside the norms of this group.

Frequently, other phrases were added, such as, "I know most of us agree" or "Most of us feel" or "We all take the position here that . . . " so that it was not simply one person who was speaking his or her own views but one person who was speaking on behalf of the group. Immediate, direct, firmly diplomatic denial of the validity of those kinds of comments was extremely important, not only in shaping the behavior of the individual in question but also, and perhaps more important, in setting group norms for future behavior.

Conclusion

Tasks and functions involve goal and process elements on the one hand and intellectual and interpersonal elements on the other. It is crucial that all four be performed simultaneously. This simultaneity and multiplicity of activity makes meetings so amazingly and enticingly complex. The management task is as challenging as any. Although meetings can be small and apparently simple, even routine perhaps, they require many dimensions of attention at the same time. Task and function management is one aspect that requires constant attention.

14

Managing Conflicting Values in Meetings

Conflict management is one of the key tasks that the meeting masters were good at, whether they were a chairperson or member. Conflict management at its most basic level involves recognizing and accepting the fact of differences and seeking ways in which parties with different approaches, goals, and investments can emerge victorious. This simultaneity of victory is conventionally called *win-win,* and it focuses attention on the available options or approaches that can provide some kinds of victory for meeting participants with differing perspectives.

A problem with many traditional conflict-management approaches is that they make some assumptions that get in the way of creating possible solutions. In particular, they often assume that individuals are clear about their values, that they have a well-ordered set of value preferences (so what "winning" is to them is clear), that they do not have any internal conflicts, and that the external set of pressures is also well ordered and clear. Usually, these assumptions are all incorrect in any specific case, though apparently only some of them need to be incorrect to create problems and difficulties.

Alternatively, it turns out people have many values, and these values—like achievement values and equality values or results values and effort values—conflict with each other. There is not only conflict between people, there is conflict within people as well. This truth may be expressed as a "dualistic theory of values." The meeting masters had an understanding of this theory (though they would not have thought of it as a theory) in general and in respect to the particulars of conflicts as they emerged in policy discussions.

The Dualistic Theory of Values

Much work on values assumes that values come in lists. Everyone has a single list. "I value this, I value that, and then, I value something else." The phrase "and then" adds a dimension of prioritization; "first, I value *X*, second, I value *Y*, and third, I value *Z*." Although popular, this approach to values does not describe the way most people think about values (or think they think about values), and although thinking about values may at first blush be an esoteric topic, it has immediate, practical ramifications in meetings in that what people often argue about with others (and more frequently than one might imagine, with themselves) are values.

A few points about values and their structure ought to be made from the outset. First, most of us hold many values—not just one or two. Second, it appears reasonable to argue that the values we hold conflict with each other—maximizing one value "costs" the other value. Maximizing competition costs the value of cooperation. Most of us believe in both competition and cooperation—it is not a question of whether we value one or the other; it is more a question of how much we value one or the other. (Quinn, 1989, presents work on a competing values theory that is a good anchor point for those who wish more information.)

In particular, a competing theory of values is most useful (Tropman, 1989; Tropman & Morningstar, 1989). The dualistic perspective suggests that the actual values we learn come in juxtaposed pairs. Competition and cooperation are one example. Competition is not the opposite of cooperation; rather, one can be highly committed to both competition and cooperation, in which case there will be a lot of conflict between the two approaches.

Some people can be highly competitively oriented and not cooperatively oriented at all; in which case, the conflict may be less severe but nonetheless present because it is often the case that the value to which we are not as committed goes to zero. Without going into a deep discussion of value conflict here, suffice to say that within most meetings one of the issues has to do with the conflict of values *within* persons as much as *between* persons. There is no secret to managing these. Rather, the secret lies in recognizing that almost all of us have conflicting commitments within ourselves. Meeting masters were able to use this insight as a way to smooth agreement and take the edge off loss.

What Are Key Conflicting Values in American Organizational Culture?

In any given culture, there are common value conflicts that are the focus of recurring debate. In American organizational culture, there seem to be nine value pairs that continually surface and thematically enter discussions regardless of what the actual discussion of the subject is. They are the following:

1. Multipurpose versus "unipurpose"

2. Pragmatism versus excellence

3. Status versus class

4. Personal versus organizational purpose

5. Empirical versus qualitative decision-making bases

6. Disposable labor versus intimate concern for labor

7. Achievement versus equality

8. Results versus effort

9. Results versus control

As with the decision rules, we bring these values from the culture at large. They are guests at our meeting table, entering, participating, conflicting, and, as always, requiring administration, management, and "executiveship."

Multipurpose Versus Unipurpose. Some individuals approach organizational decision making with a single purpose in mind—the bottom line or some other single issue. Others approach a decision from a multipurpose point of view, arguing that the organization has a range of goals to be achieved. The bottom line is one purpose, but others may involve integrity of the client base, retention of customers, increasing market share, the need for reinvestment, and so on. Our internal pressure for accomplishment tends to support a single focus—let us do something and do it now.

The difficulty here, of course, is that a unipurpose focus can lead to premature action. On the other hand, a multipurpose focus can lead to a stalling of action, in which so many purposes are simultaneously present that one is unable to choose and thus unable to act. The meeting masters were able to recognize the power and pressure of the need for "unipurposeness," and balance it with the recognition that there were other purposes to be achieved as well.

Pragmatism Versus Excellence. One value that most of us have is a pragmatic one: Let us do it; let us get it done. If there are details, possible ethical hesitancies, and so forth, let us set them aside because the most important pressures are action and accomplishment. In the business community, "ship it" is the phrase often used for this kind of pragmatic approach, indicating that even though the product is perhaps flawed or has a problem, let us get it out there. An excellence approach, on the other hand, says that we must not do anything that does not represent the highest possible quality. No performance or product is satisfactory until it has met the highest possible standards.

Obviously, there is a conflict between these two values, both of which most of us hold. There is the desire to get something done. That is the pragmatic wish—let us not worry too much about all of the entanglements; let us move ahead. But there are also questions about excellence, quality, and top-of-the-line performance—let us not ship until we are completely sure that the entire product is flawless. Naturally the first value may lead to premature action and the second value may lead to no action—yet both values have merit. Frequently in a meeting, fights occur over exactly this value: Let us move ahead on the one hand versus let us do our best on the other. Meeting masters are able to follow the difficult course between the two values, an accomplishment enhanced by the recognition of the presence and validity of both values within the group and values within each person in the group.

Status Versus Class. Some issues are decided through an emphasis on group gains versus individual ones. Sometimes the results benefit the group or corporation as a whole; these would be considered *class-oriented results.* But there are also results that benefit individuals on an independent or one-by-one basis; these are called *status results.*

Consider a meeting, for example, regarding $100,000 available for some kind of salary-compensation allocation. Some people may feel that an improvement in the fringe-benefit package (class result) or an across-the-board increase (class result) is the appropriate way to go. Others may feel alternatively that a bonus (status result) or merit increase (status result) is the way to go. The difficulty, of course, is that the discussion of the specific problem before the group—how to allocate $100,000—is confounded by conflicting commitments about how resources should be allocated. Part of the discussion will focus on the specifics at hand, but part of the discussion is a kind of morality play in which issues of a much larger compass are being argued and debated. Meeting masters were able to recognize the presence of these kinds of discussions and desires, validate them, and yet keep focus on the issue at hand.

Personal Versus Organizational Purpose. Some of us approach most issues with a single question—What is in it for me? Yet we are aware that there are implications for the organization with which we work. Others approach most discussions with a different kind of orientation—What is in it for the firm? Whether they themselves gain this time around or not is of lesser importance.

This conflict, both with respect to any specific issue and in general, is known as the *conflict between personal purpose and organizational purpose.* It is imperative that both organizational purpose and personal purpose be attended to in any discussion. All of us have some commitment to each, although the fraction varies. Meeting masters recognized each and attended to both.

Empirical Versus Qualitative Decision-Making Bases. Some people prefer to approach decisions "by the numbers." Others, as mentioned before, prefer to approach decisions by the gut. Numbers rarely tell the entire story—we often do not have the right numbers and we do not have them in time. Nonetheless, they do have some validity and merit. A more intuitive approach is often spoken of as valued and valuable. Still, it is hard to check or verify and, perhaps most important, hard to defend if one goes wrong. Yet most good high-quality decisions represent a blend of numbers and guts. Recognizing and balancing these two approaches, these two styles, was an important skill of the meeting masters.

Disposable Labor Versus Intimate Concern. Most decisions affect people, and one's view toward people is often at issue with respect to a particular decision. One view is that people are simply parts of the organization, to be used and disposed of as the occasion demands. When times are tough, people are laid off. When times are flush, people are hired. And so it goes.

There is a different approach, however, that views employees and customers as valued links to the organizational effort. These employees' and customers' interests should be represented "at the table" even though they may not be present at the meeting. Hence, decisions that would harm employees, customers, suppliers, and vendors are viewed very seriously and taken only as a last resort. Actions that might enhance the quality of life of those same groups are viewed affirmatively. One can see the conflict between these two points of view—one that takes the value of people as paramount and the other that views labor as essentially a replaceable part. Any specific issue can invoke this larger value conflict. Once again, it is imperative in achieving a decision—and the meeting masters were consistently able to accomplish this—that both points of view are regarded as valid and validated and that they are accounted for within the discussion mix.

Achievement Versus Equality. Most of us are committed to the idea of achievement. Such commitments of course create difference among people, and to some extent there is nothing wrong with creating differences, but it does create winners and losers. At the same time, we are interested in spreading resources around. Fair play is always balanced by fair share. People struggle between the goals of achievement, say, or wealth, and the goals of more equal distribution of wealth. Meetings where issues of across-the-board increases versus true merit increases is a place where this issue surfaces.

Results Versus Effort. All employers want results. However, results are not always forthcoming or possible. It is also important that people keep on trying (effort). On the other hand, again, effort alone is not enough. Balancing the relationship between results and effort is a key organizational dilemma that comes up all the time in meetings.

Results Versus Control. Results come up in another way as well. All managers want results. However, all managers want controls to be in place and procedures followed. Dilemmas occur frequently when results are produced with unorthodox methods that threaten control.

Managing Value Conflicts

The point here is not to provide an exhaustive list of value conflicts but rather to indicate the presence of these value conflicts and suggest some ways that individuals might manage them.

The first technique is *transcendence recognition*—participants in a meeting recognize that the arguments, conflicts, and differences in view involve only part of the issues immediately under discussion. The differences are also about the values that we hold. It is perhaps for this reason that trying to change individuals is so difficult—their values are not going to change. One might think one is discussing a simple bonus plan, but it is in fact discussing issues such as pragmatism versus excellence, status versus class, and so on. Recognizing this extramural presence and its power and influence is the first technique of value conflict management. (Here, again, noticing makes a difference.)

The second technique might be called the *value finesse.* The finesse involves avoiding taking on someone's values directly. It is perhaps a law of human nature that the more one pushes, the more resistance one gets. Thus, if someone tries to say to an individual deeply committed to personal purpose that organizational purpose is at least as important, tremendous resistance will be encountered—the entire progress of the meeting could be stalled or unravel. The finesse involves finding a way to work around that particular commitment.

Fortunately because commitments are not unitary, the most obvious way around them is to appeal to *other* commitments held by the same individual on that same dimension. It is not necessary, therefore, to get people to give up their commitment to personal purpose, to suggest that "in this instance" or "for this purpose" or "at this moment" they also recognize the value of organizational purpose. In effect, it involves simulating, invoking, or enhancing the other value on the same dimension or within the same matrix that individual holds.

Individuals are not being asked to give up anything but are asked to invoke something that is already present within themselves. This difference may seem subtle. I can assure you that it is not. It is powerful and has often been the key to unlocking a very positive result within a meeting.

A third technique is validation. This was mentioned in Chapter 13 and takes its cue from the well-known phrase, "I'd rather be right than president." When it comes to values, this phrase applies to many of us. We would rather be right than win. Or to put it differently, being right *is* winning.

Hence, in a discussion of allocating money if the tendency of the group seems to be moving toward bonus (a status-based approach), in conflict with some others who feel that across-the-board approaches are more valid (a class-based approach), then one might actually have a sort of two-level win. This win can occur by recognizing the validity of the value of across-the-board while at the same time recognizing the necessity of bonus in this instance. Those who value across-the-board can savor the "values victory" of having been "validated" even though they "lost" in the specific instance. Those who favor the other approach can savor a win in that, in this instance, they got what they wanted.

Such a perspective recognizes the complexity of levels that is often implied by "winning" and avoids the defeatist approach of loading all the meeting's eggs in a single basket on this issue. Rather, when a more complex picture is presented, several people can win different parts of the picture. This is a win-win that does not mean that a single decision is acceptable to both. Rather, it refers to the multiplicity of decision elements and exploits the fact that some people can win in some elements and all other people can win in other elements.

Conclusion

There are many value conflicts that are brought to the meeting table. These come from society itself and add a dimension of complexity and a layer of difficulty to the discussion of any specific issue. The presence of such conflicts suggests that the discussion of any specific issue is never such; rather, it invokes, invites, and involves other issues of a value nature. The values-conflict approach suggests both a complexity and a way out of the complexity. The complexity is that most of us have many values, each of which conflict with the other. This creates a very problematic management situation. On the other hand, even though we are committed to X, we also have some commitment to Y, and this duality of commitment can be used if the idea of win-win is phrased more generally, more inclusively such that some people can win on value grounds, whereas others win on specific implementation grounds.

The issue of value conflict, then, and its management suggests one very important and overarching observation that what happens in a meeting is not only a result of what is going on in the meeting but also a result of the traditions, cultures, and values that are brought to the meeting by the participants and by the information that is shared. It is imperative to recognize that not only is there the complexity of simultaneity—many things going on at once—but there is also a complexity of depth. The first might be called horizontal complexity or horizontal simultaneity, and the second might be called vertical simultaneity. In the former, one pays attention to interpersonal, intellectual elements, goals, processes, functions, and so forth. In the second, one pays attention to the precipitating (here and now) elements as well as the predisposing (there and then) elements.

People do not come into meetings as blank slates. People come in with values, commitments, and convictions, and the issues, important as they are, provide ways as well for individuals to express their values. Anyone who thinks that what is "on the table" is all that is on the table is sadly mistaken. Anyone who forgets, however, that what *is* on the table really is on the table is also mistaken. Vertical complexity needs to be recognized as well as horizontal complexity. The meeting masters had this richness of view, and now that the rest of us are aware of it, we can begin to undertake it as well.

15

Managing the Evaluation Rules

The whole purpose of the techniques, principles, and new paradigms introduced here has been to help meeting managers become meeting masters.
The goal of the meeting master is high-quality decisions—achieving that
combination of perspectives and actions that satisfies the largest number of
stakeholders and that has the potential for enduring over time.

Organizations, as with families and individual lives, are run out of their
decision matrix. We can look at an organization in a number of ways. In *Images
of Organization*, Morgan (1986) suggests a variety of ways—the organization
as a machine, an organism, a brain, a culture, a political system, or a psychic
prison. One additional way is to consider the organization as a decision
matrix—hundreds, even thousands, of decisions being made every day, most
of them in meetings. And of course, meetings are not only "the weekly meeting"
but also meetings with one's husband, wife, or partner, kids, parents, boss, a
subordinate here or there, and so on.

Out of this array of meetings, a decision stream emerges; the many streams
combine into a decision matrix. What the organization is, then, is the sum total
of its decisions, and anyone interested in quality or in producing quality
service comes sooner or later to be interested in the quality of decisions. As
I suggested in Chapter 4, the quality of decisions drives the quality of the
product. For this reason, high-quality decisions are not only a goal in and of
themselves but also a means toward the end of total quality meetings, which in
turn is an aspect of total quality management.

Approaching the analysis of decisions from a quality point of view is not an
easy task. There is a lot of conventional wisdom about decisions—after a meeting, people will say, "That was a good decision," and others will agree. But it is

not immediately clear, or even intuitively clear, what is meant by a good decision. The paradox, however, is that the speaker and the listener seem to have some common frame of reference for understanding what they both are talking about. It is what they are each talking *about* that is the subject of this chapter.

Many people identify decisions with results. In a way that is true. It is a result of an information-processing activity that has achieved a closure. A decision might be thought of as a plan for action. As already discussed, it is really much more a collective noun than a single thing. It is made up of a lot of small parts knit together or built into something we call a *decision*.

In that sense, a decision is a result. However much action the decision is in this sense, it is not action in the sense that action is some kind of consequence or effect from the decision, as many believe. One might call this "outcome." The decision, however, is only the first step in an equation that results in outcomes. Consider the following equation for a moment:

$$O = D + I, \text{ or}$$
$$\text{Outcomes} = \text{Decisions} + \text{Implementation}$$

As most organizational practitioners know, a final outcome or result is dependent on not only the decision but also the implementation process. Each variable in the equation has a range of values that it can acquire: A decision can be of high or low quality; an implementation can be of high or low quality. Sometimes this variation works to mask the actual underlying process. For example, a low-quality decision can sometimes be saved by high-quality implementation.

Conversely, a high-quality decision can be sabotaged by low-quality implementation (e.g., working to rule, that passive-aggressive pattern in which employees follow *every* rule, no matter how inappropriate). Perhaps the most excellent results are achieved when there is a high-quality decision as well as high-quality implementation. Again, the most god-awful results may derive from rotten decisions and despicable implementation. Consider Table 15.1. The difficulty in analysis is that there is a degree of overlap and conditionality. On the overlap side, it is often not clear where a decision ends and implementation begins, as I discussed in Chapter 10.

In particular, those who are involved in implementation have a greater say in the actual decision—hence, built-in overlap. Conditionality refers to the extent to which known downstream elements, such as implementation parameters, shape upstream decisions. Knowing, for example, what your spouse might tolerate for dinner may shape your decision about what to suggest. Alternatively, knowing the evening schedule both of you have (implementation

Table 15.1   Types of Outcomes as a Result of the Quality of the Decision and the Quality of the Implementation

Quality of Decision	Quality of Implementation	
	High	Low
High	Great outcome	Ruined by poor implementation
Low	Decision saved by great implementation	Disaster

factors) may affect your suggestion with respect to the complexity of the dinner menu itself.

Difficulties notwithstanding, it is important that we seek to analyze the series of decisions produced by meetings and see whether they are any good. There are two major approaches to this problem: the rule of decision review and the rule of decision autopsy. First, however, we need to discuss briefly the salutary effects of the evaluation process itself.

Evaluation as a Salutary System

A salutary system is one that has a positive spin-off as a result of the system itself. The purpose of introducing this discussion here simply is to indicate that the system of rules that I am about to share is good, but so are alternatives. These rules have been used in various applications in numerous settings. These rules seem to work in most settings. But other approaches might work as well, or better, and might articulate more effectively and more efficiently with particular cultures and organizational styles.

I would therefore like to urge readers not to become caught up in arguments about the validity of any particular system. Rather, I would like to emphasize the point that the introduction of a review process itself changes the meeting process and begins to improve it slowly. Because when people realize they are being evaluated, they tend to observe their own behavior with somewhat greater scrutiny with an eventual eye toward looking good. Hence, decision review provides two very useful functions for the meeting in question. First, it specifies that the result of the meeting is to be decisions; that provides great clarity right from the start. Second, by creating the future potential for oversight, it puts oversight in mind as part of the meeting process. This creates a truly unique—at least for today—set of conditions. Almost no one oversees what committees, meetings, or boards do. Having to revisit an issue from an evaluative standpoint gives one pause for thought and is almost always helpful.

Steps in the Evaluation Process

Evaluation should be viewed as a process rather than a point in time. Evaluation, as with total quality management, is a journey. It is not something that one picks up at one particular point in time and then suddenly *does*. Rather, whatever one does is based on and must include prior steps.

In the next section, I will provide some specific activities for evaluation decisions, but these are based on and require prior actions and set the stage for following ones. An important overview of those actions has already been mentioned—the announcement of an evaluation process. This announcement sets the stage for evaluative structures, creates the appropriate expectations, and builds the scene that will be played out as the evaluation drama unfolds. Without that, the sudden announcement of an evaluation of this or that appears jerky if not ill timed or ill tempered.

The Evaluation Process

Within this overall template, a series of five steps is useful to keep in mind. Taken together, these five steps represent the evaluation process. They are

1. Goal setting

2. Monitoring

3. Oversight

4. Assessment

5. Appraisal

GOAL SETTING

The first step is to begin by setting some goals for the meeting. Typically, both task and process goals are important. Task goals refer to the accomplishment of decisions and actions—getting work done. That might be described as effective meeting goals. Process goals—having a process that starts on time, ends on time, is authentic, allows for participation, and so on—are also important. We might call these goals meeting efficiency.

Effectiveness is doing the right thing; efficiency is doing things right. Neither is useful without the other. Goals established, then, we can move on to the next four steps in the evaluation process.

MONITORING

Monitoring simply refers to the ongoing review of whether things are going okay. In the case of meetings, monitoring will refer to seeing whether the meetings actually started and ended on time, whether agendas are out, whether minutes are getting out, whether reports are done according to the rule of reports, and so forth. Continual attention needs to be paid to such tasks. The feedback that monitoring provides is very useful in and of itself and leads to the third stage—oversight. You can use the Keep, Stop, Start (KSS) System mentioned in Appendix B.

OVERSIGHT

Oversight refers to the checking against standards. Throughout the book, a number of rather specific guidelines have been given. Some were just mentioned (again!)—start on time, end on time, keep a rough time order interior to the meetings, deal with items on the agenda, do not deal with items not on the agenda, and so on. The KSS provided in Appendix B can accomplish this easily. The point is that oversight allows for some correction to occur as one begins to see that some of the targets have not been met.

ASSESSMENT

Assessment involves relatively important and potentially fateful midcourse corrections. Basically, assessment occurs in about the middle of the time span in question—at the middle of an academic course or at the 6-month period if one is looking at a yearly evaluation. Say, for example, that one began to implement some new meeting technology and sat down after a 6-month period and, using material from the monitoring reports and the 3-month oversight analysis, had a serious discussion about whether all was on target and how things were proceeding. Important changes might result from this kind of meeting.

APPRAISAL

Appraisal, in the usual case, might be a year-end effort to look at exactly how the committee or the meeting series had gone over the past year. Enough time has passed to see whether some of the new technology has had some impact. A review of various rules and the extent to which they have been truly implemented is part of the appraisal process. In addition, information from the *decision audit* and *decision autopsy,* which will be mentioned in the next two sections, is also brought to bear.

At this point, the group sits back and tries to ask the question, "How are we doing?" from a process point of view as well as from a decision-making point of view. Fateful results can come from this kind of look-see. The group may, for example, entirely reconstitute itself, seeing that it has received bad marks in both areas. It may redouble its efforts, seek to identify problems and difficulties, and move on.

The evaluation process, as discussed here, refers primarily to the process of the committee, the board, and the meeting series up to the appraisal process. Appraisal means that a judgment is made based on information from monitoring, oversight, and assessment stages. Information also is brought in from the decision audit and decision autopsy and a thorough, integrated review of the meeting is undertaken.

One may feel that this process is a little bit elaborate for "just your weekly staff meeting." However, if one reflects on the costs of "just the weekly staff meeting," then these procedures will become quite justifiable. These costs include not only the actual hourly rate of the workers involved, which for executive staff is often quite substantial, but also the time spent preparing meeting materials, sabotaging as well as making the decisions or nondecisions in the group—we have not even begun to mention the costs of the actual bad decisions, the opportunities foregone because windows of opportunity were closed, and so on. And then of course there is "rework"—meeting again to fix things that were not fixed in the last meeting.

Meetings are a key decision technology. As such, they need to be reviewed and refurbished on an ongoing basis. As with any kind of technology, people tend to become sloppy and slipshod as time goes on. There is nothing evil about this process. We all do it—in driving, a golf game, and so on. Constant attention is needed, and the evaluation process provides some impetus for that constant attention on the one hand, and some techniques and technology of its own through which improvement can be accomplished on the other.

Decision Audit

If decisions are the products of the meeting, then periodically one should look at them. Linking the audit (and the autopsy discussed in the next section) to the year-end effort mentioned earlier can occur on an annual basis. The real decision about how frequently to cycle the evaluation process depends on the turbulence of the environment.

In a very fast-paced environment, the environmental cycle should be run perhaps every 6 months or even more frequently. By the time one discovers that one has been making the wrong decisions in a volatile environment, it is too late. On the other hand, in a relatively placid or tranquil environment, every 18 months or even every 24 months would be okay. If one is seeking to implement changed meeting technology within a stodgy or slow-moving system, then relatively quick cycles would be important—to reinforce the members, not because the environment is turbulent.

How then would one go about a decision audit? Here is where the minute-taking system mentioned in Chapter 4 becomes crucial for another reason. One can go back, over a 6-month period let us say, and sample decisions (perhaps 20%) and lay them out for inspection. Naturally it is important that these decisions be easily accessible.

Otherwise, it is going to be too much of a difficulty to get them, and the decision-audit procedures are over before they start. Some people who use the system of keeping minutes on a word-processing file mark or indicate the decisions with a simple ampersand or other device that allows all of the decisions to be pulled up from the files automatically One can then identify a 20% sample very easily.

If one cannot find the list of decisions easily, then it is very difficult to implement the decision audit, and that becomes a problem. The decisions are opaque and unclear, and if analysts cannot find them, then the members probably are not sure what happened either.

Given that they can be identified, they are put on the list and either one individual or a small group of perhaps two or three gives them a grade, A through F. An A is for a decision called the all-win decision; all stakeholders are ahead (although they do not have to be ahead equally). This is usually the point meant by people when they say after a meeting, "That was a good decision." They tend to refer to a decision in which everybody came out a step ahead. If this were a stock portfolio, all stocks would have gone up, although not all equally.

A B decision is a plus-minus decision with some stakeholders losing but others gaining. The judgment is that on balance, everyone is ahead with this decision. It could be, for example, a merger in which two executives are now reduced to one. The combined efficiencies and effectiveness of the new operation, however, make that sacrifice worthwhile. Again, using the portfolio metaphor, were this a stock portfolio, some stocks would have lost and others gained, but the average gain would be on the plus side of the ledger.

A C decision is the null decision. Pluses and minuses have occurred, but the net result is zero. Some people have gained, some people have lost, but the system is no further ahead than it was at the beginning.

A *D* decision is the opposite of the *B*. Again, there are some pluses and some minuses, but there may have been heavy losses in one area (something Edward Deming calls "incalculable losses"). These losses are not overcome by the positives. For this reason, if it were a stock portfolio, it would be entered on the negative side of the ledger.

Finally, there is the *F* decision, the so-called nuclear-war decision or the all-lose decision. In this scenario, every stock has lost. With respect to the decision, it is an example of one in which everyone is behind.

The analysts then sum up the grades and present a grade distribution for brief discussion. Although apparently simple, this procedure is somewhat stunning to most groups. It is the rare group, even today, that has actually gone back and looked at the decisions they have made as a group and asked if they were any good or not, on any basis. (I should add here that this system is more or less arbitrary. If you have a system of decision rating that you would prefer, by all means use it. It is as much—this point was mentioned before—the process of the decision-analysis system as the specific system itself.) Coming to grips with and looking at, in a collective atmosphere, one's past collective efforts is a lot like looking at team films after the game. One can see how things fit together—or did not.

The facilitation of this review meeting is something to which a considerable amount of attention should be paid. Every effort should be expended not to seek guilty parties. The decision audit is not a witch-hunt. If the decision making has not gone well, then efforts can be made to find out—perhaps through the autopsy—what the problems were and how they might be corrected.

The topics should be introduced by indicating that this was something we all did, and if mistakes were made, we all made them; if benefits were attained, we all share in the glory. Working through the "search for guilty parties" scenario is often an early effort in decision audit, as people seek to cover their anatomy and indicate they had always disagreed, it was not their fault, and so forth. Continual emphasis on the team—team effort, team spirit—is essential to make the decision audit work.

The Decision Autopsy

Coupled with the decision audit is the decision autopsy. The autopsy is a more detailed "taking apart" of decisions to see what really happened. Whereas the audit provides the distribution and overall score, the autopsy allows the group to look in detail at a decision in each of two categories: an *A* and an *F*; an exceptionally good one and an exceptionally bad one. Two are selected and, in effect, taken apart. There is a really in-depth analysis of what went right (and how we can continue it) and what went wrong (and how we can prevent it). This effort is not one of self-congratulation or blame assignment. Rather, it is one in which the *process* through which success or failure were achieved is deeply considered.

The autopsy is designed to provide enough detailed information to allow members of the group to really proceed with improvements in specific areas. The audit sets the stage, and the autopsy provides the tools. It is important to look at an *A* decision and an *F* decision for two separate sets of reasons: a psychological set and a theoretical set.

On the psychological side, the *A* and the *F* create the good news–bad news scenario that is more beneficial in looking at problem areas. As most readers will know from performance appraisals, it is important to say to individuals, "Here are some things that are going right and that we should continue. On the other hand, here are some things that are not going so well, that are actually going wrong, and we need to look at them in some detail and figure out together how we can improve them." Most of us naturally feel defensive when things that we are associated with have "gone wrong." There is usually an attempt to say, "It's not our fault," and to in general avoid coming to grips with our part in the issue, the problem, or the difficulty.

That resistance is somewhat lessened if it can be balanced with a section of items that are going well. Hence, that positive twist, that positive spin, can off-set, to a degree, an excessively negative spin. That is the psychological reason that the *A* and the *F* are needed, and the autopsy does help in identifying things to encourage and support and in identifying things to avoid in group decision-making situations.

THE EXCELLENCE MATRIX

The analysis of things gone right and things gone wrong for improvement purposes, however, provides us with a much deeper understanding of what excellence really looks like, and for this additional reason, the autopsy is important. Theoretically speaking, the conventional understanding of "things going right" and "things going wrong" appear to be at opposite ends of the continuum. This can be seen in Figure 15.1.

A _____ F
Success Behaviors   Failure Behaviors

Figure 15.1   A Conventional Conceptualization of the Relationship Between Failure and Success Behaviors

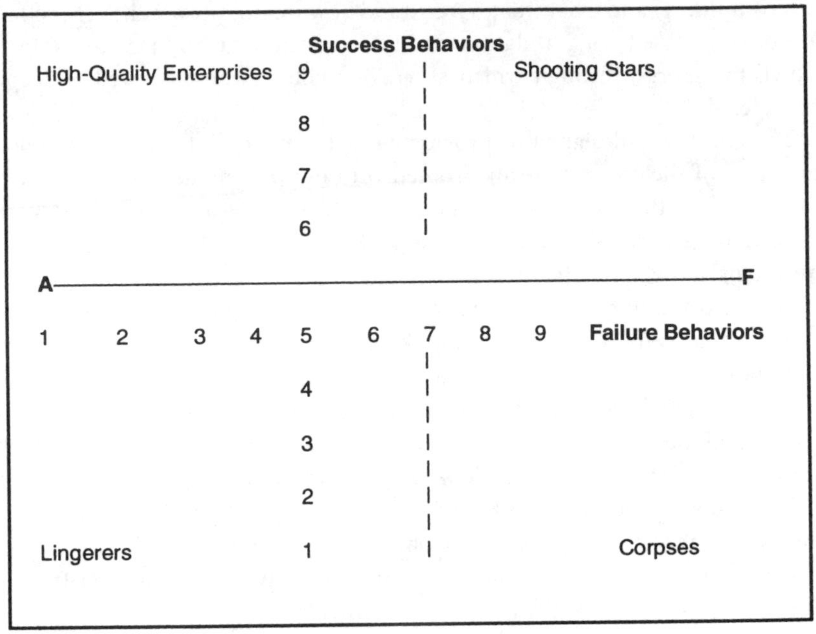

Figure 15.2   The Excellence Matrix: A Revised Conceptualization of the
Relationship Between Failure and Success Behaviors

NOTE: The vertical axis represents success behaviors, few to many; the horizontal axis represents failure behaviors, few to many.

Most of us think that doing things well is the opposite of doing things badly. We think that if we are doing things well we are, by definition, not doing things badly. That kind of linear thinking is what Figure 15.1 is designed to illustrate. A slightly more complex model, however, is more accurate, and Figure 15.2 displays this approach.

Assume that we are engaging in a range of behaviors, some of which are success behaviors and some of which are failure behaviors. We may perform a lot of each or some of one and more of another. The key theoretical point is that the behaviors are *not the same behaviors,* or to put it differently, *not the opposite of each other.* In other words, most of us do a bunch of things throughout the day, personally and in our meetings. Some of them are good, some bad. But in this more complex scenario, doing good is not the opposite of doing bad; it is the average of good-bad behaviors.

In the model described in Figure 15.2, we can look in the upper right-hand quadrant and see individuals and meetings, perhaps whole firms, who are doing a lot of things well and a lot of things badly. We might call them "the shooting stars"—they appear to be good at one point, but suddenly we do not see them. In the upper left-hand quadrant are individuals, meetings, and firms that are doing very little wrong and a lot right. These are called "high-quality enterprises," and it is important to understand that to be high quality means to do little wrong and a lot right simultaneously.

In the lower left-hand corner are the lingerers—those individuals, meetings, and firms that are doing little right, but little wrong. They seem to be waiting around for the environment to advance them or finish them off. In the lower right-hand quadrant are the corpses—those organizations, individuals, and committees that have died. (They may or may not be aware of it, however.)

In short, we think of ourselves as engaging in bundles of behaviors, the sum of which puts us in the quadrant. It is not necessarily that each behavior is either good or bad. It may be good, and then we engage in a bad behavior. Together, they may cancel each other out, or we may exhibit more good behaviors than bad behaviors.

The essential point for decision autopsy is that the F decision involved different behaviors from the A decision. Just finding out what is being done well and continuing it and even improving it, important as that is, does not address the other set of difficulties that one faces—the things that are not being done well. Those are separate and different and have to be addressed in their own terms.

The decision autopsy, then, provides information about success behaviors and failure behaviors. It allows us to pay attention to each and to continue that which we are doing that is positive—to expand it and to improve it—and adjust, change, stop, or correct that which we are doing that is negative. Decision autopsy provides information on the two sets of activities—continuing the good and cutting out the bad—that are needed for true excellence.

Conclusion

Everything worth doing is worth evaluating. Evaluation is, first of all, a process that begins with goal setting. These goals are then monitored, overseen, assessed, and appraised. As we move through the cycle, judgment and fatefulness become more prominent. Stages two and three are the "feedback" stages, in which judgment is minimized and information sharing is heightened; stage four is a part where judgment and fatefulness are high.

Evaluation can also include the decision audit and the decision autopsy. The audit looks at a range of decisions and gives them a grade. The idea is not to pin blame on people—that is to be avoided—but rather to look at the system that produced good, and bad, decisions. The autopsy looks at the good and the bad, and asks what went right that we should continue (the *A* decision) and what went wrong and we should avoid (the *F* decision). However, looked at as a package, it produces the excellence matrix, a matrix that argues that to be excellent, one has to achieve accomplishments—doing right, on the one hand, not doing wrong, on the other, and achieve as well the understanding that *they are not the same things, nor opposite of each other.* Doing right does not mean that one is not also doing wrong!

PART III

Becoming a Meeting Master: Some Tips on Application

"Now, before I give my pat answer, does anyone else have any dumb questions?"

The bad news, I suppose, is that there is a good bit of detail to learn before one can become a meeting master. The techniques can be mastered, however, and they are not difficult to accomplish. Many of the techniques readers will recognize already as things they do sometimes or occasionally or things they do in some degree. But excellence requires focusing on a distribution of detail.

Another observation might also be in order. As one studies the examples and techniques presented in this book, one might say, "This doesn't apply to me." If you say that, the likelihood is that it *does* apply.

But you might also say, "This could apply to anything." It is true, the topics are rather universal, although the detail is quite particular. They are topics of attention that are required for success in anything, and that insight, paradoxically, provides validation for their concrete application. If one said, "To be a successful meeting manager, one has to master a series of skills that are completely different from anything else you do in any other area of your life," this would create a bit of a problem intellectually and conceptually. On the other hand, if one said, "The topics or areas of attention that are required for master meeting management are very much the same as those required to be a master at anything—the details and application are different," this would seem more reasonable.

There has been discussion of what needs to be done to make meetings successful. But you might be asking about how to actually do it. Well, the good news is that it is not tough to do. It requires knowledge of *what* to do and the wish or *motivation* to apply the techniques.

It is similar to having a recommended diet—the *what*. Then there is the wish to get into shape—the *motivation*. The third element is helpful *implementation* hints, some that can help one actually have a better experience.

You are probably asking, "What are the things that I can do that will be helpful? Are there tips and hints that can make the experience easier, especially as most people still regard meetings as a problem?" Chapter 16 provides a range of ideas about how to become a meeting master. Chapter 17 provides some perspectives on application from the standpoint of a TQM (total quality meeting) approach.

16

Strategies and Tactics of the Meeting Masters

R eviewing the material presented so far, one might have the wish to step back and say, "I can't really do any of this stuff. It's not going to make any difference. People are going to do what people are going to do, and I'm simply going to continue along with what I have been doing." When you are faced with a large amount of material, it frequently does seem as if the effort is too great, too complex, and really not worth it.

In this chapter, I will take you through the very first step to develop a paradigm shift within yourself. Readers will recall I talked about paradigm shift early on in the book. Meeting masters really thought about meetings differently than others. They thought of them as occasions for excellence, and this perspective is the essential first step.

Occasions for Excellence

Most of us go through our days carrying out agendas that have been scripted heavily by our kids, our bosses, our spouses, and even our dogs. We tend to think of phrases such as "getting through the day" or "finding out what the day has in store," rather than "creating" or "crafting the day." One of the things most striking about the meeting masters was their sense of having transformed the mundane, everyday, often disgusting meeting into something that was special. I first recognized this specialness in attending their meetings. The reason it was special, however, was not because of anything magical—these leaders *made* it special.

That specialness began with a commitment to excellence. Excellence to them involved efficiency and effectiveness—and doing right as well as not doing wrong. Each of these women and men essentially shared this view in one way or another—it was basically an affirmation of self. "If I'm going to spend time in a 3-hour, 2-hour, 1-hour, or 15-minute meeting, I want it to be valuable, because I'm valuable. I don't have time to waste. And therefore, I'm going to try to make the time as profitable as possible for me."

This perspective was not a selfish perspective, although it may sound that way. It came from a sense of self-purpose, self-worth, and self-valuation that then extended to and infused the activities in which they were involved. In this sense, an anthropological-sociological phrase, "the enhancement of the mundane," becomes very tenable and very appropriate. Meeting masters developed a commitment to excellence that they applied to meetings.

The commitment to excellence, however, was really to something broader than meetings. Their commitment was to achieving high-quality decisions—a point I have stressed before. This commitment was not something that simply affirmed that things have to go well. They had to go well *because* the people there were important, the decisions were important. The decisions affected the lives, careers, and fates of individuals throughout the organizations, and this made a difference.

The difference between the electric atmosphere and communicative culture of meetings attended by meeting masters and many other meetings was like the difference between going to a terrific party and a dud. So the first step needed to become a master is a commitment to self—actually, an affirmation of the self. Flowing from this affirmation is a sense that the activities and interactions in which the self is engaged are worthwhile. That worthwhileness does not come from outside the self. It does not come from the presence of your boss or from your mom and dad. It comes from the fact that spending one's own valuable time demands a valuable result.

Success Through Small Wins

Almost universally, the meeting masters were incrementalists. Karl Weick, a well-known professor of organizational science at the University of Michigan, talks about this approach as an actual strategy. He calls it "success through small wins" (Weick & Roberts, 1993). Kanter (1983) has a similar idea. It strikes a positive note with most of us. The big bang, the smashing success, or the times we drive an opponent into the ground are few and far between. Indeed, when those do occur, there is not the sense of satisfaction that one gets from closer competition. After all, if one can be a smashing success, one's opponent must be an abysmal failure, and the lack of challenge from such an opponent actually takes away from the enjoyment of the victory.

That meeting masters felt a sense of urgency about the activities in which they participated led them to a process of constant—sometimes irritating— insistence on both doing things right (efficiency) and doing the right thing (effectiveness). But there was no single point at which these transitions occurred. Rather, it was achieved step by step, inch by inch, small improvement by small improvement. The meeting masters realized that despite their knowledge allowing for greater efficiency and effectiveness, they simply could not order it. Excellence is a developmental process—a journey, not a moment. They were therefore—paradoxically perhaps—satisfied with small wins because they saw themselves as contributing to that developmental process.

In the next chapter, I will talk about a number of specific strategies that one can use. None of them is dramatic, none phenomenal. Some will have greater impact than others. One does seek, of course, to increase one's leverage. But the meeting masters communicated satisfaction with the energy of direction rather than the magnitude of the result. "Working with people," one master said, "is always a slow process."

The Sprint-Pause Cycle

Your own mastery, however, is more likely to be jerky than smooth. As you begin to master material, you will move quickly from the novice through the beginner stages and into the stage of competence. The road, however, becomes much steeper as one moves out of competence into the expert and master stages of development. Within each of those substages, there will be times when your progress is pretty swift and you really feel that a lot of strides are being made. Other times will be slower and there will not seem to be any improvement at all. I want to call your attention to the sprint-pause cycle to alert you to its presence and to caution you against euphoria during the sprint stage and despondency during the pause stage. Only in one's imagination do things move smoothly.

The Process of Becoming Good at Meeting Management

Managing meetings well will require a bit of work, and there is some detail attached to it. As with anything else, there are things to know. Acquiring the detail and then putting it into practice is often a discouraging process, whether it is cooking, playing a musical instrument, or learning a sport. Frequently, discouragement is the victor, competence the vanquished. It therefore seems appropriate to suggest in advance the steps that one might go through in the acquisition and implementation of this knowledge.

Five steps or developmental stages are likely: novice, beginner, player, expert, and master (see Quinn, 1989). Take a look at what happens in each of these stages. While we refer to meetings, one might also think in parallel fashion about some skill that one has acquired. Learning to drive is a good example in that almost all of us will have gone through this experience. Learning another language would be an effective metaphor for some.

THE NOVICE

In the novice stage, one is at the very start. Recall, if you will, the time you first sat behind the wheel of a car and turned it on. How scary that was! The novice is consumed by rules and focused excessively on the self—his or her performance: How will I do, will I hurt anyone, can I actually do this? Actual performance is relatively jerky and quite slow. The same will be true as you apply these techniques.

THE BEGINNER

After a relatively short period of time, the beginner stage emerges. As a beginner, one has learned the basic rules and may actually begin a process of receding, a fade-out that will be completed in the next stage. We still often refer to rules, but the beginnings of automatic muscle memory reaction are just starting to show. Performance smoothes somewhat, although there are still peaks and valleys. It definitely has lost its pointy tops. This will be the next stage in meeting management.

THE COMPETENT PLAYER

The player, or competent person, is where most of us are on most things. At this stage, the rules that we have learned have faded. Readers of this passage, for example, are able to understand it because of rules of grammar, but you are not thinking about verb, noun, object, subject, predicate, and so on. Rather, you are just reading along and the rules are silently operating, coding, and connecting. Consider the following:

> If then we owe, I don't know el, I seal. Ah, ha.

This little nonsense phrase illustrates the very idea. As long as things conform to known rules, the rules remain suppressed in the player stage. If something unusual happens, they pop up: "This does not make sense," "What is he up to?" or "This must be a mistake." At the player stage, patterns not mentioned in rules begin to be noticed and emerge more fully. This process began in the beginner's stage and is now in full flower, so not only is one paying attention to the usual rules, but one has also developed an ancillary set of experiential rules that are attached to the packaged software we have already received and have implanted into our brain. At this stage, you begin to get good. The first two stages will pass relatively quickly. You will spend more time here. The learning curve gets a bit steeper.

THE EXPERT

Here, selective attention rather than total attention seems to be the name of the game. We are able to complete many projects in which we are expert, with only minimal attention to what we are actually doing. This does not mean no attention—it simply means that oversight has also gone underground, following rules. We dip in for a systems check and a temperature check periodically and are always available to rush back in if some special emergency occurs. Although screening software as well as rule software has also slipped into the background, behavior is apparently automatic, but of course tremendous skill and development have gone into bringing the individual—you, in this case— to this point. Experts do a lot right in meetings. There are also errors, missed opportunities, or distractions that cause meetings to go awry.

THE MASTER

In just one or possibly two areas, we are masters. Our performance is flawless, or very close to flawless, under a wide range of conditions and hazards. The master tennis player, for example, can use a poor racket, play on a poor court, and still look absolutely terrific. Holistic absorption is the characteristic of this stage in particular. It is a difficult concept to convey but suggests that the individual master absorbs a multiplicity of stimuli at once and virtually simultaneously orders them in terms of the importance for the next action and then acts. There is a seamless flow between presentation of stimuli and action. There does not seem to be even a trace of the jerkiness of the novice.

Even adversity—as in an aikido fall—is converted to an advantage. The master dips in here, dips in there, regularly entering the flow process, but only at the most key points and in ways that energize and improve the performance of those around him or her. Playing tennis with a master tennis player, unlike others perhaps, is an experience that allows one to improve one's game very substantially. The master tennis player knows exactly how much spin, force, or direction to put on the ball to stretch the opponent. Similarly, meeting masters display this kind of behavior. They never seem to be doing much, and one recognizes their mastery only by the experienced result of excellent meetings.

After a while, one has the sense that something is different when these people chair or when they are around. Yet it is not immediately obvious exactly what this is. Indeed, the question of "what that is" is exactly what this book is about—sharing the secrets of meeting masters such that others can, without long periods of observation, understand, What do masters really do anyway? What makes them masters?

Application

Obviously, moving from one stage to another is a process that takes some time. In my observation, one can move fairly quickly by applying the material in this book through the novice and beginner stages to the practitioner stages. At that point, the gradient becomes somewhat steeper and a bit slower. The vast savings of time that will result from achieving even player status, however—to say nothing of expert status and beginning mastery status—are certainly worthwhile.

But there are a couple of other rewards as well. One is the increased esteem that players, experts, and masters get. This is an important piece of psychic income that can motivate us all. There is yet a third reward that is perhaps the most important—the achievement of high-quality decisions. As indicated before, our families, our firms, our agencies, our bureaus, and our society are run fundamentally on the basis of the decisions we make and the actions that do or do not follow.

As I suggested, it is impossible to produce high-quality services, high-quality products, or high-quality anything while making low-quality decisions. I suppose examples could be cited in which low-quality decision making was regularly followed by high-quality results. The difficulty, of course, is that these accidents should not be taken as evidence. Accidental successes do occur, but usually orchestras that do not prepare and somehow do fantastically well are few and far between.

Appealing as it might be to follow that active "let it all hang out" stance, however, the people who perform high-quality activities over and over again in a wide range of settings are those who apply a great deal of time and thought to what it is they are doing. They practice, they experiment, they refine, they improve, and that is what the meeting masters actually did. The impressive thing about them was that instead of taking the usual view that the self-fulfilling prophecy might suggest, these experts said, "If I'm going to spend as much time and effort as I seem to be spending at meetings, I ought to really try to make them produce." They did try and the meetings did produce.

Conclusion

Becoming a meeting master begins with self-affirmation. That affirmation in turn generates a commitment to and an expectation of excellence. Those expectations, however, are tempered by a recognition of and an acceptance of success through small wins. Step by step, higher-quality decisions are accomplished. It is the progress and the rate of progress rather than the huge leap of improvement that is going to make the difference in the final analysis—at least, if the meeting masters are to be believed. One's own development may be fast at times and slow at other times, with periods of intense activity and improvement followed by plateaus and even some backsliding, but the overall path is one of progress.

Preparation of the self, however—one's attitudes and paradigms—is only the first step. There are several specific implementing activities in which one needs to engage. The next chapter addresses this implementation, putting some of the material—the tips, the hints—into practice.

Then there is the recognition that there are stages in the development of skill, stages that run from novice to master. These stages are recognized in anything we do, from learning a language to meetings. But, with the right attitude and the appropriate bag of skills, mastery can be achieved.

17

Implementing Total Quality Meetings (TQM)

How can one actually bring about total quality meetings (TQM)? The answer is easier than you might think.

The first step is to familiarize yourself with what the meeting masters have done. It is always good to understand the best practices. The fact is, however, that if one has read a book on riding a bicycle, it does not mean that one can leave the house, jump on a bike, and perform as an expert.

So the second step is experimentation here and there. After one has a fair grasp of the recipe, then one needs to try out pieces of that recipe. In part, this is to get a feel of what is actually going on when you do it. Another reason is to explore, in particular situations, those techniques that you find easier and those that you find more difficult. Everyone has his or her own take on this.

The third step is to secure a confederate. Often, individuals in the organization share your disappointment and the irritation, frustration, and even anger that you feel about meetings. Involve those individuals, share that material with them. Get those persons interested and begin to conspire about ways, situations, and occasions in which you can make meetings better around your shop.

Familiarize Yourself

It is one thing to read through a book and get an overall sense of what you ought to do. My hope is that you have already done that and are now at the point of saying, "I wish there were some ways that I could implement some of this stuff." Now is the time to browse through the volume. Note the rules. Note the chapters that seem to make the most sense to you.

Before you do that, develop your own list of pet peeves, the things that are most irritating to you in the meetings in your firm or agency. With that list in hand, take a look at some of the techniques and see which ones can make the most difference, given the particular difficulties that trouble you in your setting. For example, if lack of agenda really upsets you, obviously the rule of halves and the rule of three fourths (discussed in Chapter 2) would be especially important to you.

Or suppose you are particularly frustrated by the lack of decisions in meetings you attend. In that event, it might be wise to familiarize yourself with Chapter 10 on managing decision rules, as well as Chapter 11 on managing decisions and choice. That material is complicated but definitely usable, and it might be a place for you to begin. In other words, what I am suggesting is that you take the material and apply it to those things that are most troubling to you, for starters. Familiarize yourself in more detail with that particular piece of material that addresses less specific concerns. It is a place to start.

Practice a Little

Once you have figured out one or two techniques that address some of your most pressing concerns, for initial practice think about trying out some of these ideas in a meeting or group that is not really as fateful as the workplace might be. There might be a volunteer group or a church group that would welcome your offer to do an agenda or take some minutes. Or there could be a parent-teacher organization that is in desperate straits for volunteers to help out with some of their subcommittees. There might be some voluntary group at work that would be a good place to begin as well. I am suggesting this mostly for insight, because there needs to be some initial familiarization in the action situation with the techniques.

I am not suggesting that you take too long at this, because you are going to want to get going and implement it in your shop. After all, that is what it is all about. Recall, however, the old caution against trying out a recipe you have never made before on the most important guests in your life—you want the opportunity to prepare it first and see how it works in your kitchen.

For a good many of the rules, you can try them out immediately and see how it goes. There is one caution, however, that has to do with the rules of decision crystallization and the implementation of decision rules in a decision-crystallization episode. Because of the complexity and difficulty of these rules,

I found it very helpful to suggest careful observation of a target group before implementation.

Say, for example, that your concern in your shop is about lack of decisions in a particular meeting series that you attend. You have read the material on decision rules and managing decision and choice and it instantly sounds right to you. You are thinking, "I could do this" or "Someone could do this. We could actually have some outcomes for starters and, maybe soon, some positive outcomes at that."

The problem is that these techniques must be applied with a certain degree of delicacy and a tremendous emphasis on timing. In a lot of ways, it is the difference between retyping a joke and telling a joke. Thus, the first step in this case is to analyze the behavior of others and perform that analysis against the template of decision rules and choice management. Now that you know some of the details of decision and choice management, it will be much more clear to you that if so-and-so had said such-and-such, then your group probably would have moved forward. Because no one vocalized or risked an action hypothesis, however, you skipped over the decision point, moved to the next item, and actually "escaped" making a decision at all. Developing an appreciative sense of what is needed through observing what is missing is an essential first step in the application of techniques that require delicacy and a light touch.

Implementing the basic techniques requires practice. A non-threatening setting is a way to get started. For more complicated techniques, observation and a little bit of thinking through about how things could have been different were these techniques to have been applied are helpful. It is somewhat similar to watching game films before you actually jump into the fray.

PHASE ONE: GET A FRIEND

After the initial personal investment, you need to broaden the involvement. Meetings are community activities; one might even call them community theater, if one views the workplace as a type of community. It is a lot easier to change if you have some allies. No doubt, in your wandering around the organization, you have identified individuals, perhaps friends of yours or perhaps only acquaintances, who are as frustrated, as irritated, or one might even say, as "ticked off" about the time-wasting, decision-avoiding, repetitive meetings as you are and have voiced some of these troubles to you. Those are the individuals to target. If you suggest going to lunch or for a cup of coffee and mention that you have material that really promises to be helpful if it can be implemented, they might agree to join you. The point, however, is that you cannot do it alone; you need others to work with you, to assist you, to conspire with you, and to help you make the change happen.

PHASE TWO: ESTABLISH A TARGET MEETING

Once you have identified some workplace folks who are willing to assist you in conspiring to improve your meetings, you can map out a strategy. The workplace strategy should consist of several steps.

The first step is to identify a target meeting, one that you can influence and one that might have some "visi-posure," a combination of visibility and exposure. With the tools you have learned in mind, you can begin to implement change processes in that target meeting. The hope, of course, is that you will gain experience on the one hand and provide an example of how things can be different on the other.

The second step is to do a meeting assessment. There are a number of ways to perform this assessment, but the simplest way is to ask people who attend the meeting regularly to share with you some of their pet peeves. This can be done either in writing (in an anonymous fashion) or in the meeting itself. The point is that one must begin an effort to change with a mandate from those affected. It is difficult to get a mandate if people do not know things can be better. In effect, one can construct a mandate from the obvious discomfort and difficulty expressed by people in a particular meeting, however. Thus if individuals say, about the target meeting you selected, "We don't have good agendas, we don't reach decisions, we don't do this, we don't do that," then that provides you with the legitimacy to say, "Well, perhaps there are some new things we could try and see how they work for us."

Once the target meeting has been selected and some kinds of discomfits or pet peeves are identified, you have the legitimacy to begin trying something different. The meeting masters advised me not to try too many things at once. Apparently, we become as attached to bad practices as we do to good ones, and we continue to stick to bad practices even though we know better. There are a number of examples of this—failing to exercise when we know exercise is better, drinking too much when we know we should drink less, failing to adjust our diet when we know that the greasy potato chips we are eating are definitely not good for us, and so on. A caution, therefore, is in order here: That one knows better practices and that in some sense, on an intellectual level at least, people would agree that it would be great if we had an agenda, it would be great if we tried to keep our meetings to a time schedule, and so forth.

At this point, the success through small wins makes a great difference. For meetings to go well and high-quality decisions to emerge, there has to be a commitment on the part of the members or participants in the meeting. The benefits must accrue to those sitting around the table first. Peer pressure needs to be developed to enforce rules. Thus picking one or two rules that seem to be helpful, implementing them first, and letting the benefits of that application roll out for a while is a very good strategy for beginning.

One can also use some kind of meeting assessment. The Keep, Stop, Start System, or KSS, mentioned in Chapter 15 and explained in Appendix B is good here. Individuals using such an assessment form do not need to know all of the details about the rules. That can come later, if need be. One can simply distribute the KSS questions to the participants and say, "I have passed around some questions for feedback because I have a feeling that there is some dissatisfaction with the meetings that we've been having. I'd like to ask you to fill out the three areas of the paper anonymously. One says, 'What about these meetings should we keep? What's positive, what's valuable, what would you like to see us continue doing?' Second, there is a place for things that you would like to see us stop doing. Make whatever list there you wish. And finally there is a section for things you would like us to start doing."

Then say, "I'm going to pull this feedback together and I'll ask for some help from a couple of you here, and we'll see if we can't develop some techniques and approaches that will enable us to retain what is valuable, stop what is harmful, and begin what is needed." It is not rocket science, but it works very well.

PHASE THREE: EMPLOY PATIENCE

You and your colleagues have been working to introduce some new techniques into your target meeting. It is going to be difficult for you to wait for some of those techniques to have an effect. This waiting period is especially troubling if there seems to be no progress at all. It is now time to recall the sprint-pause cycle from the previous chapter and apply it to meeting progress.

In the previous chapter, the sprint-pause cycle was applied to your own development; here, one can think of it as applying to meeting development. As people are learning new techniques, it takes a while for them to show progress. Your role, and that of your coconspirators, is to express support for the small improvements (success through small wins applies here, too) and at the same time not express overdue disappointment or hostility at the lack of progress. Even though people do not make progress, they know they have not—they do not need you to point this out. What they do need, what is valuable and helpful, is reinforcement and celebration of the positive directions that they are taking.

Some of the meeting masters even developed little buttons to reward people. TQM is one example. Others had "good job" printed on little cards and some even had Post-its made up with phrases such as, "Remember meeting excellence" on them. There is no question that a number of these are hokey. Nonetheless, they serve to set a pace, keep up the drumbeat of expectation, and use pulling rather than pushing as an important motivational tool.

PHASE FOUR: CONDUCT A PERIODIC EVALUATION

After a period of 3 to 4 weeks, it might be time to sit down with the group, use the KSS System again, and ask participants how things are going. The purpose of the evaluation is as much ritualistic as it is informational. Doubtless one will get information from it, and anything that is evaluated is attended to. Hence, one wants to set up the evaluation time within a reasonable period, without necessarily taking it too far. It also allows for midcourse correction, the introduction of small improvements, and the opportunity to let others make and try out suggestions over relatively short time frames about ways that they think things could be improved. This builds commitment and participation.

PHASE FIVE: ENCOURAGE CONTAGION

Simultaneously, with developments and improvements in the target, individuals are beginning to have their eyes opened. Things do not have to be the way they have been: They can be better; they can even be outstanding. At this phase, the truth of the saying, "Nothing motivates like participating in and contributing to excellence" becomes clear. There is absolutely a building sense of excitement, and participants shift from converts to apostles. As their own experience of excellence begins to hit home, they want to implement it in other places. Thus, there is the contagion of success.

One person tells another, "We're doing some stuff in the engineering group that is really great, and I'd like to try a little bit of that—I think I know enough to begin to get things going." At this point, the meeting masters began some encouragement by wandering around—they encouraged this innovation here and that innovation there. It almost does not matter if the innovations are really working as well as they could. Indeed, here the skill of the master is revealed.

Some people, in their processes of wandering around—people we might call "lesser masters"—cannot resist telling people how to do it better. The excitement of individuals in this process is sucked away as some outside expert comes in and says, "If you'd have just done it this way, everything would have turned out all right." Rather, the meeting masters would not say much at all. Or they might say, "Looks good. There might be some other ways to do it, but I can't think of any at the moment." (Even though, of course, they could think of 100 different and better ways.) They realized that key was the motivation of the individuals. That had to come from inside.

Conclusion

Implementation is the assembling of a thousand details in the appropriate sequence and juggling, burnishing, nudging, and pushing to get everything to work just so. One cannot do this on a computer-assisted design screen. People are involved, and thus constant on-line, real-time attention is needed. Meeting masters, I think, got tremendous satisfaction out of helping high-quality decisions to be achieved in their own groups. They got even more satisfaction from helping others achieve high-quality decisions. The same rewards are available to you.

PART IV

Strategic Perspectives on Meetings

"*Can you pray again in a couple of hours? He's in a meeting.*"

Now that we have some ideas about how to really make things better, some readers may want to think a bit more about the paradox and persistence of lousy meetings and the connections meeting improvement may have in the larger questions of running and managing bureaus, organizations, and agencies.

The paradox of meeting misery is that in North America and Europe meetings abound. Much, if not most, managerial work is conducted in and through meetings. Most of the time, meeting participants do not feel these meetings go well. Problems abound.

There is certainly a continuum of meetings, from the informal one-on-one in the office to task forces, teams, committees, and decision groups and from new product teams, new product task forces, and other such organizational creations that make up the bulk of executive work to the heavily scripted and almost completely theatricalized presentations for top corporate CEOs. These kinds of meetings take up the vast bulk of the daily activity of many executives. If meetings do not go well (well = decisions are made, there is little rework, the decisions are of high quality, and participants have fun!), the chances are the organization is not doing well either.

If anything, the cost of the meeting itself is increasing rapidly. Employees travel all over the country and the world to attend meetings. In a period of increasing competition, the time and cost alone of meetings, in personnel time and travel cost, is a factor to be considered in most big and small organizations. This is not to mention the problems that compound these costs when the results are of poor quality.

We need to understand a bit more about what actually goes wrong in meetings and develop a perspective on why this happens. Such a broader understanding will make the perspectives and principles of the meeting masters more understandable and easier to apply. And of course, it is great to have better meetings. People feel better, and there is not the grumbling and grousing that characterizes so many workplaces today.

But there are larger goals that are actually achieved here. As I suggested in the High Quality Decisions Principle (p. 19), the goal is not only to have a better meeting in some narrow sense but also to have a decision-making system that is efficient and effective. Meetings can be seen as an information-processing system. The output is a decision stream. It is that decision stream that runs the company and that produces, finally, organizational success or failure. In short, meetings, or more specifically the policy products of meetings, can be a signal of organizational health or illness.

Organizational policy is the result of a series of decisions, which are made in a series of meetings. Successful organizations are driven and informed by successful policy, which requires a successful series of decisions that in turn needs successful meetings. So often we fail to achieve these goals, however, and fail to see the connections among meetings, decisions, and policy.

In Chapter 18, the dismal background of "meeting lore" is explored. Chapter 19 details some of the popular explanations about the problems in meetings. Chapter 20 examines why things often go so wrong in meetings. Chapter 21 connects the total quality perspective to meetings and decisions, linking total quality meetings with total quality decisions. After all, bottom line, the purpose of the meeting is to use a group to do better what we as individuals do all the time—make decisions.

18

The Meeting

Lore and Legend

The famous John Cleese movie short *Meetings, Bloody Meetings* opens with a shot of Cleese's character in bed with his wife. The wife is reading a novel, and Cleese is lying there surrounded by papers from the office. His wife looks over at him and says, "Why can't you do your work while you're at work?" "There isn't time," he replies. "I have to go to meetings." She asks, "Would it make things easier if I came and slept at the office?" "Why don't you come and sleep at the meetings?" he suggests. "After all, if it weren't for the sleep we got at meetings, I'd never be able to work this late."

The very mention of meetings in contemporary management circles seems to send shivers down everyone's spine. Conventional wisdom suggests that no work gets done at meetings. "I didn't get any work done at the office today—I spent the whole day in meetings" is a commonly heard phrase. Somehow meetings have come to be defined as equal to "not-work."

We are almost ashamed at the gratitude that washes over us when a meeting has to be canceled, similar to the sense of release that occurred when a professor did not show up for the exam. There is the same sense of nervous apprehension, of heads turning and faces questioning, "Can we go now do you think?" And like dominos falling, one, then the rest, we get up to leave.

This freedom—from the now-canceled meeting and its roles and difficulties—is mixed with the same resignation that exists in the classroom—the exam will still have to be taken; the meeting will surely be rescheduled. Although transitory, the sense of relief may as well be enjoyed, because it will be over too soon.

Approach and Avoidance

What is it about meetings that gives us these feelings of approach avoidance? "Thou shalt meet" was not one of the Ten Commandments. Presumably the world could get along without meetings, yet in the corporate sector they seem to be an almost daily irritant. The time spent in meetings is substantial and increases as executives ascend the corporate ladder.

Could we just *stop* meeting? Clearly meetings have some attractant. We are drawn to them almost as surely as the moth to the flame or the rat to the cheese in the trap. Many, many meetings have equally fatal results. Unlike the moth and the rat, however, we sense and even discuss the difficult results that are to follow. It is almost as if, in some perverse way, we enjoy the bad meetings, the boring times, and the nondecisions. Perhaps, as in a self-fulfilling prophecy we may even, because of our attitudes of negativism, go a step toward creating some of those very results that we claim to abhor.

Our aversion to group activity of particular kinds extends beyond the meeting. Meetings are usually singular events, with necessary connection from one to another. Even if a structural connection exists—such as the corporate staff meeting—there is no overarching assignment or focal task to be accomplished. Committees—and boards, another well-known group form—suffer an even worse reputation (if possible!) and have some of these overarching yet often loosely specified responsibilities and tasks.

Boards of directors, too, are similarly characterized as old fogies and inept. Sometimes they are corporate boards, which rule the larger and smaller organizations of corporate America. At other times, they are the governing boards that Houle (1989) writes about in his book, *Governing Boards,* which tends to our voluntary associations, educational institutions, and other philanthropic endeavors. (We will be talking about boards in Part V.) Or they are our government coactivities—city council, the school board, or Congress itself.

Poking fun at the ineptitudes of these groups has long been an American sport. Will Rogers poked fun at the Congress all the time. The Ann Arbor, Michigan, City Council in 1994–1995 took to meeting until the wee hours of the morning. They regularly violated the rule that suggests that "The mind cannot absorb more than the seat can endure."(If you meet for too long a time, participants get a condition known as *comitosis rectus,* in which a paralysis begins in the lower back and travels up the spinal column to the mind. The first system to go is the eyeball controllers, and the pupil slips down and is hidden behind the lower lid. As you look out over your group, there are only whites of eyes looking at you. If you notice this, it is perhaps best to adjourn promptly!)

THE KISS OF DEATH: MEETINGS, COMMITTEES, AND BOARDS

Despite their potential value, however, this value seems realized too infrequently in practice. Meetings seem dreary and endless, and then—as if to add insult to injury—pointless.

Committees and meetings drone on, often accomplishing little. In fact, the phrase "Let's appoint a committee" or "Let's have a meeting" is almost universally recognized as the "kiss of death."

A "terminal fantasy" was voiced by a corporate executive I interviewed some time ago, who was told by everyone he would go to heaven immediately because of his good deeds. As we were chatting about this, he said, "You know when I get to heaven, I have one wish." "What's that?" I asked him. "I hope the Lord will grant me a meeting room of my own construction. It will float gently on a piranha-filled river. Each seat will be perched upon a trap door, operated by buttons concealed under my table. The next time someone says, 'Well, Sam, I don't mean to object, but . . . ' I'll say 'You sure don't, Ted' and push the button, dropping him into the drink. We'll let the little nippers have at him." Such hellish fantasies from a heavenly expert suggest some of the difficulties that most of us must experience on a daily basis.

Surely as management analysts review the decline of American business, some attention will be paid (although not much has been as yet) to the lackluster role of boards of directors. To some extent, the horrible story of the burglarizing of America by greedy executives will be the story of manipulated boards of directors, of decision-making groups that did not or could not decide or were so consumed by self-interest and so unschooled and untrained in their responsibilities and the nature of their trustee role that they simply caved in to manipulation by aggressive executives. (But, as I mentioned, boards *are* improving.)

Meetings, committees, and boards are central to the operation of our commerce and policy, yet viewed with aversion and distaste. Board "malperformance," committee ineptitude, and meeting meandering have not yet come out of the closet as legitimate foci for management attention. And it is difficult to find someone who can help improve the quality of decision making in your meetings, committees, and boards.

AMERICA VERSUS THE GROUP

America, in particular, has always been ambivalent about groups and the group process. Individualism has been our hallmark, it is more than individualism—it is "rugged individualism." "Rugged collectivism," or "rugged groupism," does not have the same ring to it. From the mountain man to the captain of industry, it is lonely at the top. Why is it lonely? No one else is there, that is why.

Our individualism even has a posthumous quality to it—in some religions, souls experience upward and downward mobility after death. With such powerful strains in our culture, it is no wonder that group-related activities suffer.[1]

POSITIVE FUNCTIONS

The positive role that groups play in our culture was pointed out early on by no less than Alexis de Tocqueville (1945), who talked about associations as the backbone of American society. Probably, those members of wagon trains who settled the West would have agreed with him. Although the mountain man obviously did some exploration, it was the wagon train that brought the folks in large numbers to settle the West. Indeed, this collective experience of participative plains crossing may have created a different ambiance for the collective and public weal. Boorstin (1965) suggests it imprinted a different consciousness on the westward movers from those who had originally come East. The original settlers were passive residents in a boat run by others, as opposed to active participants in a convoy that contained their own belongings as well. Joint decision making of the sort de Tocqueville would have understood was a factor in the westward settlement, and perhaps much less so in the move from the Old World to the new.

As troublesome and problematic as meetings, committees, and boards are, and as much as we would like to avoid them, they have their inexorable appeal because of the functions they perform for us. Yet this very multifunctionality creates its own set of stresses.

One key function, of course, is representation. America has norms about representation, meetings, and committees, and boards are one venue that allow for a plurality of interests to be at the table. Apart from its value support, such plurality has practical value. In today's complex decision-making world, there is most often the need for several points of view.

A second function is decision-rule balance. As noted in Chapter 10, a decision rule is an agreed-upon standard that makes decisions legitimate. The problem is that each decision rule—and there are several—favors one set of interests or type of interest over another. No decision rule is neutral.

Hence, our most famous decision rule—the one person–one vote rule—favors the breadth of preference and does not pay any attention to the depth of involvement or intensity of emotional commitment that one has toward an issue. Nor does it pay any attention to the expertise or power of the individual voter. Typically, a high-quality decision must satisfy several decision rules, and it is in meetings, committees, and boards that the dynamics of difference are ironed out. Those majoritarian types that have the votes will simply call for a vote. Minorities would be foolish to call for a vote—they would always lose. Hence, they must appeal to other bases of decisional legitimation and argue their case in the context of collective decision making.

The intensity of involvement in the delivery process can, under certain conditions, help build commitment to carrying out the decisions after they are made. The lack of that development is one of the main reasons why one manager complained, "We don't do much, and when we do, nothing happens anyway."

The group process can, of course, foster a competitive spirit with respect as the reward, and again, under certain and proper conditions, these tensions can sharpen and heighten the quality of performance. (See Zander, 1982, for more detail.)

DECISION QUALITY

Most scholars who study decisions point out that groups make better decisions than individuals. There are a couple of aspects to this conclusion. One is that individuals are prone to errors that lead to bad decisions.

One error is the *selective perception error*. In that situation, individuals simply do not see all that there is to see in a situation. They all have blinders on, and because of the blinders, do not recognize their blinders. A second problem is the *review-for-proof-only error*. In this case, individuals have looked at a situation and come up with a preliminary assessment or opinion. Then they are asked to look again at the situation, to see if their answer holds up. Almost none of them will actually look afresh; indeed it may be impossible to look afresh. Rather, they review the situation with the perspective of seeing if they can verify their answer. This action is called review-for-proof-only, and it is the cause of lots of errors.

Usually these two errors lead to a third error—the *premature commitment error*. Having found an answer (error one) and checked it (error two), individuals feel confident that they are right and proceed as if they are. Often sadness rather than quality prevails.

Conclusion

Meetings, committees, and boards have a bad reputation in American society. In such an individualistic culture, this result is not surprising. Yet they occupy so much time, relate to so many key functions, and cost so much money that the efficiency and effectiveness are essential, and improving them is a task of high importance. A negative meeting culture is on everyone's lips.

Note

1   All group activities are not ignored. Professional sports have many "team" activities.

19

The Negative Culture of Meetings

So many things go wrong in meetings that we ought to look at the kind of complaints people have about meetings. It will be important for us to understand what goes wrong to understand what makes things go right.

Pet Peeves

To see where you stand in this discussion, it would be good to take a minute to list your pet peeves about meetings, the things that really make you mad when they happen. Take a separate sheet and make a list of things that trouble you in the meetings you attend. Do not think just about one group of meetings (e.g., those at work), though be sure to include them. Rather, think about work meetings, church meetings, civic meetings, or PTO meetings. Do not think just about recent ones; think about the meetings you have attended over several years, so you can develop a good list. Then you can compare your list with the ideas I have compiled over the years.

Compare your list with the list I've compiled and presented in the following sections. The items are pet peeves or problems that others have shared over the years or are problems that I have seen as a participant observer. This is not my full list (which runs to several pages), but it will give some idea of what meeting participants think. The difficulties fall into several categories. Key categories where problems occur include structure, process, people, and leadership.

Structural Problems

Some of the pet peeves on your list probably fell into the category of structural problems. The structural problems most frequently mentioned include the following:

- Unclear meeting time
- Lack of agenda
- Emergency meetings causing the need to cancel other appointments
- Meetings that occur at inconvenient times, especially between 6:00 a.m. and 9:00 a.m. or 4:30 p.m. and 7:00 p.m., and meetings that go on after 9:30 p.m.
- "Check" or "trap" meetings—held at 8:00 a.m. on Monday morning or 4:00 p.m. on Friday afternoon, which are really designed to see if people are coming in on time or leaving early and have no other functional purpose
- Problematic physical settings, which include insufficient numbers of chairs, poor ventilation, and so forth

These are the problems that come up most frequently in the group surveys that I have made. There are dozens more that are common but that cannot be mentioned here because of space limitations.

Process Problems

A whole other set of frequently mentioned problems occur with the process of meetings—what happens when people actually sit down together and attempt to make decisions. The following complaints are the most common:

- Dominating people—somebody dominates the discussion
- Quiet people—some participants remain silent during the meeting and then complain later outside the meeting
- Improper physical expressions—participants do not say anything in words but use body language, such as eye rolling, long sighs, scowls, frowns, and furious writing of notes to indicate that they are displeased and they do this at inappropriate times
- Bombing—the "bomber" lands a missile of negativism on any new suggestion, often commenting, "We've tried that before, it won't work" in response to a new idea offered tentatively to get discussion going
- No decisions—lack of closure on key items
- Lack of common understanding about what was really accomplished
- Socializing—excessive sharing of personal concerns and issues, showing family pictures, etcetera.
- Food problems—permitting noisy food to be eaten, which becomes a distraction to other participants

- The plump packet—copious amounts of written material are handed out at the start of the meeting and followed by the incessant question, "Well, what do you think?"
- Time problems—not starting on time, not ending on time, taking too long on trivial items, and having no time left for important items

Some of these issues overlap with the people category to be mentioned in the next section, but they really focus more on the process of the meeting itself and what happens during it. Although good process obviously does not make for a good meeting, bad process can ruin almost any meeting, and participants' complaints clearly indicate that this is a bothersome category of items for them.

People Problems

Individual people often are singled out—sometimes appropriately, sometimes as a scapegoat—for a whole range of meeting problems. Their foibles are frequently handy hooks on which to hang the blame of meeting malperformance. Indeed, meeting books abound with characterizations of rotten types, each of whom we recognize and each of whom contributes her or his own thorn to our meeting side. Among the frequently mentioned types are people such as the following:

- Thelma Talk-a-Lot
- Sam Stall
- Don Domineering
- Nick Negative
- Ted Theorizer
- Nelly Nuts-n-Bolts
- Jim Just-a-Little-Bit-More-Info-on-This-Topic-Please
- Herman Hypochondriacal
- Yolanda You're-Not-Going-to-Believe-What-Happened-to-Me-Yesterday

There is no question that individual behavior bugs us. Part of the problem, of course, comes from the very personalities of the people themselves. But part of it comes from the first set of problems mentioned in this chapter, structural problems. If there is no agenda, individuals' particular personal peculiarities have full scope for expression.

If Thelma really does like to talk a lot, the absence of an agenda or any particular topic is certainly grist for her mill. If Herman Hypochondriacal likes to tell you about his most recent illnesses (what one of my colleagues called the "organ recital"), then the absence of structure and focus gives full rein to his aches and pains. Doubtless there is a balance between individual characteristics on the one hand and structural presence or absence on the other. Nonetheless, the personalities as they are expressed in meetings do bother people, and some of the items on your list no doubt reflect this concern.

Leadership Problems

It is almost impossible to have a meeting without a leader. Sometimes this person is called the chairperson, sometimes the facilitator, sometimes the coordinator, sometimes the convener, and sometimes the boss. These words bring us to a dilemma, though. That the meeting has a central figure does not mean that leadership is present. As will be discussed later, one apparently needs both positional skills and role skills—both meeting head skills and leadership skills—to manage successful meeting management. Complaints over the meeting head position-leader role area are significant. Among the most popular include the following:

- The chair does not chair.
- The chair is a footstool.
- The chair lets the meeting get out of control.
- No one is leading our meeting.
- We float from point to point without any guidance or direction.
- The chair lets the aggressive members get away with murder.
- The chair never calls on people if they do not jump up and down and scream for attention.
- The chair actually hinders us, because just as we are about to come to a decision, the chair seems to become scared and says, "Do we really want to do this?" at which point everybody backs off.
- The chair attacks and makes fun of members in the group.
- The chair never lets anyone talk.
- The chair opens each topic with a negative bombastic comment and then invites others to share their views; no one does, of course.

People reporting on these problems seem to expect some kind of direction or guidance from the person who has called the meeting or is supposed to be the chair. They call this deficit a lack of leadership. When leadership is not forthcoming, they become restive and blame the absence of leadership for meeting malperformance.

There is a reciprocity to the leadership issue, however—followership. When I ask chairpersons what their complaints are, a rather different list emerges. They share things such as, "Nobody says anything," "Nobody will take any responsibility," "I thought I had entered Madame Tussaud's wax museum," and "When I ask what anyone thinks, half the people look at the ceiling, and the other half look at the floor."

Somehow leadership and followership are missing when one looks at the positions of chairperson and member participant. The participants obviously expect the chairperson to take leadership. From their point of view, this is essential when one is in the chairperson role. The chairperson, on the other hand, expects leadership to be shown by the participants, as issues shift throughout the course of the meeting. The participants do not seem to have a clue about this expectation and simply shut up. The result is that no one's expectations are satisfied and few are happy.

Results

Possibly as a result of these problems, and other ones you may have mentioned, meeting participants as well as chairpersons often complain about the absence of results for time invested. It is a summary category in which people are saying that the value of the meeting is "less than zero." Although individual respondents may have different reasons for putting the meeting in this category, it comes down to the following set of complaints: "We met for hours and nothing happened," "I thought we had finished this item last week after great difficulty. Lo and behold, it pops right up again this week, and we spend the entire two hours on it!" "I can't recall when we've made a decision. Everything seems to have been decided already so I don't know why we even come to meetings like this," "We seem to decide things okay in the meeting, but nothing ever happens, ever, as a result of what we did."

Although participants appear to be willing to tolerate occasional lapses in closure and occasional and even semi-regular episodes of decision avoidance, they react strongly to a pattern of inefficacious behavior that is characterized by some meeting series.

Negative Mind-Set

These complaints are just a sampling of thousands like it that I have heard. It usually takes focus groups about 10 minutes to come up with a list of about 25 or so pet peeves. As each one is mentioned, affirmative nods and mutters ripple around the table. Frequently, many of the contributions have seven or eight asterisks as other members of the group get enthusiastically on board with someone else's contribution. Trashing the meeting is great fun and very validating. What they are mentioning, however, is the precipitating problems in meetings, the things that are on the surface of their discontent. Not once has anyone mentioned that one problem is that we accept all this chaos, disappointment, and time wasting. People view a bad meeting like bad weather—it just is. This underlying acceptance of meeting "rottenosity" is one of the predisposing causes of awful meetings. What we would not accept in a restaurant, at a concert, or in many other venues are considered "God's will," more or less, in meetings.

The negativity of meeting culture is a two-level problem, then. At the precipitating level, there are many specific problems and peeves that people readily cite. At a deeper, predisposing level, however, is our acceptance and tolerance of this malperformance, including, of course, our own malperformance. At the end of the day, meeting negativity occurs because we allow it and contribute to it. Surface change will never address the problem. Surface change is the "binge/purge" of the meeting world. We can, and must, do better and more fundamental work.

Conclusion

These pet peeves suggest the range of things that can go wrong in meetings. It is a pretty impressive list, and most people with whom I have talked can quickly come up with a couple dozen peeves that they have. Some of them go well beyond that. With such dissatisfaction so close to the surface, there obviously is a job to be done in improving the efficiency and effectiveness of the decision-making meetings in which we spend so much time. What is even more important, however, is our acceptance of the inexorability of bad meetings. Change needs to start there.

20

But Why Do *Things Go Wrong?*

Most of us can share pet peeves easily, and sometimes we think that the peeves are actually the reasons why things go wrong. This is especially the case with our peeves about individuals. I am frequently asked if I cannot help a group to "get rid of" a particular member who is regarded as very troublesome. But it is not the person. It is the system.

I already mentioned the acceptance of meeting rottenosity and its inexorability at the end of the last chapter. But there is more. Meeting complexity and lack of complexity management are the two prime candidates. From a more analytic point of view, one could divide the reasons why things go wrong into two major categories. One deals with complexities of the meeting process, and the second deals with lack of management of these complexities.

The Complexities

What do the complexities include? First, hidden functions of a societal nature are a part of the meeting agenda. They don't often surface directly, but are deep within our own consciousness. Second, there is our own value system of individualism and the misperception of high-quality, individual decision making. These values and misperceptions lead to a failure to recognize the limitations of individual decision making. Third, there are problems in group decision making that become overemphasized. Fourth, there is our lack of training and preparation for the meeting activity—most of us have not learned the basics of group process. Finally, these combine to create an engine that produces what we fear. It is called the *self-fulfilling prophecy.*

HIDDEN FUNCTIONS

Understanding the hidden functions of meetings involves understanding the complex structure of meetings and the social and organizational functions meetings fulfill. Hidden functions include finding, sorting, and prioritizing preferences; organizing the social aspects; implementing diversity; achieving "representation"; and dealing with complexity.

Finding, Sorting, and Prioritizing Preferences

One key function of meetings is the finding and sorting of preferences. When the preferences of everyone are secured in a voting mode, this is referred to as the one person–one vote rule and it reflects the extensiveness of preference. (Recall the material on decision rules in Chapter 10.)

The problem is that, in all groups, the breadth of preference is only one of a number of dimensions that have to be considered. Depth of preference is also something that is of great importance. Human society is always interested in how strong its members feel about particular elements within it. Managing these emotions, as Hochschild (1983) speaks of it, is something of great importance (see Chapter 8). Meetings serve as occasions to explore both the breadth and depth of preference along particular dimensions or with respect to particular issues. Issues of expertise, power, and who might implement the decision are also involved. Once these preferences are identified, then priorities need to be attached to each basis of decision. It's a tough task.

Organizing the Social Aspects

Meetings have other hidden duties as well. These functions are sometimes organizational in nature. Meetings of groups can be thought to have social or societal functions that add to the burden of tasks that have to be managed.

Implementing Diversity

Another key function involves pluralism and diversity—the presence of different kinds of people and opinions. Managing pluralism and diversity has long been a feature of American society. Because many of the "plurals" and "diverse" are minorities, majority rule does not always meet their needs. Thus, it is through the association and meeting network that they make their views known and their needs expressed. That is at the civic level.

Within organizations, the same kind of issues appears. Groups are looked at to see whether they contain diverse and pluralistic memberships. Increasingly, the "all-white, male group" is becoming anachronistic and is a relic in many places, replaced by representation from both genders and multiple ethnicities and interests.

Achieving "Representation"

Pluralism and diversity lead to another issue of considerable difficulty with which meetings must deal—representation. In 1982, John Naisbitt suggested in *Megatrends* that we are moving from a society of representation to one of participation, in which people hesitate to delegate their presence and want to see it and do it for themselves. This trend has been seen in meetings as well, with larger groups and more participation. A remaining problem, however, is that not everybody can be present all of the time for all the matters that might concern them.

Some degree of representation has to be established. Yet within the nongovernmental arena, there is no formal or really legitimate way for achieving this goal. The pluralism of interest of a group may have representativeness but their influentials may not be represented. Jews are present, but not the Jews who count. African Americans are present, but not the African Americans who count, and so forth. Representation deals with the ticklish issue of the extent to which one group member at a meeting can speak for other members of that group. Can Sheila speak for women? Can Sam speak for African Americans? Can Saul speak for Jews? The answer, of course, is a complex one and requires skills at meeting management, because it is, finally, "yes," "sometimes," "maybe," and "no." The quality and nature of the answers differ.

In the sharing sense, anyone can represent the views of other groups. One does not even have to be a member of a particular group to convey the views of that group, especially if one has access to public opinion data, customer referral slips, and so on. Credibility is added, however (or seems to be added), if one is a member of the group in question. The issue of whether such a member has a legitimate right to convey that view is often raised and sometimes becomes a factor in problematic meetings.

In addition, individuals often flee from and disabuse the representative function. Some individuals object to and resent, and thus avoid, representativeness. When asked, "What do women think on this issue?" Sheila might angrily reply, "I don't know! I'll be happy to tell you what I think, but as to what women think, why don't you ask them?" Sheila may, of course, take exactly the opposite route and claim that she is speaking on behalf of what women think today when, in fact, it is what she thinks instead. Both avoidance and false assumption of representativeness must be considered. The meeting manager must be aware of the presence of these problematic issues and work to ensure a balance between them.

Dealing With Complexity

The last hidden social function of meetings is dealing with the complexity of the current scene. Most proposals that come before commercial groups involve legal, financial, manufacturing, shipping, delivery, design, market, and corporate interests, just to name a few. All of these interests want and need to have some kind of say in what is going on, but the timing, sequencing, ordering, and weighting of their views become a management process in their own right. Yet increasingly, individuals can no longer have all or even most of the information needed to bear on crucial decisions. How to get relevant people involved in a way that is real, meaningful, or useful becomes one of the critical difficulties of the meeting manager, not because it is good to make people happy, but rather because their input is essential in making a high-quality decision.

These societal functions create a set of reasons that explain in part why meetings fail: because we have a variety of purposes, what Merton (1958) called "latent functions," that are present and sitting with us at every meeting. It becomes a problem to fully understand the totality of what is going on at meetings. Several levels of activity may be occurring simultaneously. One could be at a societal-governance level in which people are challenging and responding to each other based on pluralism, representativeness, and complexity. At another level, business may be taking place with individuals placing and accepting orders, assignments, and responsibilities, and trying to do that within the context of these other conflicts.

Furthermore, depending on which societal function one takes as determining in a given instance, the composition of the group may vary. A group one would put together on the basis of intensity or extensiveness of preference is not necessarily the same group that one would put together on the basis of pluralism and diversity or on the basis of representativeness or yet again on the basis of complexity. The meeting manager is often the master juggler, attempting to balance a wide array of interests.

Lack of Complexity Management

Meetings and decisions are complex matters involving the interaction of ideas and people. Management of this complexity is very important.

INDIVIDUALISTIC VALUES AND THE MISPERCEPTION
OF HIGH-QUALITY INDIVIDUAL DECISION MAKING

In addition to the hidden functions, another major reason for the complexities that arise in meetings is that, from the start, our culture does not like meetings. Zander (1982), I think, says it best:

[We] are not all that interested in explaining or improving group life. . . . Individuals feel that the organization should help them; it is not the individual's prime job to help the organization. [B]asic values . . . foster the formation of groups that put the good of the individual before the good of the group. In Japan, in contrast, important values foster interdependence among persons, courtesy, obligation to others, listening, empathy, self-denial, and support of one's group. (p. xi)

This individualistic focus is part of the reason why we tend to blame individuals when things go wrong in meetings. We fail to see the corporate, the collective, or the systemic elements in behavior and instead single out their manifestations in an individual act or action pattern and target it for intervention. Individualism has many positives—and that needs to be said. It releases energy and it creates a certain degree of self-reliance. Yet, it also creates the notion that it is really only the individual who does things.

As noted earlier, a very common saying in the American work force is something similar to, "I didn't get any work done today; I spent the whole day in meetings" or "I can't wait to get out of this meeting so I can get back to work." Somehow, work and meetings are connected by an unequal sign. What happens in meetings is somehow not work and is defined as such. Thus one cannot expect that much work will go on there, in that almost by definition, work is not expected to go on there (Wetlaufer, 1994).

What is expected? That is unclear—and it is developing this clarity that is part of the skill of the meeting masters. Our whole history of "mountain-men" heroes tends to be about individuals—the Lone Ranger, Superman, Batman, and so on. Although these individuals had helpers (Tonto, Silver, Lois Lane, Robin), they all tended to occupy subdominant positions in the script and in society as well. This individualism now appears to be changing, and there appears to be a rebalancing of our perceptions and norms, allowing for a greater recognition of interdependence as well as independence. Nonetheless, we have a legacy of individualism that has created an anti-group climate. In that meetings and committees and boards are part of "groups," they are affected by this historical, normative pattern.

Parallel with the view that group decision making is a piece of nonwork is a view that suggests that individual decision making is likely to be better.

Box 20.1   A Thought Experiment in Individualized Decision Making

Readers are invited to consider all the digits from 0 to 100 lying in a row.

1. Please count the nines and write your answer down somewhere.

2. Check your work to be sure you have the right answer.

3. Given that you have 10 bucks in your wallet, how much would you bet of the 10 you have the right answer?

Now compare your answer to the correct one.[1]

This perspective, flowing out of the commitment to individualism that is a characterization of this society, embraces a conviction that, while recognizing the possibility of flaws in others, secretly believes that for one's own self, errors are few and far between (if they exist at all). So powerful is this perception that it is appropriate to give a small example of the foibles of individual decision making that can be quickly experienced by the participants. It is an exercise (Box 20.1) quick enough to administer here.

This simple exercise, of which about 1% of the people I have administered it to get correct, suggests three perils in individualized decision making.

First Peril: Selective Perception

With selective perception, we simply do not see the things that are before us. This point needs to be driven home through the exercise—otherwise, we simply would not have believed it. To this day, I have difficulty understanding why I proceeded as I did. As with most people, I went up the right-hand column and found, quickly, ten 9s. Then I looped over and picked up the other 9 in 99.

That is the most common approach—it is the most common answer. Why did I not go back down? I don't know. But one is faced with the troubling question, "If you missed this many 9s in a simple exercise, what might you be missing in a more complex meeting interaction when decisions need to be made?" That was not the end of my mistakes. I made two more.

Second Peril: Review for Proof Only

Readers will recall that I asked you to check your work. I was asked to check my work. I did not, nor does almost anyone who takes the exercise actually change his or her answer after arriving at an initial estimate. I reviewed for proof only. I had just found 11. I therefore *knew* there were 11.

Checking, under those conditions, was simply a matter of validating that which I already knew, hence, the phrase "review for proof only." Indeed, finding 11 again strengthened my conviction that I was right. How often we are guilty of this sin, coming to a decision or a view that something is the case and then finding additional reasons to bolster that case rather than being open for the additional pros and cons.

Third Peril: Premature Commitment and Added Certainty

How much did you bet? I "bet" you were pretty certain. I "certainly" was. The added certainty that came from the bogus application of review led me to become overly committed to my answer. I was having lunch with a colleague who was showing me the exercise when he asked me, "How certain are you?" I replied, "Certain enough to bet lunch and drinks." Needless to say, I paid for both lunch and drinks. He asked me several times, "Are you certain? Do you want to check again?" In no sense did he force me to do it. My commitment came out of my own conviction that I was headed to a free lunch. Actually I was right—it is just that it was his free lunch.

How often this scenario characterizes us—premature commitment stemming from selective perception and reviewing for proof only. In my case, and in this simple example, the good news is that it is not hard to get out of it. I pay for lunch and that is that. But in a meeting situation or a betting situation, sometimes that overcommitment can escalate.

In poker, for example, *see, raise,* and *call* can force you to a betting level far beyond what you had intended to get into. This happens in meetings as well, where the spiral of commitment, once started, rises precipitously. It is a scenario all too common in individualized decision making and one that, despite the fact we know about it, needs to be carefully controlled. What it suggests is that individuals are, on balance, far less likely to make high-quality decisions than groups. Although groups and individuals can make mistakes, groups, because of the features of error-correcting mechanism, social support, and competition for respect, are more likely to come up with something of high quality—provided, of course, that they are properly managed.

GROUPS DO MAKE BAD DECISIONS

Individuals often believe that, in fact, groups make terrible decisions. It is true. There are bad decisions (and, indeed, there are categories of bad decisions) that come from groups. Some of these group-decision problems have names that have entered the popular language. One of them is *Folly,* a second is *Groupthink,* a third is the *Ersatz Decision* (popularized by the Abilene Paradox and the Garbage Can Model), and a fourth is the *Nondecision* (popularized by the parable of the Boiled Frog). It would be useful to look briefly at each one.

Folly. Tuchman (1984), in her book *The March of Folly,* has written a historical treatise on essentially awful group decision making. She describes Folly as a situation in which (a) a decision to take action was made, and action was taken in which there were clearly defined alternatives; (b) more than one person was involved; and (c) the process existed over more than a single political entity. She talks about the Spartans taking in the Trojan horse and continues on through a variety of historical examples up to the Vietnam War. There is no question Folly exists. There is no question, either, that some of the examples of Folly have been major. The space shuttle *Challenger* disaster, in which individuals were trying to make a decision late at night on the phone and important information had apparently been suppressed, is a more recent example. That some decision processes, even over historical time, are badly managed does not constitute evidence that group decisions are worse, however, only that some group decisions are bad.

Groupthink. Groupthink is a concept popularized by Irving Janis (1983). It essentially describes the situation in which everyone agrees with a proposal because the group members do not want to disrupt the cohesion of a group or make people feel bad. Sometimes the proposal is advanced by a powerful individual. In point of fact, everyone hates the idea. For a variety of social, structural, and personal reasons, individuals hesitate or are unable to speak out. Later, however, the decision is often sabotaged in the implementation phase because, really there was no buy-in from the start.

The Ersatz Decision. The Ersatz Decision, or fake decision, has some similarities to Groupthink. Everybody "more or less," "sort of," decides to do something. It is popularized in the story of the Abilene Paradox (Harvey, 1974) in which an entire group actually decided to do—and did—something that nobody wanted to do. The difference between the Ersatz Decision and Groupthink is that people, to a certain extent, actually agree. There is a lack of crispness and crystallization, however, and the decision is sometimes a process or a rolling decision in which action builds as time moves along. In any event, there is still the absence of frank discussion and honest shakedown of opinions, and there is a lack of willingness to grab hold of alternatives and say, "No, I really don't want to do this, and I think we ought to look at some other alternatives."

The Garbage Can Model. Michael Cohen, professor of political science at the University of Michigan, coauthored an impressive article a number of years ago called "A Garbage Can Model of Organizational Choice" (Cohen et al.,

1972). It helps us understand the complexities of information processing. Cohen argued that organizations (communities, families, etc.) have four types of individuals within them and that decision making of high quality requires that these four types be present in the same room at the same time.

1. The first type is problem knowers. They are individuals who understand the problems the organization is facing and articulate them well. These individuals may not be the usual kind one would expect to see at a meeting. They could be secretaries, janitors, or people who work at the fringes of the organization. Such people know how customers think, and what problems the customers are having.

2. The second type is solution providers, individuals who are able to think up solutions to problems—creative, innovative types. But they may not know the actual problems, so they are limited. Similarly they may lack the authority to move ahead with solutions.

3. The third type is resource controllers. This is a group of individuals familiar to us all in most organizations. They sign off on the allocation of people, money, and other organizational resources. They do not necessarily make the final decision, but their approval is often needed. They are often thought of as road-blocks within the organizational framework, partially because they are never brought in at an early enough time. They are a crucial part of the organizational "foursome" to which meetings must respond.

4. The fourth type is "decision makers looking for work." Cohen and his colleagues identified the concept of "management by walking around" long before it had achieved commercial popularity. They basically saw the decision maker as a floating point within the organization, sometimes here and sometimes there, dealing with issues as they came up and as they were brought to them for termination. To be effective, however, the decision maker obviously needed the opinions of the problem knowers, the solution providers, and the resource controllers. If all of these seem somehow aligned, then the role of the decision maker might simply be to give the green light. If, on the other hand, there was a difference of alignment or a strategic conflict among the three groups, then choice might be needed.

Furthermore, although it appears from this example that the decision maker comes at the end of the line, that is really not always the case. Sometimes the decision maker operates in the beginning, middle, and end, setting crucial parameters, reviewing midrange alternatives, advancing some and blocking others, and then ratifying or selecting the final one. Bringing the decision maker in only at the end often creates considerable problems and difficulties. What Cohen suggested is that quality decisions need all of these types in the same room at the same time, interacting, sharing, talking, and creating, hopefully synergistic effects. Most of the time, he argued, they are thrown together randomly as if tossed into a garbage can, hence his title.

A typical meeting might contain two problem knowers and a resource controller. If solution providers are absent and decision makers are not there, it is difficult for the group to proceed. On the other hand, another type of meeting might contain some solution providers, some resource controllers, and some decision makers but nobody who really knows or understands the problem the organization is facing. Thus, decisions might actually get made, but they would be of low quality because they would be the wrong decisions, about the wrong thing, and at the wrong time.

The Nondecision, or the Boiled Frog. Tichy and Sherman (1993) argued that if one takes two frogs, places them in a petri dish full of water, and very slowly brings that water to a boil, the frogs will boil to death. Why do they not jump out? The "just noticeable difference" in their environment is not enough to cause them to act. One frog asks the other, "Do you think it's hotter?" "Not really," the second frog replies. They both croak!

Tichy and Sherman point out that there are whole segments of American industry—auto, steel, consumer electronics, as well as fishing tackle and musical instruments—that have "croaked." They did not see the environment changing. They did not change; they died. Think of how many meetings and committees these firms must have had (and still have) that went nowhere or made things worse.

So groups do make bad decisions. These have been some of them. But that does not mean groups always do this or that the group is the reason. More often it's our own lack of training.

LACK OF PREPARATION AND TRAINING

Most individuals lack preparation and training for decision making within groups. Most of us come to group participation with no training of how it should occur or what our positions and roles should be. When one is appointed to be a chairperson, one usually has no idea what a chairperson should do. If one is lucky enough to have hooked up (formally or informally) with an outstanding mentor, it would be possible to imitate that behavior when one had one's own chance.

Most of us, though, did not have good mentors or teachers with respect to this behavior, and we, therefore, simply replicate the old behavior. It is almost as if bad patterns were lying in wait for an opportunity to be exercised. The lack of training partly comes from the point previously mentioned—the devaluing of group activity in general. But whatever the reason, the people sitting around the table at any particular meeting are very unlikely to have had any kind of briefing, background, or suggestion as to how they might behave or what things might be expected of them.

No football coach would send a team out so ill prepared. No symphony orchestra would begin a performance in such a lackluster fashion. Yet meetings are run over and over and over again precisely because many of us, quite frankly, do not know what we are doing. To make matters worse, a subset of the "us" group is in a position of power, which allows us to intimidate others and sometimes we fail to hear the helpful feedback that could guide and direct our performance to improved levels.

SELF-FULFILLING PROPHECY

Lack of preparation and training stimulate the operation of the self-fulfilling prophecy. Most of us know what that is, but let me review it quickly. It has four steps.

1. As the self-fulfilling prophecy begins, one believes that a certain situation or fact is true or false, which in reality is neither true nor false. Examples might be "I can't lose weight," "I can't stop smoking," and "Meetings are rotten."

2. This initial belief in the reality of a certain situation causes the taking of actions consistent with that reality. Therefore, I do not join a weight-loss clinic, I do not sign up for a smoking clinic, and I do not try to do anything to improve my meetings.

3. It follows almost inexorably that the feared result occurs. Now it is quite possible that the feared result would have occurred anyway. If one does not join a weight-loss clinic, if one does not join a smoking clinic, if one does not seek deliberately and systematically to improve one's meetings, however, then it is quite likely that weight will not be lost, smoking will continue, and meetings will continue to be bad. In this sense, our behavior contributes to the continuation of the very feared result, but we do not often see it that way. Instead, we use the manifestation of the feared result as proof for Point 4.

4. We were right in the first place.

This cycle is very neat, very tight, and very powerful. That is the bad news. The good news is that it can work on anything, so if we begin to take a different view and say, for example, "Meetings can be productive and exciting," that may lead us to take certain steps consistent with that view, which in turn may create a great improvement in meetings, which may in turn serve as a validation for our original premise. It is the hope of this book that the self-fulfilling prophecy can be made to work in the opposite direction from the way it is working now.

WHY GROUPS CAN MAKE BETTER DECISIONS

The problem illustrated by these complexities and difficulties discussed in this chapter certainly confirms that bad decisions can be made by groups, as well as individuals. Despite this contempt, it is not all bad. There is a less prominent but vigorous sense of appreciation for collective efforts in meetings, committees, and boards. Houle (1989) speaks of nonprofit boards as a "repository for American voluntary values." Like it or not, in this complex world, at some level we recognize that the decisions that affect our lives are made by meetings, committees, and boards. There is some social scientific evidence that suggests the possibility that group decision making, if properly orchestrated, can be superior to individualized decision making. But this requires attention. If unattended, groups can make some really rotten decisions.

However, as a structure, groups, if properly run, have a better potential. Why is that so? Zander (1982) suggests at least three reasons.

First, groups provide an error-correcting mechanism. Other people with other perspectives ask questions such as, "How about this?" and "How about that?" which open up new doors of consideration and review that might have been closed.

Second, groups provide social support for ideas and contributions. Frequently, we engage in self-doubting behavior when we have a new or good idea. Instead of thinking of it from its positive points of view while recognizing that there may be some difficulties, we think that it probably would not work. Social support can often get us over this hurdle and can suggest a new approach that might have great merit.

Third, groups foster competition for respect. That competition, if properly channeled and handled, is a very positive force. We all want to show others what we can do. As long as the competition is within bounds, is not grandstanding, and does not involve the destruction of others in the group, it can be a positive force. Improperly handled, it can contribute to any one of the problems above. The potential, therefore, is there—the actuality remains to be developed.

Conclusion

Meetings become complex for many reasons. The more complex they are, the more management they require. Most of us fail to understand that a meeting is a complex social form with manifest social and organizational functions as well as latent ones. Not only are there many of each type of function, but there is often a simultaneity about them—several are operating at once. To make matters worse, they point in different directions. Hence the "solution" to the "problem" of meetings is more complex than "kicking ass and taking names." It involves, first, an appreciation of the manifold complexities that are potentially present, and the ability to discern which among the many possible ones are actually operative at the moment. These assessments must be continuous, and done in real time, for the most part. Individuals—meeting masters—need to be able to *create* solutions more or less on the spot. Lack of management of these elements is the fundamental reason why so many meetings are so chaotic.

Note

1 The most common answer, and the one that I got when I first learned this exercise, is 11. Other common answers are 10, 9, and 1. The correct answer is 20.

21

Quality Management Equals Quality Decisions

Even though most of us may not really know why so many things go so wrong in meetings so often, one thing is clear: Meetings are a despised activity on the organizational pecking order. Indeed, they are so low, they may even get into the negative zone. Being in the negative zone means that not only is an activity nonproductive (time cost), it prevents you from doing some things you might otherwise be doing productively (opportunity cost), and it actually irritates you so much that you get less done overall than you otherwise might have accomplished. This perspective is particularly unfortunate in that meetings, committees, and boards are actually—for better and most often for worse—in the center of organizational life and represent a particularly important component in the developing movement toward total quality management.

Recall that the excellent meetings run by the outstanding meeting masters had the following four common features already mentioned in the Introduction of this book:

1. Decisions got made.

2. They were of high quality.

3. There was little rework.

4. People had fun.

I mentioned before that meeting masters were among those who felt their own time was worth more; they would not accept, tolerate, or sponsor poor-quality results. Without expressing it, they were embracing total quality management.

What *Is* Total Quality Management?

Total quality management is a perspective on organizational life that suggests that organizations should aim to turn out the highest-quality products or services possible for both external customers (the usual suspects) and internal customers (anyone downstream from you in the workplace). In the initial forays into total quality management, it appeared to many thinkers in the quality field that quality products were the goal. Thus, turning out a flawless widget, automobile, violin, or check-in procedure seemed to be exactly what the company needed to do to compete nationally and internationally.

To accomplish this goal, organizations instituted a multiplicity of checks on the actual product. The goal, it was felt, was to find where the flawed products were and remove them and then find out where the flaws were and fix them. Within this context, it also seemed to be reasonable that there would be individuals or small groups of individuals that would be responsible for the individual and systemic flaws. Those individuals should be removed from the production process.

Little *q* and Big *Q*

This initial attempt to produce quality goods and services was found to be flawed for two fundamental reasons. First, it contained too narrow a definition of quality, and second, it misconstrued what was required to produce quality—that is, it misperceived the essential nature of the quality process. Although important, the production of high-quality goods and services has come to be known as little *q* and, as thinking progressed, depends on total quality management or Big Q.

What is quality? Or what is excellence? One firm uses the following definition: Doing the right thing the right way the first time. Others give a more academic or grade-based definition as follows:

> *F* products or services: The company tells the customer to take the product or service or leave it. If many of them leave it and the company goes out of business, it gets an *F*.

> *D* products or services: The company will try to improve or repair a defective product or service but only under considerable pressure from the customer. The

company may have a niche in or lock on some market segment and thus is able to act in a fairly high-handed manner.

C products or services: The company has a policy of repairing or replacing defective products but does not make them right the first time.

B products or services: The customer is anticipated; rather than waiting for customer demands, companies producing the B product or service seem to anticipate what it is the customer might want and try to meet that need ahead of time.

A products or services: The customer is delighted and amazed; the company goes beyond outreach and anticipation to a plateau at which considerable value is added to the products or services. It often involves the integration of a number of disparate parts.

Looking in more detail at the A level of quality helps us understand why looking at the quality of a specific product or service, as opposed to the total customer experience, misconstrued the nature of the quality process. Building a fault-free automobile is as essential to the quality process as offering a perfectly good meal at a restaurant. People's overall satisfaction and sense of amazement and delight, however, only begins with fault-freeness in a car or an excellent meal in a restaurant. In addition, there are the hundreds of little touches within the automobile itself that add value—coin-changers, arm rests for your right elbow, and so forth—and create that added sense of the special and unique.

Furthermore, there are things that the manufacturer does not control—such as shipping protocols that stress not chipping the paint on the delivered car, or the whole dealer ambiance and the buying experience through which the car moves from the manufacturer to the customer, and so on. In the restaurant, there is not only the meal, but also the ambiance and the timing and pacing of the waitperson. We have all had the experience of a wonderful meal that has been ruined by our inability to catch the waitperson's attention to get that second cup of coffee or a fresh drink, and we are all aware of the sense of irritation and pique that builds during that process. The flow of our dinner conversation is interrupted. The pleasure of owning a wonderful vehicle can be dashed by a crummy situation at the dealership.

Total Quality Management = Total Quality Meetings

What does this discussion about quality suggest for and about meetings? Achieving total quality requires total quality management or Big Q. Total quality management is required because customer satisfaction does not depend solely on one single part of the product but rather on the product ensemble, as in the case of the automobile or dinner. All parts need to be attended to, and no one person is responsible for any specific part.

Thus the problems are the integration and coordination and the simultaneous and sequential attention to the millions of details that create the total quality experience for customers. Big Q is driven, therefore, by management processes— perhaps it *is* the management process—and it is at this juncture that quality discussion, effective decision making, and effective meetings link up. Total quality management requires total quality decisions. In essence, the interior of the organization is driven by the matrix of decisions made throughout the course of days, weeks, and months by a variety of individuals. High-quality decisions require high-quality meetings.

Just as it is very difficult, if not impossible, to produce high-quality products with low-quality processes, it is very difficult if not impossible to produce high-quality decisions with low-quality meetings. Hence, the following relationship: High-quality products and services require high-quality management; high-quality management requires high-quality processes; high-quality processes require high-quality decisions; and high-quality decisions require high-quality meetings. We discover that meetings become not peripheral to but absolutely central to the achievement of organizational goals in the new total quality management environment. It is for this reason that running high-quality meetings is essential. It is not because it will make people feel better, although it might. It is because high-quality meetings are an essential feature of the total quality management system in any organization.

"Quality is Free"

Within the quality movement, there is a famous saying, variously interpreted, that quality is free. What can this mean? In this context, it means that whatever the costs of putting in a quality program, not only will they be saved but also additional savings will be recouped because of the lack of inventory of bad products and a lower need for rework. If a substantial proportion of a plant's cost is focused on rework or if a substantial portion of a staff's time in a certain industry is made up of listening to and dealing with customer complaints of one sort or another, then an entire person's salary, two persons' salaries, or the salary of the entire complaint and repair department may actually be changed and saved because they will no longer be needed.

A very similar point can be made about meetings. The meeting experts suggested that they spend about 25 to 35% less time in meetings than their colleagues. In fact, one of the things that originally called the meeting masters to my attention was that they seemed paradoxically both busy and free, in the sense that they were extremely active and almost fully booked but they almost always seemed to have time in their schedule for another crucial piece of this or that. It is the old adage, "If you want something done, ask a busy person."

If one thinks about a 35% savings, or even a 25% savings, in one's time allocation, the significance of efficient meetings comes quickly to the fore. But it was even more than that. It was not just that meeting masters got things done quickly—they got them done better. In the famous efficiency and effectiveness definition, they not only did things right (efficiency), but they also did the right thing (effectiveness). They made decisions on time and made decisions that held up over time.

In today's era of staff and resource reductions, even doing the same with less is not sufficient. One has to do more with less. Saving time within the meeting framework, through both efficiency procedures (shorter meetings) and effectiveness procedures (failing to have to rework decisions at the next meeting), is a considerable cost savings. Furthermore, it creates a work environment where individuals feel the excitement of efficacy, and this in turn creates a positive work climate.

Conclusion

The mundane meeting, then, turns out to be a (or perhaps *the)* hidden driver in producing total quality within the organization. It is at the meeting where organizational representatives from different parts of the organization get together in cross-functional coordination or, all too unhappily, cross-functional conflict. Meeting masters not only prevent this from happening but also create a positive, upbeat climate. This is sustained not only by the pleasure of the interaction itself—that is part of it—but also by the good feeling that is actually generated by a job well done. Efficient and effective decisions, therefore, become the sine qua non of total quality management. That is why total quality meetings equals total quality management.

Part V

Leadership in Family Meeting and Civic/Community Meeting Decision Making

"Before we begin this family meeting, how about we go around and say our names and a little something about ourselves."

A s I have mentioned, meetings are seen to be awful, but this awfulness is accepted as if it were a force of nature. Time after time, I have exposed people to better ways of doing meetings, whether through a training exercise, a training film, or helping them to experience an actual meeting that goes really well. Their response is appreciative, respectful, envious, and one in which they express admiration for the tools and skills of the meeting master. The odd part about it, however, is that they somehow do not see it as anything they could do.

It is sort of like looking at a million-dollar house—people say, "Gosh, I wish I could have a house like that." The difference here, of course, is that they *can* become meeting masters. The techniques in this book are not rocket science— they can be mastered, at least up to the level of competency or beginning expert, relatively easily. For some reason, the mindset of the typical person with whom I talk is that the acquisition and application of such knowledge and techniques is impossible. What this mindset means is that change and improvement in meeting culture is truly an uphill battle.[1]

Negative phrases abound. "We have tried this before." "It will not work." "There is no point . . . " "I do not have the time . . . " I am sure readers can fill in the blanks here.

But meeting negativity is not the only source of change resistance. In a weird inversion, many of the awful practices are seen, perversely, as beneficial. Time after time, we go to meetings where there is no agenda, and nothing happens. At the end, someone usually says, "Well, it is always good to get together" (after which someone usually mutters, sotto voce, "To see if there was any point in having gotten together!"). Absence of agenda is seen as "offering freedom from structure." Wandering, pointless discussion is argued to "provide an open environment of expression" and on and on.

"Meeting negativity" and "perverse benefits" are not the only sources of opposition to meeting process improvement. A third source might be called "It's not really a meeting." I am referring here to other settings where meetings and decisions occur: family meetings, civic meetings, board meetings, and community meetings.

While we are obviously meeting all the time with family members around a variety of issues, only the most somber occasions and suggestions for improving family group decision making, such as someone having to go into a nursing home, would be called a "family meeting." If I tell colleagues that I have a meeting with my wife Penny, they regard the comment as a humorous aside, and "just the kind of thing John would say." Times when one gets together with family members, in pairs or groups, to process information and make decisions, are not thought about as "meetings." Hence, family meetings are approached in a haphazard manner. Discussing the family context as a meeting context is a book in its own right. However, I can provide some beginning thoughts and suggestions for improving family group decision making.

Civic meetings are a second source of concern. Perhaps—and it is just a thought—lousy meetings are driving citizens away from civic participation. There are PTO meetings, citizen action meetings, paint up/fix up meetings, block club meetings, subdivision meetings, stamp and coin club meetings, fishing club meetings—literally millions of meetings. How they go reflects the social fabric of America itself.

Then there are the boards of directors of the million plus nonprofit organizations in the United States. These unpaid, volunteer directors "run" a significant sector of the country. How are they doing? Generally, they are doing poorly. The performance of these directors has recently come under much scrutiny and criticism, as has been the case with for-profit directors. Meetings are lackluster and casual, decisions are deferred and delayed, and individual members (directors) fail to take the statesperson role and use directorship as a personal platform. The list goes on.

Each of these groups—the small clubs and associations and the more formal nonprofit organizations—come together in a loose network in American communities to enact "community decision making." The quality of our communities depends, to a large extent, on how well they function. As with the family, community group decision making is an entire area of study and work. However, as with the family, I can provide some helpful thoughts and tips.

Note

1   Actually this mindset and battle are not all that unusual. When I talk with organizational consultants and coaches about introducing innovative practices in companies and firms, they say the same kind of reaction is visible—an awed appreciation of the success of "the other firm" coupled with an odd sense that "We could never do that *here*, of course."

22

Family Group Decision Making and the Family Meeting

No one would find it an odd statement to say that families make decisions. Getting together in the first place, buying a house, staying in or changing a job, career choices and trade-offs, having children, saving, and spending are a few of the important decisions families make on a routine basis. Then, of course, there is the daily decision concerning "What shall we have for dinner tonight?" The problem is that, for most families, decisions are arrived at in haphazard and very often counterproductive ways.

What Are the Problems With Family Decision Making?

The decision problems in family group decision making are the same, generally, as those in firms, but with a twist for the worse. Many of these typical problems I have already discussed earlier in the volume. Problems such as the following will be recognized by every reader:

- Poor decision recognition (are we deciding something here, or just talking about it, or hearing about it? *Exactly* what is going on here?)
- Failure to explore alternatives well (too much black-and-white thinking; not enough gray thinking; premature closure)
- Failure to actually decide anything (rediscuss, and rediscuss, etc.; closure avoidance psychosis or Zeno's Paradox)

- Failure to "partialize" the problem (the presence of too many decisions at once; everything impacts everything else)
- Failure to address partialized problem elements in the right sequence
- Failure to set and articulate decision criteria
- Failure to address problems at the right time (for the problem, or time of day, or both)
- Abilene Paradox (everyone deciding to do something nobody really wants to do)
- Groupthink (domination by a powerful person)
- Defensive routines (some topics are not/never discussed and their "nondiscussability" is not discussed)
- Decision rework (the decision made poorly, then reworked again and again)
- Poor decision evaluation (no audit; no autopsy)

To add to these problems, there are a few things that make family decision making generally more problematic than organizational decision making.

First, there is the emotions factor. Families have ideas about who has authority, who should be involved, how much say they should have, and so on. Of course, everyone in the family does not see it the same way. Second, in the intimate family circle, "payback" for "disloyalty" or "taking another view" can be immediate and devastating. The intimidation factor, including self-censoring, is very high. Then there is the problem of history, something that is harder to escape in family decision making than in organizational settings.

Finally, what families often do not realize is that they are having a meeting to make a decision. In organizations, employees will say, "We had a lousy meeting." There is the beginning sense, at least, that there was some process that *should* have produced some result, but did not. In families, that is not a phrase one hears. Hence, there is not the recognition that there is a flawed process. There is recognition that there is a flawed result, but usually from the result itself.

Decision making is often embedded in an ongoing stream of family interaction—daughter mentions to dad on the way out to the school bus that she needs the car tonight; dad asks mom something while she is feeding baby; a couple exchanges opinions while in the bathroom in the early morning.

This process is well illustrated in the training film about the Abilene Paradox.[1] Those of you who have seen the film recall that everyone in the family "agreed" to go to Abilene for some food, something that no one really wanted to do. Because of flawed decision and family meeting processes, they "made" an awful decision. They had an awful, hot trip into town, a bad experience in town, and an awful, hot trip back home, only to find that *no one wanted to go in the first place.*

The film illustrates many of the problems with family decision making. It is often informal, with no points of crystallization. While in this case all the players were sitting on the porch, in many cases of family group decision making the process is stretched out over time and space, with only some of he players involved at any one time. Family group decision making may be more illustrative of the random process of decision development described by Cohen et al. (1972) in "A Garbage Can Model of Organizational Choice." Families, like firms, have problem knowers, problem solvers, resource controllers, and decision makers looking for work (perhaps more appropriately called "blessers" in a family group decision-making context). High-quality decisions need all the contributors in the room at the same time.

This random approach is manifest in many ways in family group decision making. Appropriate family members are assembled (or consulted, or "touched base with," or whatever) in a series, that is, one at a time, over time, as Cohen et al. (1972) have observed in other contexts, rather than all at the same time.

We can do better in family group decision making than we do. Consider the following as a beginning.

A Starter Menu for Improving Family Group Decision Making: The Family Meeting

Improving family group decision making requires the same two steps that are vital in organizational decision making. The first step is to improve the setting of decision making—the family meeting. The second step is to improve the process of decision making itself. Improvement of the meeting setting needs to come first, because without a setting where decisions are made, it is hard to improve the process.

CREATE A FAMILY-MEETING MINDSET

Families have meetings, or whatever each particular family calls them, to process information and make decisions. Put differently, they have meetings for the same reasons that business organizations and civic organizations do. Family decision making may start out with a dyadic meeting of the nuclear spouses or partners; these meetings may expand as the family grows and children need to be taken into account. Nuclear families may continue to have dyadic meetings with the primary pair, and expand to other sets of meetings with different topics as the family grows.

At the same time, other meetings with the extended family are held. Members of the extended family may include at times moms, dads, in-laws, brothers, sisters, and their spouses and partners. Nuclear family meetings deal with all the big issues—money, sex, food, division of labor, kids, and so forth. They also deal with vacations, preschool, school, camps, etcetera. The extended family meetings may deal with family reunions, care of elderly parents, family emergencies, funeral arrangements, and so on.

The first hurdle that families need to surmount is the idea of having a family meeting itself. Everyone is accustomed to the weekly meeting at work, but few are accustomed to the weekly meeting at home, though some families do have them. It does seem a little odd, though, to think about having a family meeting. Families, after all, are supposed to be loving and connecting. Does not the "meeting" idea sound a bit on the formal, corporate side? While there are families that have formally declared meetings, most people I talked with about family meetings associated them with some family disaster or huge problem.

So the first step for family meeting improvement is to acknowledge that we *are* having a meeting. This acknowledgement announces that there is a need for a more formalized decision process.

ADDRESS FAMILY DECISIONS AT THE RIGHT TIME

Family group decision making is plagued by poor timing, both macro timing and micro timing. Macro timing refers to the problems of addressing problems at the right time over the course of the week, month, or year. Deciding what to have for dinner is better done in the morning, because anything that is needed can be acquired during the day. Waiting till a few minutes before dinner narrows options. (Of course it can be decided *earlier* than the morning before. My grandparents had the same meal every day of the week: Mondays was one thing, Tuesdays another, Fridays was fish, so there was no decision making needed! Such gastronomical routinization is not my recommendation, however.)

Micro timing refers to the time within the day when family group decision making occurs. Poor micro timing refers to an inconvenient time of the day or night within the family flow when decision making occurs. Often, one family member will initiate a decision sequence at his or her own convenience, but at a time that may be inconvenient for other members of the decision set.

Finding family time for mutual discussion and decision is a huge problem. Two-earner couples with kids have almost no time during the day to get together and may have only the evening hours, when each may be exhausted. Finding—indeed making—time for family decision making is crucial. Trying to deal with important items "on the fly" is a sure recipe for poor decisions, if not disaster. Families might be well advised to develop family-decision times when families can coalesce.

IMPROVE FAMILY-DECISION AGENDA DEVELOPMENT

Episodic meeting times mean that families have difficulties developing an agenda and that the agenda is more or less random. There is usually no agreed-upon way for the family members to get their input into the meeting.

If there is a dyad, it is not so bad. But for larger families and extended families, someone has to find out what is on people's minds. This is what I called the rule of halves in Chapter 2 (getting material for the next meeting half way between the meetings, or at least before the meeting, so that the agenda can be properly built).[2] While that rule might be a bit on the formal side for family meetings, some checking about areas of interest and some notification of a time and date for a family meeting would help.

Setting a time for family meetings allows for individuals to enter items. It could be as simple as a square on the fridge where yellow Post-it notes with items for discussion are hung. A small improvement here can and will yield large dividends.

ADDRESS FAMILY DECISION-MAKING ITEMS IN THE RIGHT ORDER

Once topics for the family meeting are identified, they need to be organized in some fashion for discussion. The agenda bell is helpful here. Without creating a formal agenda (though that can be done), the general principles of the agenda bell—easy stuff, the hard item, and future items—can really be of help in a family meeting.

There are many more things that could be done to improve family group decision making. However, the purpose here is to initiate thinking and create a beginning awareness of family meetings *as* meetings.

A Starter Menu for Improving Family Group Decision Making: The Decision Process

Getting your family meeting ducks (members, items) in a row is the first step. The second step to improve family group decision making is to improve the decision process. Doing that improves the potential for building high-quality family decisions. However, as this whole book suggests, efficient meetings do not necessarily mean effective meetings. Doing things right (efficiency) does not really help if you are not doing the right thing (effectiveness). Perhaps a good place to start would be the use of the decision rules or bases that make decisions okay. These rules, or bases (explained in Chapter 10), are always present when decisions are made, however unacknowledged. As families process information and preferences to achieve a decision, it helps to keep the following five rules in mind:

1. The extensive rule—breadth of preference, or what would be best for the whole family

2. The intensive rule—depth of preference, or who will be most affected and what does that person or persons want

3. The involvement rule—implementor preference, or who will carry out the decision and what does that person think

4. The expert rule—expertise, or what does expert opinion (realtors, investment counselors, doctors, etc.) say and do we have it

5. The power rule—influence, or what are the most influential family members' goals and how they can be addressed while taking the other four rules into account. Powerful family members could be, for example, the family bread-winners, the spoiled child who always gets his or her way, or the grandparent patriarch (though rarely is this person powerful in a family unit in America)

There are, of course, many other ways to improve the quality of family group decision making. Again, the purpose here is to simply introduce the idea of quality in family decisions and suggest one way (using the five decision rules) to approach their improvement.

Conclusion

Families are undergoing a set of huge changes. The very definition of family has diversified and become complex. In terms of marriages, about one in two break up. Many couples, referred to as the sandwich generation, care for both kids and elders.

Educational costs for family members are huge, not only for children (private schools, charter schools, college), but also for older family members going back to school for long-desired degrees or for a second career. Family members are living longer and lives need to be reinvented after retirement, or perhaps there is a return to work in the works. All of these elements, from getting married to leaving marriages, and so on are, among other things, decisions. Perhaps some family problems can be seen as resulting from bad family meetings and bad family decision making. If so, a little work can make it better.

Notes

1 *The Abilene Paradox* is a motion picture originally released in 1984 and is available on video through CRM Learning, 2215 Faraday Avenue, Carlsbad, CA 92008. The film is based on the original journal article (Harvey, 1974) of the same name.

2 While this approach may seem a bit odd to families, they already actually use it in other areas. "Mom" (or "the cook") tries to get food preferences for upcoming meals so that appropriate planning, shopping, and preparation can be accomplished.

23

The Eclipse of Community and the Civic Meeting

From Bowling Alone to Meeting Alone

M any people today lament the "fact" that communities are, well, less "communal" than at least they recall. The "good old days" seemed to be more interactive. Home newspaper subscriptions are falling rapidly, some indication at least that our need to know what is going on around us maybe is less. Street-level interaction seems to be waning. Things that we used to do together outside the home now seem to be done inside the home.

The physical home structure is expanded to thousands of square feet so that there is plenty of interior space. The veranda or front porch, which faces out toward the street and invites interaction with passersby, has been replaced by an ugly protruding garage. The current trend is to have a deck that faces an interiorized backyard. In many neighborhoods, tall, opaque fences cut off any view of, or interaction with neighbors. Almost everything can be done *inside* the home—video centers can produce high-quality entertainment, food can be delivered, and catalogue shopping supplies the home with products. Faith Popcorn called this "cocooning." Community activities truly seem to have really thinned.

Bowling Alone

Robert Putnam (2000), a political scientist at Harvard University, has been a major voice in the "collapse of community" hypothesis. He created quite a stir a few years ago when he introduced his "bowling alone" hypothesis. His argument was captured in the image that there are more bowlers and fewer leagues than in years past. To him, this meant that America's vaunted individualism was running amuck. Social networks and social capital in American communities were being effaced. Perhaps the word *amuck* is too strong, but he sounded a theme familiar to social and cultural commentators, priests, ministers, rabbis, professors, and others. Individualism was, perhaps, too strong.

A Bit of History

America has always experienced a tension between the individualistic mountainman metaphor—our preferred mantra—and the collectivist "wagon train." While each is vital, and a balance absolutely necessary for a vital and productive community, we prefer the idiosyncratic, unique explanation of things.

This point was one that W. Edwards Deming (1986), the father of the quality movement, had the toughest time infusing into American business psyche, which of course is a large part of the American psyche. Ultimately, he failed to convince us that the person at the end of the line was the messenger of bad news, not the maker of bad news. Hence, this individualism of ours has always been poised for dominance, and ready for victory.

On the other side, though, our ability to work in groups has, perhaps, been an unacknowledged, or under-acknowledged part of our greatness. The just-mentioned wagon train was *the* vehicle (literally and figuratively) that settled the West. They were little communities moving west. And Alexis de Tocqueville, that peerless observer of American culture, observed that as well. His comments on "associations" are generally well known. Putnam (2000), however, begins Chapter 3 of *Bowling Alone* with the following quote from de Tocqueville that points to the social importance of associations:

> Americans of all ages, all stations and all types of dispositions are forever forming associations. They are not only commercial and industrial associations in which all take part but others of a thousand different types—religious, moral, serious, very general and very limited, immensely large and very minute. . . . Nothing, in my view, deserves more attention than the intellectual and moral associations in America. . . . (p. 49)

If de Tocqueville was right, and associations—civic groups, stamp clubs, political action organizations, and so forth—are the vital part of American life, then their decline would indeed be an illness striking at the very core of the American way of life. And Putnam (2000) provides an avalanche of evidence that, indeed, such a decline is well underway. The PTA is losing membership and activity (Table 9, p. 57) and philanthropy is down—overall among Protestants, Catholics, and United Way contributors (Figures 31 and 32, pp. 124–125). I need not go on; his voluminous data (much reported in appendixes) says it all. In Chapter 15, he sums it all up, and guesstimates the weights of these social changes that have caused this decline in social investment.

He begins with pressures of time and money. This is a work variable. In this category he includes, as well, the pressures of two career families. He weights this cause at 10%.

Cause two, also at 10%, is "suburbanization, commuting and sprawl." This pressure is sort of an ecological one, which makes "being there" less attractive as "getting there" becomes problematic and stressful.

Electronic entertainment—cause three—weighs in at 25%. Being entertained in your home as opposed to going out is easy, convenient, and comfortable. Like the house, entertainment systems get bigger and bigger.

Cause four achieves a 50% weight. It is generational change. A generation raised on the importance of civic engagement is being replaced by less-engaged children and perhaps even less-engaged grandchildren.

We have 95% so far. In his summary, Putnam (2000, Figure 79, p. 284) has an "other?" category. I think I can fill this in.

Awful Meetings as a Cause of Associational Decline

At least with respect to the associations that de Tocqueville was talking about, the work of those associations occurred in meetings. So banal and so obvious is this point that neither de Tocqueville (1945) nor Putnam (2000) talk about the meetings in which "social capital" is built.[1] If my argument here is correct, that meetings are an important social form or forum through which accomplishment is generated, then awful meetings, which proved limited or negative accomplishment (negative accomplishment means that things are worse off after the meeting then before), would be a huge turnoff. The bottom line is that poor meeting process and results may be the missing factor in Putnam's analysis. As individuals experience the pressures and costs that Putnam details, each of us may be more and more sensitive to the "true value" of the activities we do choose to participate in.

The focus groups on meetings that I have held over the years signal this theme, and the following story confirms it:

> When my daughter was in the 2nd grade, I joined the PTO at her school. We had 17 standing committees that reported every month (so you can imagine the excitement that began to build as the meeting date approached). I was chair of the Capital Expenditures Committee—we approved every expenditure over $25.

At the November meeting, we began with the report from the Ice Cream Social Committee. Now the Ice Cream Social Committee does no work till May and June, but nonetheless, we did not want to make the chair feel bad. Her committee had not actually met yet, but she did not want to be caught "reportless" so she lied.

She said, "The Ice Cream Social Committee met, we had coffee, we had tea," etcetera. And then she did something we all do when we lie. At the end of the lie, she added a factoid: "We had a rather nice, new tea, actually." That is supposed to make the listener feel more okay. However, in this case—you know what is coming—someone asked, "What kind was it?" and we discussed the lied-about tea for a while. It was not a long discussion, but it set the stage for what was to come.

Next up was the Principal's report. He mentioned that the popcorn popper in the teacher's lounge had burned out, and asked if we could "pop for a new popper." This was a phrase that delighted him for many minutes. As chair of the Capital Expenditures Committee, I was up. After a brief consultation with my other members, I moved that we allocate $25 to pay for a new popper.

As in many groups, the suggestion of actual action stuns them. After my motion, there was a silence. I really do not know what they were waiting for, but finally, a teacher spoke up. "If you are going to get a new popper," she said, "get one that pops all the kernels. The last one popped only about half of them and I broke a tooth; it cost me more than $800 for a crown." That led to a somewhat longer discussion about reconstructive dentistry.

At that point, the discussion really got underway. One person offered, "If you really want to pop all the kernels, it is the oil that matters." He mentioned peanut oil, as something that cooks at a higher temperature. We discussed oil for about 20 minutes, in spite of repeated attempts to get back on track. Then someone said that it was not really the oil, but (and again, you know what is coming) the kernels. This was the most vigorous part of the discussion, with strong opinions on white and yellow kernels, boutique mixes, and the like.

By this time, I was out of my mind. We were about 40 minutes into this discussion when I moved that we appoint a PTO subcommittee to come into the school at each instance of popcorn popping to remove the "unpopped" kernels by hand. The motion died for lack of a second. We were not able to get to any of the other business that evening due to time.

Usually, I do not have to tell the whole story at all; I just tell the first part, and the listeners finish the rest. It is like call and response. Everybody knows the rotten meeting script.

When one thinks, "Should I go to the 'name-your-group' board meeting tonight," and she or he thinks back over the past desultory record of accomplishment, the idea of watching television—attractive to begin with—is significantly enhanced.

After all, people are still active in spite of Putnam's five causes of disaffection. They are just in activities that do not involve them in meetings. At the workplace, we feel trapped in meetings. Mandatory or not, we sort of have to go. We think, "I have a couple of meetings coming up this week (which means any week). I am going to suffer two hours of non-accomplishment for each one. Why, then, should I *volunteer* for additional pain and non-accomplishment in the evening?"

Putting in the "Fix"

We are really talking here about the range of groups de Tocqueville was addressing—big and small groups, moral and affinity groups, religious councils, temple boards, parish councils, etcetera. The fix would be to take rotten meetings seriously as an important cause of the social malaise that troubles us all. That alone will be a difficult task, because it would be difficult to give the lowly committee or meeting such social weight.

But meetings are where the work of voluntary organizations gets done. Hence, meeting training could save social lives as CPR courses save physical ones. And like CPR, there are right and wrong ways to do the job. The Red Cross holds classes and certifications for CPR and lifesaving because it is important to society that people know the right way to do these procedures and are capable of doing them. A similar "Meeting Master" certification could be developed as well.

Lets go a step further and say that no one could be on a board if they were not "board certified." This proposal may seem draconian. However, excellence, in my view, is never an accident. The people interviewed for this work clearly knew better ways to do meetings. Better is not a matter of "I feel like doing this. . . ." Rather, it is a set of relative standardized practices, customized to be sure, but standardized nonetheless—like the agenda bell—that really work and truly make meetings go better and assist in the accomplishment of high-quality decisions. We owe it to our volunteers and the health of our "social sector" to do a better job and make the PTO meeting something I want to attend.

Conclusion

By all accounts, American individualism is becoming even more dominant than it has been in the past. "I vant to be alone" is an increasing refrain. This interiorization with "each tub on its own bottom" appears to be having significant social costs. Increased demands at work, sprawl, generational changes, and attractiveness of electronic media are offered as prime causes. Those things are doubtless in play, but let us not forget that building social capital through associational interaction and participation must provide a sense of accomplishment to the participants and add value to them and their lives; otherwise, other choices will be made. The work of associations goes on through meetings, and rotten meetings push people away from associational choices there and into other arms. Developing and offering a meeting training program that certifies people to participate, as with CPR and lifesaving, could be an important answer

Note

1   Neither de Tocqueville's *Democracy in America* nor Putnam's appendix in *Bowling Alone* mention meetings.

24

Crisis in Governance

Problems With Boards of Directors

In the previous chapter, I explored some of the reasons why social capital might be "draining down." That is a serious social problem. Though I briefly mentioned boards, boards of directors are a social form that requires special attention.

Why Boards of Directors Matter

Boards of directors matter because they collectively represent the governance structures of the for-profit and not-for-profit sectors. How boards function—that is, how *well* boards function—is a vital issue for the country as a whole. For our society to flourish, boards must function well. In the corporate sector, it is vital that they provide the oversight and direction for the top team.

Most corporate boards are a combination of "inside" and "outside" directors—a mix that creates its own set of challenges. Nonprofit boards—and nonprofit agencies—exist because the society has decided to make tax expenditures and donations in exchange for civic contribution.[1] The boards' mission is to craft and explain what that contribution is to the community and to see to it that the mission, as thus articulated, is carried out. In addition, both for-profit and not-for-profit boards need to be aware of the problem of social exploitation—of achieving their purpose through exploiting the environment or their employees.

From a 21st-century perspective, it seems to most Americans that significant questions can be raised about whether or not boards are performing appropriately. More directly, there seem to be serious problems in corporate and nonprofit board performance. Without going into a litany of troubling examples, let me mention just a couple of examples from each sector. Most readers will be familiar with the Enron debacle of 2001 and counting. The collapse of that entity is significant not only because of the immense problems it created for its shareholders and employees, but because the ripple effects have been enormous, akin to a sort of social nuclear explosion. Problems in the American Red Cross and the United Way of America (and not a few local United Ways) as well as other nonprofits (arts and human service organizations) suggest that nonprofit boards are not much better off.

Both corporate and not-for-profit boards are deeply flawed. Those flaws matter because they cause or allow our institutions to malperform, whether they are for-profit or not-for-profit.

Advisory Boards

The boards already mentioned are the legally constituted entities we call boards. There are other kinds of boards, many of these organized by governmental entities as ways to increase citizen improvement. Frequently called advisory boards, these boards have no decision-making authority (though some of the governmental ones may be statutorily created). These entities are given the name *board* I suspect to provide apparent strength (as opposed to, say, advisory *group*). However, the focus groups that I have talked with universally report that these boards stumble along, hobbled by the usual problems of group meetings. To these problems, we can add unclear mandate and poor understanding of and handling of the role of advisor. These boards, or quasi-boards, exist in a sea of frustration and underaccomplishment. They, too, need work.

Improving Board Function

To improve the functioning of boards, two kinds of improvements are needed. First, directors need to know what they should do. Second, they need to know how to do it. Following is a discussion of what boards of directors should do. Insights for how to improve board function are presented in the next chapter.

WHAT SHOULD BOARDS DO?

Boards have eight main functions. They are not simple, but they are also not impossible. These main functions are as follows:

1. Promote and manage the interests of the stockholder, stakeholder, or civic purpose

2. Articulate the vision, mission, and goals

3. Make and oversee policy

4. Choose and evaluate the CEO

5. Stimulate innovation

6. Introduce and support strategic change

7. Establish and ensure the proper structure and process

8. Evaluate themselves and their decisions

Each one of these main functions is examined in the sections that follow.

Promote and Manage Interests and Purpose

Directors need to be aware that they are trustees. That is, they are not working for their own purposes. Corporate directors usually receive handsome compensation; however, that is more in the way of reimbursement than remuneration. Directors need to be statespersons, not partisans. Obviously, there are times when individual directors need to push for change and take up the cudgel. However, the wider community interest of stockholders, stakeholders, and citizens needs to be the point of reference.

The problem here is that each of the groups of reference—stockholders, stakeholders, and citizens—is a somewhat different point of reference. Corporations will pay most attention to stockholders, then to stakeholders (such as employees, ex-employees, families of employees, etc.), and perhaps then to citizens. Nonprofits will, on the other hand, look first at stakeholders— they have no stockholders—and then to citizens at large. In both cases, there is the question of whether the organization is adding value to the stockholders' or stakeholders' investment.

Articulate the Vision, Mission, and Goals

Boards, with management, need to articulate the vision, mission, and goals of the organization. If the highest level of the organization does not know "what business it is in," than no one else can be expected to know it either.

Make and Oversee Policy

Boards make organizational policy. This area always has been, and always will be, a contentious one because there is no clear line between policy and administration. There is always something of a "gray area" existing between the two. Policy is the area on which management and executive committees work, or should work. (Often executive committees become a sort of faux board, deciding things that are then rubber-stamped by the larger board.)

Perhaps most contentious is the area of policy oversight. This is the heart of the Enron case, and the heart of the United Way cases as well. What was the board *thinking* when these organizations' many problems were going down? What did they know, when did they know it, and if they did not know, why not?

Choose and Evaluate the CEO

This area is probably the most contentious and most badly done in most boards. First, it does not happen that often, so boards have less experience with it than other areas. (Although, with the average tenure of CEOs decreasing, boards are becoming more experienced.) Second, it is very time intensive, which sometimes makes it difficult for certain directors. Third, there are always the departing conditions of the old CEO. Sometimes the old CEO hangs around, offering to help (this is not always bad; however, it is like your first husband or wife hanging around offering to help). Sometimes the outgoing CEO has been fired. Then the search process is laced with blame and recriminations. For most boards, this event—the search—is one good time to get professional outside facilitation, not only for the search process itself, but also for the meetings.

Evaluating the CEO is another vital function for boards. This should happen yearly, and the process should begin with an examination of the organization's strategic plan and an invitation to the CEO to propose a series of activities and emphases for the coming year that he or she will undertake with reference to that plan. These activities are then reviewed and accepted by the board, and become the basis for the CEO's quarterly feedback sessions and yearly evaluation. Usually it is good to have a committee developed for this purpose.

Stimulate Innovation

Most organizations exist to provide regular products; organizations can only survive, however, if they provide new products as well. There is, therefore, a tension between what the organization does in the here and now and what the organization needs to do to survive for the long run. While there is no hard-and-fast rule for how much of each organizations should do, it is axiomatic that "daily routine drives out innovation." Hence, boards need to make and enforce an innovation policy.

A good rule of thumb is to follow the practice of some of America's more innovative companies—85% and 15%. The regular activities of the organization should be accomplished with 85% of the resources, and the remaining 15% should be devoted to innovation. These goals are accomplished through activity review and budget review. On occasion, it is the organization that wants to move ahead and the board that is dragging its feet. If that is so, then the board needs to change.

Introduce and Support Strategic Change

Stimulating innovation is one thing. Changing the organization to accommodate change is another thing. Introducing change regularly involves a number of problems including the following five that occur commonly:

1. Inertia

2. Self-interest

3. Entrenched culture

4. Noninvolvement of those affected by the change

5. Not credible or insufficient rationale explanation for the change

Boards need to be aware of these problems and work with management to overcome them and assure innovation and progress. Sometimes the board has to prod management to become more forward thinking. Sometimes the board has to challenge itself, and sometimes it is the board itself that is the stick-in-the-mud.

Establish and Ensure the Proper Structure and Process

In order to accomplish these goals, the board needs to do two things. One of them is ensuring proper structure and process. The other, mentioned in the next section, is engaging in self-evaluation. Proper structure means that the board needs to have committees for each one of the strategic plan's substantive elements and for each one of the points mentioned here.

Board work is basically committee work. In a small board, it can be a committee of the whole, but standing committees are better. Then, of course, the board, in its overall meetings and in its subcommittees' meetings, has to ensure that good meetings occur. While high-quality meetings do not guarantee high-quality decisions, poor meetings most certainly guarantee bad ones.

Evaluate Themselves and Their Decisions

Boards, of course, need to evaluate themselves. This process needs to be rigorous and regular. Several kinds of evaluation are required. One is an evaluation of the directors themselves. Each director should be assessed by all other directors and management. Then, the board as a board needs to be assessed as well. This assessment means the board *meetings* require evaluation as well as the board *decisions*.

Conclusion

Boards are the social infrastructure of the American pattern of self-governance. Those who rail against "big government" or "whatever government" might do well to ask themselves about the vitality and quality of "governance." Corporate and not-for-profit boards provide a vital component of decision making—for good or ill—that affect the lives of every American. My personal observation—coming from years of working with boards and executives—is that boards are functioning, but at a level that is barely adequate to sustain confidence and integrity. Already, in 2003, because of well-publicized board failures (Enron, for example), the country is wondering whether or not we can really trust the impartiality of directors. And the answer, all too often, seems to be "No." Our society can, and will, do better than this judgment implies.

Note

1 A tax expenditure is the amount the government would have collected in taxes if the organization paid taxes.

25

Leadership in Community Decision Making

Problems in family group decision making, in civic groups, and in structures of governance represent a series of important problems in American society today, and poor meeting skills add considerable difficulty. To these, we need to add problems in community decision making. Communities are more loosely coupled systems than organizations and firms, so decision making is more entangled, less precise, not as easy to follow, and generally more opaque.

Leadership

Leadership can be defined as achieving change without crisis. Crisis has two meanings in this definition. One is that leaders act *before* crises force action. Changing when a crisis is upon you is a lot easier than changing before the crisis arrives. The problem with waiting is that the options available as the crisis actually unfolds are far fewer and usually much less appealing that the options available in the precrisis period. Leaders are able to articulate for us the "gathering storm" and enable us to act before crisis restricts us.

The second meaning of crisis here refers to the amount of crisis change creates. When change happens, it creates a certain amount of crisis. If change is stimulated by an active crisis itself, organizations and persons undergoing change face a double crisis—the crisis that required the need to change in the first place and the crisis of changing itself. Leaders are people who help us avoid the double crisis and manage the crisis of change.

Leadership can exist everywhere and anywhere—in the firm, in the family, and in the civic association. It is not associated with a position as such, though common parlance often makes that association. We talk, for example, about senior managers as organizational leadership, we expect moms and dads to exercise family leadership, and we think of clergy as religious leaders. This misconception needs correction. Leaders are, as defined above, people who help us to change. They sometimes are those who occupy positions of power, but often they are not. Indeed, many individuals in high positions continually disappoint in the leadership dimension.

One of the most important areas where leadership is needed today is in the broad area of community. Community—the unity that comes from commonness of interest, identification, commitment, geography, or concern—can be local, regional, or national. For our society to prosper and grow, citizens must take and encourage leadership in every kind of community. Communities are aggregations or constellations of many specific groups. They tend to be "organizations of organizations" rather than a single organization itself.

The Ends and Means of Community

Vibrant communities enhance the quality of life of their members while not detracting from the quality of life of other communities. We are all members of many communities. Communities of interest range from stamp clubs to gun safety clubs to the Mothers of Multiples association. Communities of identification could include the Jewish community, the Italian community, the Chinese community, the African-American community, and so forth.

Communities of commitment focus on things people care about. "Green" communities bind together people interested in ecological improvement; the healthy lunch coalition involves those persons and groups interested in school nutrition and healthy eating in school. People committed to breast cancer awareness, stopping road rage, and improving nursing homes are all over the country. And of course, there is the common interest that comes from living near others. *Northern Living* is a magazine for people who identify with living in northern Michigan.

The "ends" of communities, for many, is like-to-like—the simple opportunity to be with those who value the same things, wear the same type of clothing, participate in the same rituals, and listen to the same music. Being there is much of the fun because it seems, for humans, that we generally enjoy what we do better when we do it with others. In many communities, means become ends.

Community Task and Process

While a significant part of community life and participation involves being there, almost all communities at some time, and some communities many times, have to accomplish some tasks or reach some goals. For example, a stamp club needs to organize the yearly stamp fair. This means working within its own membership to prepare, working with other clubs and vendors to produce the event, and so on. Community task accomplishment—as community is used here—means a loose coordination among community organizations is achieved, standards for the community are set (what is a healthy lunch?), and overall community goals are articulated and planned. Sometimes community action is needed to force relevant organizations to comply—the school board may need pressure to look at the lunches the school is providing and to ask about the health of that lunch.

There is another result that community membership produces, however. Process accomplishment means that the participants themselves gained through the work of the community group, and learned how to be better, more effective participants in the next round of community work. Members of the community have an opportunity to express themselves on issues and engage with other members of the community, through which learning occurs. We all need to learn how to work and play well together in the community sandbox.

Conclusion

Communities are the most ephemeral social groups in which we exist. But they provide a vital locus for activity and meaning. Communities are, in some sense, constantly being created, and re-created. It is for this reason that leadership is vital. Without leadership, communities wither and atrophy. It is far easier to cop out or avoid participation in the more populous community than it is in the tighter-knit and more visible family or board of directors.

The argument of this chapter, and of this section, really, is that the quality of family life, board life, and community life depends heavily on the ability of those entities to know what they are about and make consistently good decisions with respect to their multiple missions. Those decisions come largely in meetings. In the case of the board of directors, the meeting locus is relatively clear cut—the board meeting and meetings of the subcommittees of the board. In the case of family meetings and community meetings, the very meeting occasion is unclear and uncertain. The straightforward techniques presented in this book can assist motivated individuals to clarify uncertainties and move forward to more meaningful meeting outcomes within their group, organization, family, board of directors, or community. The bottom line is that better meetings lead to better decisions and better decisions lead to better quality of life for us all.

Appendix A

Writing Samples

High-Quality Decisions
3568 River Pines Drive • Suite 100
Ann Arbor, MI 40103
734 • 663-3411

John E. Tropman, Ph.D.

President

Sample Agenda

Memo to: Staff

Memo from: John

Re: Staff Meeting

Date: Monday, 10:00-12:00

1. Announcements   10:00-10:10
   Penny, Sarah, Matt, Jessica, Jared, Evelyn, Daniel, Ethan

2. Minutes from last Monday's meeting   10:10-10:15

3. Easy Items (Discussion and Decision)   10:15-10:35
  3a. Office decoration—Penny   10:15-10:25
      Review of new furniture
  3b. New software—Matt   10:25-10:35
      Matt recommends MS Office 2000

4. Moderately Tough Items (Discussion and Decision)   10:35-11:05
  4a. Training and consultation coverage—Sarah   10:35-10:50
      Holiday/vacation coverage
  4b. Film archives—Jessica   10:50-11:05
      Review and approval of new information
      system (Attachment A)

5. The Toughest Item (Discussion and Decision)   11:05-11:30
  5a. Hourly versus batch pricing—Penny
      A proposal to use both hourly and batch
      pricing methods (refer to previous report)

6. Blue Sky Items (Discussion Only)   11:30-12:00
  Looking at new markets
  6a. The music business—Matt
  6b. Libraries and museums—Jessica
  6c. The health care system—Sarah
  6d. Child Care—Jared and Evelyn
  6e. Mothers of Multiples—Daniel and Ethan

Snack follows at noon!

High-Quality Decisions
3568 River Pines Drive • Suite 100
Ann Arbor, MI 40103

John E. Tropman   734 • 663-3411

President

Sample Report

EXECUTIVE SUMMARY

The Problem
Key material in the firm is stored in several locations. A master file system has not as yet been set up. There is lack of understanding about what *should* be stored.

The Options

1. Let things stay as they are for now.

2. Plan to revisit this problem in 6 months.

3. Ask Jessica to develop an information storage and retrieval plan.

The Recommendations—Option 3
Jessica should be asked to develop a plan. Any delay means more will be lost and the job is tougher.

High-Quality Decisions
3568 River Pines Drive • Suite 100
Ann Arbor, MI 40103

John E. Tropman   734 • 663-3411

President

Sample Minutes

STAFF MEETING

Monday

1. **Announcements**
   Penny announced the new parking lot was ready. Sarah announced a new program at Woman Health, Inc. Matt announced he would be at a software meeting on Friday. Jessica announced new materials for the library. There were no other announcements.

2. Minutes from last Monday's meeting
The minutes for the last meeting were accepted.

3a. Office decoration
The new furniture setup for the reception suite was reviewed.

Decision: Penny was given approval to purchase new desks and chairs as well as proceed with the general scheme of decorating.

3b. New software
Matt reviewed the advantages of the new Windows suite.

Decision: It was decided to purchase the new Windows suite.

4a. Training and consultation coverage
Problems have occurred in providing enough coverage for weekends, when many groups like to do training sessions. Sarah had worked out a 1.5 to 1 plan. Each Saturday/Sunday would count as 1.5 days. These days would go into a day bank; draw outs would be negotiated at Staff Benefits.

Decision: The 1.5 to 1 Bank Plan was approved.

4b. Film archives
Jessica reported that there is no more room in the film archives. Some pre-1994 films need to be destroyed.

Decision: It was decided to maintain only a current film archive, with 1995 as a base for the current year, and advancing each year (next year 1996, etc.)

---

5. Hourly versus batch pricing
Questions often come up about how to price. The idea is to price in "package" or "batch" mode for larger customers, at $1,750 per day and on an hourly (somewhat higher) rate for small ones (see report), at $250 per hour.

> *Decision: It was decided to go with the proposed dual-rate system, $1,750 per day, $250 per hour, for 6 months.*

Different views were expressed. Some favored the dual-rate systems. Others felt a single, hourly rate was best.

6. **Blue Sky Items —New Markets**

   A lively discussion of new markets (music, libraries, museums, and health care settings) was held. Each of these seemed very promising. More discussion will be held next week.

   6a. **The music business—Matt**

   Matt sees small bands—for example, the Brass Band of Battle Creek—as a customer.

   6b. **Libraries and museums—Jessica**

   Jessica sees the need to develop information software for nonprofits generally and libraries and museums in particular.

   6c. **The health care system—Sarah**

   Sarah pointed out that, with the health care system expanding, many project leaders need training in effective group decision making.

   6d. **Child care—Jared and Evelyn**

   Jared and Evelyn explained that there is a lot of small (ish) child care institutions that could use customized decision-making tools.

   6e. **Mothers of Multiples—Daniel and Ethan**

   Dan and Ethan pointed out that there are numbers of organizations where parents of twins and other multiples get together. That could be a great decision-making market.

Appendix B

Sample Evaluation Sheet

The Evaluation Process

Have the members of the group set up an evaluation process that includes the following five main steps:

1. Goal setting—where we want to go to, by when, etcetera. What outcomes do we seek? Establish a time line (say, a year) for goal accomplishment

2. Monitoring—periodic checking in to assess progress

3. Oversight—milestone review

4. Assessment—quarterly judgments about the quality of progress

5. Appraisal—final judgment about how well the project was completed

Keep, Stop, Start—KSS

At the end of each meeting, pass out a sheet that asks three questions to each member:

What in this meeting went well and should be KEPT?

What in this meeting did not go so well and should be STOPPED?

> What did not happen at this meeting that should be STARTED?

It will really help you!

Decision Audit

Take a sample of decisions from the minutes. Assign a small group from the larger group—one or two will serve—to give decisions one of the following grades:

A An all-win decision—all stakeholders advanced, though perhaps not equally.

B Some stakeholders advanced and some did not. On balance, however, the result is positive for the system (organization, community, or family).

C Some stakeholders advanced and some did not. Basically, there is change in winners and nonwinners, but the overall result is neutral for the system (organization, community, or family).

D Only a few stakeholders advanced and many did not. Overall, the result is negative for the system (organization, community, or family).

F The nuclear-war decision—all stakeholders are worse off than previously. The system is grievously harmed.

Present and discuss your grades with the larger group. Do not worry too much about being right. It is the discussion of the decisions and their review that really counts.

Decision Autopsy

Take an *A* decision and an *F* decision for examination. Ask of the *A* decision, what went right and how can we keep this up?

Ask of the *F* decision, what went wrong and how can we avoid it in the future?

Remember that this is not a search for *blame;* it is a search for *understanding* and *improvement.*

References

Boorstin, D. (1965). *The Americans: The national experience.* New York: Random House.

Cohen, M., March, J. G., & Olsen, J. (1972). A garbage can model of organizational choice. *Administrative Science Quarterly, 17*(1), 1-25.

Deming, W. E. (1986). *Out of the crisis.* Cambridge: MIT, Center for Advanced Engineering Study.

De Tocqueville, A. (1945). *Democracy in America.* (H. Reeve, Trans.; F. Bowen & P. Bradley, Eds.). New York: Knopf. (Original work published 1835).

Egan, G. (1995). *Working the shadow side.* San Francisco: Jossey-Bass.

Goffman, E. (1959). *The presentation of self in everyday life.* New York: Doubleday.

Harvey, J. B. (1974). The Abilene paradox. *Organizational Dynamics,* pp. 17-43.

Hochschild, A. R. (1983). *The managed heart.* Berkeley: University of California Press.

Houle, C. (1989). *Governing boards.* San Francisco: Jossey-Bass.

Janis, I. (1983). *Groupthink: Psychological studies of policy decisions and fiascoes.* Boston: Houghton Mifflin.

Janis, I., & Mann, L. (1977). *Decision making: A psychological analysis of conflict, choice, and commitment.* Glencoe, IL: Free Press.

Jay, A. (1976, March/April). How to run a meeting. *Harvard Business Review, 54*(2), 43-57.

Kabat-Zinn, J. (1994). *Wherever you go, there you are.* New York: Hyperion.

Kanter, R. M. (1983). *The change masters.* New York: Simon & Schuster.

Katz, D., Gutek, B. A., Kahn, R. L., & Barton, E. (1975). *Bureaucratic encounters: A pilot study in the evaluation of government service.* Ann Arbor: Institute for Social Research, The University of Michigan.

Lucas, G. (Producer), Spielberg, S. (Director), & Kasden, L. (Writer). (1981). *Raiders of the Lost Ark* [Motion Picture]. United States: Paramount Pictures.

Merton, R. (1958). *Societal structure and process* (Rev. ed.). Glencoe, IL: Free Press.

Morgan, G. (1986). *Images of organization.* Beverly Hills, CA: Sage.

Naisbitt, J. (1982). *Megatrends.* New York: Warner Books.

Putnam, R. D. (2000). *Bowling alone.* New York: Simon and Schuster.

Quinn, R. (1989). *Beyond rational management.* San Francisco: Jossey-Bass.

Rittel, W. J., & Webber, M. (1973). Dilemmas in a general theory of planning. *Policy Sciences, 4*(2), 155-169.

Tichy, N., & Sherman, S. (1993). *Control your destiny or someone else will.* New York: Doubleday.

Tropman, J. E. (1989). *American Values and Social Welfare.* Englewood Cliffs, NJ: Prentice Hall.

Tropman, J. E., & Morningstar, G. (1989). *Entrepreneurial systems for the 1990s.* Westport, CT: Quorum Books.

Tuchman, B. (1984). *The march of folly: From Troy to Vietnam.* New York: Knopf.

Weick, K., & Roberts, K. (1993). Collective mind in organizations: Heedful interrelating on flight decks. *Administrative Science Quarterly, 38,* 357-381.

Wetlaufer, S. (1994, November/December). The team that wasn't. *Harvard Business Review, 72,* 22-26.

Zander, A. (1982). *Making groups effective.* San Francisco: Jossey-Bass.

Bibliography

Benedict, R. (1946). *The chrysanthemum and the sword: Patterns of Japanese culture.* Boston: Houghton Mifflin.

Bramson, R. M. (1981). *Coping with difficult people.* Garden City, NY: Anchor Press/Doubleday.

Braybrooke, D., & Lindblom, C. E. (1963). *A strategy of decision: Policy evaluation as a social process.* New York: Free Press.

Carver, J. (1990). *Boards that make a difference: A new design for leadership in nonprofit and public organizations.* San Francisco: Jossey-Bass.

Cleese, J. (1988, May 16). No more mistakes and you're through. *Forbes, 141*(11), 126-128.

Clifton, R. L., & Dahms, A. M. (1980). *Grassroots administration: A handbook for staff and directors of small community-based social service agencies.* Monterey, CA: Brooks/Cole.

Cohen, M., & March, J. G. (1974). *Leadership and ambiguity.* New York: McGraw-Hill.

Conrad, W. R., Jr., & Glenn, W. E. (1983). *The effective voluntary board of directors: What it is and how it works* (Rev ed.). Athens, OH: Swallow Press.

CRM Films (Producer). (1991). *Groupthink* [Motion picture]. Available from CRM Learning, www.crm-learning.com, or 2215 Faraday Avenue, Carlsbad, CA 92008.

Daft, R. (1992). *Organization theory and design* (4th ed.). St. Paul, MN: West.

Flamholtz, E. G. (1986). *How to make the transition from an entrepreneurship to a professionally managed firm.* San Francisco: Jossey-Bass.

Goodman, P. S., & Associates (Eds.) (1986). *Designing effective workgroups.* San Francisco: Jossey-Bass.

Greenleaf, R. (1973). *Trustees as servants.* Peterborough, NH: Windy Row Press.

Griggsby, C. (1972). Separable liabilities in directory trusts. *California Law Review, 60* (4).

Hackman, J. R. (Ed.). (1990). *Groups that work (and those that don't): Creating conditions for effective teamwork.* San Francisco: Jossey-Bass.

Hart, P. (1990). *Groupthink in government: A study of small groups and policy failure.* Amsterdam: Swets & Zeitlinger.

Janis, I. (1972). *Victims of groupthink: A psychological study of foreign-policy decisions and fiascos.* Boston: Houghton Mifflin.

Janis, I. (1989). *Crucial decisions: Leadership in policymaking and crisis management.* New York: Free Press.

Johansen, R. (1988). *Groupware: Computer support for business teams.* New York: Free Press.

Kahneman, D., Slovic, P., & Tversky, A. (Eds.). (1982). *Judgment under uncertainty: Heuristics and biases.* New York: Cambridge University Press.

Kieffer, G. D. (1988). *The strategy of meetings.* New York: Warner Books.

Kleindorfer, P. R., Kunreuther, H. C., & Schoemaker, P. J. (1993). *Decision sciences: An integrated perspective.* New York: Cambridge University Press.

March, J., & Simon, H. (1958). *Organizations.* New York: Wiley.

Margolis, R. J. (1989, September). In America's small-town hospitals a patient isn't 'just a number.' *Smithsonian*, pp. 52-67.

McCaskey, M. B. (1982). *The executive challenge: Managing change and ambiguity*. Boston: Pitman.

Mills, C. W. (1956). *The power elite*. New York: Oxford University Press.

Mosvick, R. K., & Nelson, R. B. (1987). *We've got to start meeting like this: A guide to successful business meeting management*. Glenview, IL: Scott, Foresman.

Mueller, R. K. (1977). *Metadevelopment: Beyond the bottom line*. Lexington, MA: Lexington Books.

Mueller, R. K. (1981). *The incompleat board: The unfolding of corporate governance*. Lexington, MA: Lexington Books.

Myers, R. J., Ufford, P., & Magill, M. S. (1988). *On-site analysis: A practical approach to organizational change*. Etobicoke, Ontario: On-Site Consultants Associates (OSCA).

Naisbitt, J., & Aburdene, P. (1985). *Re-inventing the corporation: Transforming your job and your company for the new information society*. New York: Warner Books.

Nakane, C. (1970). *Japanese society*. Berkeley: University of California Press.

Oleck, H. L. (1980). *Nonprofit corporations, organizations, and associations*. Englewood Cliffs, NJ: Prentice Hall.

Ott, J. S., & Shafritz, J. M. (1986). *The facts on file dictionary of nonprofit organization management*. New York: Facts on File.

Parkinson, C. N. (1957). *Parkinson's law and other studies in administration*. Boston: Houghton Mifflin.

Plous, S. (1993). *The psychology of judgment and decision making*. Philadelphia: Temple University Press.

Portnoy, R. A. (1986). *Leadership: What every leader should know about people*. Englewood Cliffs, NJ: Prentice Hall.

Quinn, R., Rohrbaugh, J., & McGrath, M. R. (1985, Winter). Automated decision conferencing. *Personnel Journal*, pp. 49-58.

Sayles, L., & Chandler, M. (1971). *Managing large systems: Organizations for the future*. New York: Harper & Row.

Schmid, H., Dodd, P., & Tropman, J. (1987). Board decision making in human service organizations. *Human Systems Management, 7*(2), 155-161.

Schwartzman, H. B. (1989). *The meeting: Gatherings in organizations and communities*. New York: Plenum Press.

Sills, D. (Ed.). (1968). *The international encyclopedia of the social sciences* (Vol. 4). New York: Macmillan.

Simon, H. (1957). *Administrative behavior* (2nd ed.). New York: Macmillan.

Sims, R. (1992). Linking groupthink to unethical behavior in organizations. *Journal of Business Ethics, 11*, 651-662.

Thurow, L. (1985). *The management challenge: Japanese views*. Cambridge: MIT Press.

Tichy, N., & Devanna, M. A. (1986). *The transformational leader*. New York: Wiley.

Tjosvold, D. (1986). *Working together to get things done*. Lexington, MA: Lexington Books.

Toffler, A. (1980). *The third wave*. New York: Morrow.

Toffler, A. (1990). *Powershift: Knowledge, wealth, and violence at the edge of the 21st century*. New York: Bantam Books.

Tropman, B. J., & Tropman, J. E. (1987). Voluntary agencies. In A. Minahan (Ed.), *Encyclopedia of social work* (pp. 825-842). Silver Springs, MD: National Association of Social Workers.

Tropman, J. E. (1982). The decision group: Ways to improve the quality of meetings and decisions. *Human Systems Management, 3*, 107-118.

Tropman, J. E. (1984). *Policy management in the human services*. New York: Columbia University Press.

Tropman, J. E., Erlich, J., & Rothman, J. (Eds.). (1995). *Tactics and techniques of community intervention* (3rd ed.). Itasca, IL: F. E. Peacock.

Waldo, C. N. (1985). *Boards of directors: Their changing roles, structure, and information needs.* New York: Quorum Books.

Waldo, C. N. (1986). *A working guide for directors of not-for-profit organizations.* New York: Quorum Books.

Whetten, D., & Cameron, K. (1995). *Developing management skills* (3rd ed.). New York: HarperCollins.

Zelman, W. (1977). Liability for social agency boards. *Social Work, 22*(4), 270-274.

Electronic Bibliography

Readers are encouraged to hop on the Web and search for "effective meetings." There are many entries available, too many to cite here. Readers can get lots of useful and customized information from this source. Therefore, I suggest the following:

www.effectivemeetings.com
www.toolpack.com/meetings.html

Print References

Boorstin, D. (1965). *The Americans: The national experience.* New York: Random House.

Cleese, J. (1988, May 16). No more mistakes and you're through. *Forbes,* pp. 126-128.

Cohen, M., March, J. G., & Olsen, J. (1972). A garbage can model of organizational choice. *Administrative Science Quarterly, 17(1),* 1-25.

Egan, G. (1995). *Working the shadow side.* San Francisco: Jossey-Bass.

Goffman, E. (1959). *The presentation of self in eve?yd4y life.* New York: Doubleday.

Harvey, J. B. (1974). The Abilene paradox. *Organizational Dynamics,* pp. 17-43.

Hochschild, A. R. (1983). *The managed heart.* Berkeley: University of California Press.

Houle, C. (1989). *Governing boards.* San Francisco: Jossey-Bass.

Janis, I. (1983). *Groupthink: Psychological studies of policy decisions and fiascoes.* Boston: Houghton Muffin.

Janis, I., & Mann, L. (1977). *Decision making: A psychological analysis of conflicti, choice, and commitment.* Glencoe, IL: Free Press.

Jay, A. (1976, March/April). How to run a meeting. *Harvard Business Review* pp. 43-57.

Kabat-Zinn, J. (1994). *Wherever you go, there you are.* New York: Hyperion.

Kanter, R. M. (1983). *The change masters.* New York: Simon & Shuster.

Katz, D., Gutek, B. A., Kahn, R. L., & Barton, E. (1975). *Encounters with bureaucracy.* Ann Arbor, MI: I. S. R.

Merton, R. (1958). *Societal structure and process* (Rev. ed.). Glencoc, IL: Free Press.

Morgan, G. (1986). *Images of organization.* Beverly Hills, CA: Sage.

Naisbett, J. (1982). *Megatrends.* New York: Warner.

Quinn, R. (1989). *Beyond rational management.* San Francisco: Jossey-Bass.

Rittel, W. J., & Webber, M. (1973). Dilemmas in a general theory of planning. *Policy Sciences,* 4(2), 155-169.

Tichy, N., & Sherman, 5. (1993). *Control your destiny or someone else will.* New York: Doubleday.

Tropman, J. E., & Morningstar, G. (1989). *Enterpreneurial systems for the 1990s.* Westport, CT: Quorum Books.

Tuchman, B. (1984). *The march of folly: From Troy to Vietnam.* New York: Knopf.

Weick, K., & Roberts, K. (1993). Collective mind in organizations: Heedful interrelating on flight decks. *Administrative Science Quarterly, 38,* 3 57-381.

Wetlaufer, 5. (1994, November/December). The team that wasn't. *Harvard Business Review* pp. 22-26.

Wherten, D., & Cameron, K. (1995). *Developing management skills* (3rd ed.). New York: HarperCollins.

Zander, A. (1982). *Making groups effective.* San Francisco: Jossey-Bass.

Electronic References

http://www.EffectiveMeetings.com
http://www.effectivemettings.com/
http://store.yahoo.com/esistore-store/mangroupdynv.html
http://www.toolpack.com/meetings.html
http://edweb.sdsu.edu/courses/edtec670/Cardboard/board/e/effectivemeetings/keymeetins. html
http://www.triangle.org/howto/meetings/elements.html
http://www.speaking.com/articles_html/JoliAndre_852.html

Index

About the Author

John E. Tropman is a Professor of Nonprofit Administration at the School of Social Work and an Adjunct Professor in the Organizational Behavior and Human Resources Development Program at the University of Michigan Business School in Ann Arbor. He also teaches in the Executive Education Program at the University of Michigan Business School and in the Executive Education Program at Carnegie Mellon University. He received his undergraduate degree in sociology (major) and in government and classics (minor) from Oberlin College, his master's in social work from the University of Chicago, and his Ph.D. in social work and sociology from the University of Michigan. He presents and consults widely on issues of effective group decision making, transformational leadership, and organizational governance.